RACING THE GREAT WHITE WAY

D1593052

THEATER: THEORY/TEXT/PERFORMANCE

Series Editors: David Krasner, Rebecca Schneider, and Harvey Young

Founding Editor: Enoch Brater

Recent Titles:

Racing the Great White Way

BLACK PERFORMANCE, EUGENE O'NEILL,

AND THE TRANSFORMATION OF BROADWAY

Katie N. Johnson

UNIVERSITY OF MICHIGAN PRESS

Ann Arbor

For questions or permissions, please contact um.press.perms@umich.edu

Published in the United States of America by the
University of Michigan Press
Manufactured in the United States of America
Printed on acid-free paper
First published July 2023

A CIP catalog record for this book is available from the British Library.

Library of Congress Cataloging-in-Publication data has been applied for.

ISBN 978-0-472-07578-2 (hardcover : alk. paper)
ISBN 978-0-472-05578-4 (paper : alk. paper)
ISBN 978-0-472-90360-3 (open access ebook)

DOI: https://doi.org/10.3998/mpub.12340544

Open access edition funded by the National Endowment for the Humanities.

The University of Michigan Press's open access publishing program is made
possible thanks to additional funding from the University of Michigan Office of
the Provost and the generous support of contributing libraries.

for Georgia, Lise, and our ancestors of the prairie;
for my Irishman, Timothy;
and for our son, Liam, whose star is rising.

Contents

Digital materials related to this title can be found on the Fulcrum platform via the following citable URL: https://doi.org/10.3998/mpub.12340544

Illustrations

Acknowledgments

There are numerous people who had a hand in shaping this project, which has taken more than a decade of work in dozens of archives, on two laptops, and in multiple writing spaces. Thank you to all who helped me, whether it was locating obscure photographs in an archive, hunting down citations, or providing funding for research.

This book was supported by a National Endowment for the Humanities Summer Research Award; an American Society for Theatre Research Grant; a Wardlaw Research Fellowship from the Texas Collection at Baylor University; and a Tao House Travis Bogard Writer in Residence Grant. Without this assistance, this book could not have been completed. I am profoundly grateful.

Miami University has generously supported this project with an Assigned Research Leave, a Grant to Promote Research, and a Summer Research Grant. I am also grateful to the Office for Research and Innovation at Miami University for providing me with a publication and reproduction grant to cover the costs of securing images, an index, and permissions.

Numerous librarians and archivists have assisted me: Jennifer Meeham, Susan Brady, and Naomi Saito from the Beinecke Rare Book & Manuscript Library at Yale University; Jeremy Megraw at the Billy Rose Theatre Collection, New York Public Library for the Performing Arts; Andrea Felder at Rights and Reproductions at New York Public Library; John Tomasichhio at the Metropolitan Opera Archives; Aime Oliver from Baylor University's Texas Collection; and Alison Clark Bodden and Mary Camezon from the Eugene O'Neill Foundation Archive. Lynn Lafontaine from the Library and Archives of Canada was helpful in tracking down film versions of *The Emperor Jones*. I am grateful for email exchanges with Scott MacQueen at the University of California, Los Angeles Film Archives; Bill Gorman at the New York State Archives in Albany; Josie Walters-Johnston, reference librarian at the Moving Image Section of the Library of Congress; and George R. Willeman, Nitrate Film Vault manager at the Library of Congress National Audio-Visual Conservation Center. A big thanks to those who helped in special collections at the Schomburg Center for Research in Black

Culture in New York City. My gratitude goes to Camille Billops and James V. Hatch for opening their home to me to conduct research. I have not forgotten the rich conversations, nor the croissant, that were so graciously offered. At Miami University Libraries, I've been supported by Adrianne Hartsnell, Ed Via, Mark Dahlquist, and Laura Sheppard. Thank you all.

I'd like to thank my incredible colleagues at the Eugene O'Neill Society, the Eugene O'Neill Foundation, and the New Ross Festival in Ireland, who have encouraged me to think beyond the horizon.

My work has been aided by many keen editorial eyes: Jennifer Parker-Starbuck from *Theatre Journal* whipped an essay on Habib Benglia into an award-winning article. I thank also Gary Totten from *MELUS* and William Davies King and Alexander Pettit from the *Eugene O'Neill Review*. The editorial insights from the late Kurt Eisen on parts of this project have made an enduring mark—his guidance will be greatly missed. I am particularly thankful to LeAnn Fields, John Raymond, and Marcia LaBrenz from the University of Michigan Press, and the readers who gave such thoughtful reports. Thanks also to Mary Hashman for indexing the book.

I thank my students, who remind me why I am writing this book, and who inspire me to keep writing.

Thanks to members of Miami University's Film Studies Research Cluster and the American Cultures Working Group, who read versions of this essay: Ann Elizabeth Armstrong, Marianne Cotugno, Andrew Hebard, Michele Navakas, and Lindsay Schakenbach Regele. I am grateful for comments from Mary Jean Corbett, Jim Creech, Madelyn Detloff, Kerry Hegarty, Peggy Shaeffer, and the late Paul K. Jackson. My gratitude goes to Gail Barker and my yoga and tennis family, who have kept me centered and well. Special thanks goes to Stefanie Kyle Dunning and Elisabeth Hodges for their perceptive feedback on numerous drafts. The English department has graciously supported research trips and indexing cost—thank you. I am also grateful to Jeanne De Groote-Strauss, Elisabeth Hodges, and Michel Pactat for help with French translations— *Merci beaucoup!* Thanks to Miami University research apprentices Emily Sharrett, Samuel Fouts, and Rylee Jung for their hard work.

Finally, I am most indebted to Timothy D. Melley, who is not only the best reader of critical work (ever), but also generous with his time and intellect.

A Note about Language

Racing the Great White Way documents the transformation of racial regimes in theater and cultural production during the early twentieth century. The book aims to provide an accurate historical record of racist structures while preventing the repetition of offensive language and its injurious linguistic force. For this reason, racial epithets in textual quotations have been omitted or redacted. When the specificity of a word or phrase is necessary—for example, to document the debates concerning offensive language and actors' efforts to change it—dashes have been used within the original word (such as "n——r"). If contemporaneous racialized vocabulary has been retained, surrounding commentary is provided in order to contextualize terminology within specific historical and cultural settings.

Introduction

In conventional theater history, all roads lead to Broadway. Traffic never seems to go in other directions. Until recently, scholarly work on U.S. theater has focused mostly upon mainstream white dramatists, actors, and venues. Hence, the "Great White Way"—a phrase that originally described Broadway's electric marquee lights—has always had an uncanny racialized meaning.

Racing the Great White Way challenges the widely accepted idea that Broadway was the central creative engine of U.S. theater during the early twentieth century. Focusing on playwright Eugene O'Neill and the actors who performed his work, this book reveals a complex system of exchanges between the Broadway establishment and vibrant Black theater scenes in New York and across the Atlantic. Productions of O'Neill's plays are ideal case studies for examining race in modern theater, not merely because O'Neill is the one of the most celebrated American playwrights (and the only Nobel Prize–winning one), or because his plays have foregrounded discussions of racial hierarchies, but also because performances of his work relied upon extraordinary, and underappreciated, traffic between Broadway and Harlem—between white and Black America. *Racing the Great White Way* shows how O'Neill's dramas, especially when performed by actors of color, transformed modern theater, as they broke color lines, moved productions to alternative venues, cut alternate film versions, and revised scripts through Black performance practices and dramaturgical framings.

To tell this story, I invite readers to wander away from the gleaming lights of Broadway toward gritty theaters in Greenwich Village or the lively Lincoln Theatre in Harlem, where groups like the Provincetown Players and the Lafayette Players engaged in unprecedented theatrical and social experimentation. Venues adjacent to, and far afield from, Broadway were not only major sites of theatrical production but also crucial venues for challenging hegemonic theater institutions during the first part of the twentieth century. Encounters on such stages enacted social change within U.S. society itself, rehearsing not only experiments in democracy, as Cheryl

Black and Jonathan Shandell maintain, but also resistance to racialized hierarchies through the restaging—and altering—of popular scripts.[1] While such productions have often been seen as mere sideshows to a more influential Broadway, they were in fact important performative vehicles for the reimagination of race relations in the United States and beyond. *Racing the Great White Way* examines a rich archive of such performances, and examines their role in a society grappling with modernization and persistent racism.

As W. E. B. Du Bois memorably asserted in 1903, "the problem of the Twentieth Century is the problem of the color-line."[2] While Du Bois was concerned with racial barriers throughout American culture, he was particularly attuned to the theater and had written more than once about Eugene O'Neill's engagement with racial politics. His essay "The Negro and Our Stage," which was reprinted in the playbills for *The Emperor Jones* and for *All God's Chillun Got Wings* in 1924, proclaimed that O'Neill was "bursting through by creating a mine of dramatic material . . . ready for the great artist's hands."[3] If O'Neill's dramas were a source of raw material for African American theater artists to excavate, then they provided the repository for theatrical productions that repeatedly broke color lines on Broadway, at the Metropolitan Opera, and on stages around the world. As important as it was to shatter such barriers, Du Bois also understood that structural reform was necessary. "DuBois's simple yet trenchant words" about the color line, notes Brandi Wilkins Catanese, articulated it "as 'a problem' that could not or would not be solved through incorporation into the dominant society."[4] *Racing the Great White Way* examines theater's "color-line problem" in two distinct ways: first, this book documents noteworthy ruptures of the color line on and beyond Broadway with O'Neill dramas, with fresh discoveries from multiple archives. As the following pages aim to make clear, productions of Eugene O'Neill's plays were instrumental in advancing a more diverse modern theater not only in the U.S. but also across the Atlantic. Second, *Racing the Great White Way* attends to the Du Boisian caution that we must critically examine institutional structures of race, especially how American theater in general—and Broadway in particular—has long upheld, and produced, racial hierarchies.

This book argues that Eugene O'Neill's emphasis on racial themes and conflicts, especially in his early dramas, opened up extraordinary opportunities for Black performers to challenge racist structures in modern theater and cinema. By changing scripts to omit offensive epithets, inserting African American music and dance, or including citations of Black internationalism, theater artists of color used O'Neill's dramatic texts to raze barriers in American and transatlantic theater. It is no accident that Obi Abili, Habib Benglia, Jules Bledsoe, Rex Ingram, James Earl Jones, Dora Cole Norman, Paul Robeson, John Douglas Thompson, Denzel Washington, Forest Whitaker, and Frank Wilson all made their mark in the theater through O'Neill plays. The first Black leading actor in a serious role on Broadway widely seen as breaking the color line? Charles Gilpin in O'Neill's *Emperor Jones*.[5] Broadway's first interracial kiss? O'Neill's *All God's Chillun Got Wings*. The first Black performer to break the color line at the Metropolitan Opera House? Hemsley Winfield in *The Emperor Jones*. The first Black director on Broadway? Charles Gilpin, directing *Jones*. The first Black lead in a major Hollywood picture? Robeson in *The Emperor Jones*. Which play integrated the twentieth-century London stage? *All God's Chillun Got Wings* in 1929. The *Pittsburgh Courier* headline celebrating Jesse Owens's triumph at the 1936 Berlin Olympics? "All God's Chillun Got Wings." The inaugural play for London's Black Unity Theatre in 1944? *All God's Chillun Got Wings*. The first two plays chosen for Brazil's Negro Experimental Theatre in 1945 and 1946? *The Emperor Jones* and *All God's Chillun*. Which play did Habib Benglia choose to launch his Parisian "troupe noir" in 1950? A revival of *L'Empereur Jones*. And Denzel Washington's first role? Brutus Jones. These artistic breakthroughs have had lasting effects beyond the stage: from Habib Benglia's involvement in the Négritude movement to Robeson's political activism. As these case studies demonstrate, in spite of the dichotomous (and at times problematic) representation of Blackness, O'Neill's dramas were utilized by Black theater artists to disrupt racial barriers within U.S. and transatlantic stages and cinemas.

My claim about breakthroughs with the theater of Eugene O'Neill by no means intends to obscure or erase the pioneering work of actors and playwrights of color who came before him. The case of Ira Aldridge (1807–67) immediately comes to mind: an American-born Black actor who made his career in Britain by performing memorable roles in plays such as *Othello*, *The Merchant of Venice*, and *King Lear* in the first half of the nineteenth century. Known as "the first important black American Shakespearean actor," Aldridge apprenticed with the African Company in minor roles before emigrating to England in 1824.[6] He never returned to the U.S. to perform. Another important touchstone in the history of African American theater was the African Grove Company (known as the African Company), the nation's first Black theater company founded by William Henry Brown in 1821; its actors challenged stereotypical presumptions about race on American stages.[7] Their unforgettable production of *Richard III* in 1822 rivaled a British touring production starring Junius Brutus Booth to great acclaim.[8]

Unfortunately, the theater burned down in 1823 under enigmatic circum-stances and Black entertainments shifted elsewhere, often to different genres such as minstrelsy, musical revues, or comedic theater. Vaudeville and musical theater productions made inroads to Broadway with produc-tions written and performed by Black theater artists like *In Dahomey* (1902) and *Bandanna Land* (1907–9), featuring George Walker, Bert Williams, and Aida Overton Walker. In terms of the emergence of serious drama, a sig-nificant development was *Three Plays for a Negro Theater*, a series of one acts that featured all-Black casts that ran for three weeks in 1917. While notable for featuring Black performers, these short plays were not considered sub-stantial works, received mixed reviews, and were created by two white theater artists: Ridgely Torrence (who wrote and directed) and Robert Edmond Jones (who designed).[9] In the 1920s there were five plays by Black playwrights on Broadway, but all of them came after O'Neill's *The Dreamy Kid* (1918) and *The Emperor Jones* (1920), with more limited runs.[10] As I clar-ify more below, companies in the Harlem Little Theatre Movement offered exciting work, often performing Broadway hits in whiteface on Harlem stages. In spite of this artistic activity, as Susan Curtis notes in *The First Black Actors on the Great White Way*, "officially and openly, black actors remained barred from the so-called legitimate theaters"[11] and Broadway was largely closed to them in meaningful roles—until O'Neill.

Writing about Black experience was part of O'Neill's repeated efforts to document voices that had been mostly absent from American mainstream drama. Like the Irish, Swedish, and Norwegian immigrants who popu-lated his early plays, African American characters were part of O'Neill's vision to craft a new American drama featuring diverse stories. His experi-ments with characters of color began in plays such as *Thirst* (1913), *The Moon of the Caribbees* (1917), and *The Dreamy Kid* (1918), and became central to works such as *The Emperor Jones* (1920) and *All God's Chillun Got Wings* (1924); his last Black character appeared in *The Iceman Cometh* (1939).[12] As Deborah Wood Holton observes, "O'Neill created, between 1913 and 1939, sixteen black characters—six male and ten female—who appeared in a total of six plays, the majority of them on stage between 1916 and 1924."[13] Prior to these early O'Neill works, white dramatists mostly relegated Afri-can American characters as one-dimensional servants, slaves, mammies, Uncle Toms, or tragic mulattoes. In a representational regime dominated by plays like *The Octoroon* by Dion Boucicault, *The N— —r* by Edward Shel-don, *Uncle Tom's Cabin* (adapted by numerous dramatists), and *The Clans-man* by Thomas Dixon Jr. (the text on which the film *The Birth of a Nation* was based), the arrival of O'Neill's work was a remarkable step forward.

Most importantly, O'Neill's dramas about Black life broke through because of their innovations in modern (if not modernist) drama. "Never had a Broadway audience seen a black at the head of an all white company performing serious drama," until *The Emperor Jones*, writes John G. Monroe in his study of Black theater in New York.[14] Indeed, Monroe begins his record of Black Broadway with *The Emperor Jones*.

Despite the innovations his work inspired, Eugene O'Neill is not an unproblematic figure in the history of racism on the Great White Way. While O'Neill was the first major American playwright to write Black characters with complexity, he also relied upon stereotypes and forms of primitivism that continue to provoke criticism.[15] Commentary on O'Neill's work was divided on its racial politics from the beginning. Harlem Renaissance intellectuals including Du Bois, Montgomery Gregory, James Weldon Johnson, and Alain Locke praised O'Neill's portrayals of African American characters in the 1920s, although some would later become more critical. In a theater world that had paltry roles for African Americans, *The Emperor Jones* provided new opportunities for actors of color. In evaluating the inroads of Black theater artists into American theater, Alain Locke praised the "sensational successes of 'The Emperor Jones' and 'All God's Chillun Got Wings,'" noting the "fine craftsmanship and clairvoyant genius of O'Neill and the acting gifts of Charles Gilpin and Paul Robeson."[16] In his essay "The Drama of Negro Life," Montgomery Gregory (activist, critic, and founder of the Howard Players) concurred: "Eugene O'Neill, who more than any other person has dignified and popularized Negro drama, gives testimony to the possibilities of the future development of Negro drama."[17] Reflecting on the development of Black drama in *Black Manhattan* (1930), James Weldon Johnson wrote that with *The Emperor Jones* "another important page in the history of the Negro in the theatre was written."[18]

Yet, the mere appearance of complex Black protagonists on the American stage was hardly a solution to the long-standing issues of concern to writers like Langston Hughes, Johnson, and Du Bois. Throughout early twentieth-century American culture, Black intellectuals and theater artists debated the fraught role of white playwrights in creating "negro art."[19] As Locke put it, there was an obsessive, if not misplaced, emphasis on O'Neill's so-called race plays:

> But the preoccupation, almost obsession of otherwise strong and artistic work like O'Neill's *Emperor Jones, All God's Chillun Got Wings* . . . suggests that, in spite of all good intentions, the true pre-

sental [*sic*] of the real tragedy of Negro life is a task still left for Negro writers to perform.[20]

Locke captured a dichotomy crucial to the argument of this book: while O'Neill's dramas were perceived as strong artistic works that challenged entrenched racist conventions, they were not without their flaws and thus highlighted the need for Black theater artists to shape a corpus of dramatic writing. Having achieved "a kind of notoriety and fame for his 'race' plays," O'Neill agreed with Locke, realizing that it was not a position for him to necessarily occupy.[21] In a piece published in the African American magazine *Messenger* in 1925, O'Neill encouraged Black playwrights to create innovative dramatic writing to reflect their own ambitions and experiences, and not imitate white theater.

If I have one thing to say—(and I grant that "I" is a presumption)—to Negroes who work, or have the ambition to work, in any field of artistic expression it is this: Be yourselves! Don't reach out for *our* stuff which *we* call good! Make *your stuff* and *your good*! . . . There ought to be a Negro play written by a Negro that no white could ever have conceived or executed. . . . *your own*, an expression of what is deep in you, *is* you, *by* you!![22]

In spite of his somewhat paternalistic tone, O'Neill's call for Black drama echoed Du Bois's plea for a new "Negro" theater "about us," "by us," and "for us," and "near us," in an essay published in 1926.[23] Until that writing arrived, it was the combination of O'Neill's bold embrace of racial themes and this desire for self-representation that made O'Neill's work such a prominent vehicle for Black innovation in theater.

Even as O'Neill turned away from writing about racial themes after *All God's Chillun Got Wings* in 1924, he was still contributing to, and supporting, a corpus of Black writing. For example, at Du Bois's request, O'Neill judged the 1925 Spingarn Play Competition sponsored by *The Crisis* and in 1931 O'Neill joined the Du Bois Literary Prize Advisory Board (the nominating committee included Du Bois and James Weldon Johnson).[24] As late as 1941, Locke included O'Neill's *The Emperor Jones* and *All God's Chillun Got Wings* in a list of an "impressive succession" of plays that marked "the vital place of the drama of Negro life in contemporary American drama."[25] With *The Iceman Cometh*, O'Neill penned the last of his Black characters (Joe Mott) and turned his attention to crafting masterpieces about his Irish American family. While O'Neill had moved on to other topics, his earlier plays featuring African American characters were revived for decades on stages all over the world, breaking color lines and raising questions about white supremacy in the theater, the role of imperial power, and Black sovereignty.

RACING BROADWAY

Throughout this book, I use the term *racing* in multiple ways. First, while my primary focus is on performative interventions by actors of color, I also bring to light the investment in Blackness by Irish-American interpreters of O'Neill (including actor Dudley Digges, director Dudley Murphy, opera singer Lawrence Tibbett, among others). As the following case studies show, there are compelling reciprocities between minority cultures in the Black and green Atlantics—seen especially in the theater of Eugene O'Neill.[26] O'Neill had a track record of creating works that featured Black life as a way of negotiating his own Irishness, at a time when Irish Americans were just beginning to be seen as white. Whiteness has long been an arbitrary racialized category whose ontological parameters had shifted over the years. Anxieties about "race suicide" had shaped how new immigrants were seen as threatening the fabricated notion of whiteness in late nineteenth and early twentieth-century U.S. culture.[27] Insofar as "the construction of race is predicated on its obsessive performance," as Robyn Wiegman has observed, performances of O'Neill's dramas troubled some of the racialized binaries so crucial to conceptualizations of race in the U.S.[28] While the Irish were "an oppressed race in Ireland," observes Noel Ignatiev in *How the Irish Became White*, once they emigrated to America, they were seen as racialized minorities, "commonly thrown together with free Negroes," until they inched their way toward whiteness. Thus, "in becoming white the Irish ceased to be Green."[29] Productions of O'Neill's plays examined here reveal the messy through lines and realignments of Irishness, Blackness, and whiteness as registers of ever-evolving sociopolitical and racialized discourses in U.S. culture.

Second, "racing" references the ways in which African American actors changed the landscape of American theater through their embodied practices on the stage and beyond by incorporating resistant performance practices to recontextualize meanings of O'Neill's dramas. Numerous Black theater artists utilized O'Neill's plays as launching pads to break through color lines and challenge what Cedric J. Robinson calls "regimes of race" on the Great White Way and beyond.[30] At its core, *Racing the Great*

White Way is a book that attends to the interventions by theater-makers of color both on and off the stage; it is about how they "raced" O'Neill's dramas with citations of Black diasporic power. Racing is therefore not merely a figurative trope but also *performative*, enacting cultural work that is inscribed upon the contours of performing bodies and within cultural practices. This concerns not only the characters on the page but also the actors' embodied practices. In shifting my analysis away from the text (or, archive)—and turning toward the repertoire, as Diana Taylor would say—I show how actors constituted alternative embodied archives by racing mainstream stages through O'Neill.[31] Paul Robeson's performance of Jim Harris, a character who repeatedly fails the bar exam and is destroyed by racism in O'Neill's *All God's Chillun Got Wings*, for instance, was offset by three other performative framings: the invocation of Black diasporic rulers in the production, Robeson's commanding performance of *The Emperor Jones* on alternating weeks, and the well-known fact that Robeson had earned his law degree from Columbia University. To take another example, Habib Benglia's reclamation and revision of the iconic Witch-Doctor character from *L'Empereur Jones*, which he performed in his own Montparnasse nightclub, offered a counterperformance to the colonial imaginary seen during Paris's 1931 Colonial Exposition. And Robeson's portrayal of the famous revolutionary in C. L. R. James's *Toussaint Louverture: The Story of the Only Successful Slave Revolt in History* performatively cited O'Neill's Black emperor. These productions shared so many similarities, I show in chapter 1, that publicity photos of *Toussaint Louverture* in the Museum of the City of New York are mislabeled as images from *The Emperor Jones*. Robeson's invocation of American and diasporic leaders (John Henry, Toussaint Louverture, and Marcus Garvey) cemented his authority as a cultural icon in the U.S. and abroad, opening up a circum-Atlantic critique of imperial power with performative citations of Black sovereignty.

My focus on "racing" moreover attends to the disruption of normative casting practices such as blackface and the racial hierarchies that governed hegemonic entertainments. Following Brandi Wilkins Catenese's notion of racial transgression, I argue that the practice of "racing" American and transnational theater with O'Neill's dramas broke color lines to "expose the limits placed upon racial discourse in order to violate them and force the possibility of progressive action."[32] By attending to archival findings, I bring to light actors who "raced" Broadway and other mainstream venues: those theater artists who transgressed and exposed racial privilege in mainstream entertainments during the first part of the twentieth century. Many of the actors and artists discussed in this project can be viewed as what Daphne A. Brooks might call "bodies in dissent," artists who rose up against racialized constraints both on and off the stage while performing in O'Neill's plays.[33] By telling some of their stories, *Racing the Great White Way* accounts for dissenting performances in breakthrough performances: from the 1923 Paris production of *L'Empereur Jones* to the 1929 production of *All God's Chillun Got Wings* that integrated the British stage.

Racing the Great White Way attends to a fourth connotation of "racing" by documenting the kinetic force of theater productions *in motion*: performances that moved across space and time while dragging the rubble of racism and also carving out new terrain. Racing moreover encapsulates the importance of embodied velocity of "race in motion" to investigate the historiographical traces of bodies moving among and between racialized contexts.[34] A theater piece is never static, nor singular, but ever changing: an index of culture in motion. *Racing the Great White Way* therefore investigates momentum, whether it involves an artistic production moving across the cartography of Manhattan, an advertisement shifting from the back of the newspaper to the front, or radical casting changes on national stages. Productions of O'Neill's dramas raced up and down Broadway, among diverse racialized spaces, and across the Atlantic: from the 1921 prison theater performance of *The Emperor Jones* to the 1945 inaugural Brazilian production of *All God's Chillun Got Wings*; from the Metropolitan Opera House to Harlem theaters; from Broadway to London. My argument applies to cinema as well. The 1933 film adaptation of *The Emperor Jones*, I show in chapter 5, was a film-in-motion, cut differently for spectators in the North and South, and again for Black audiences, who objected to the use of racial epithets in the film.

Most importantly, *Racing the Great White Way* attends to productions that ply a layering of time periods—and their citational tugs. Each chapter in this book therefore charts the performative afterlives of O'Neill plays and their adaptations (as drama, film, opera, and dance), as they move across space and time and among genres and continents, serving as dramaturgical vehicles for actors' interventions. Performances traverse not only space but also time, such that the past is *"on the move . . . co-present, not 'left behind.'"*[35] This is the radical promise, Dwight Conquergood reminds us, of shifting our mode of analysis away from *poesis* to *kinesis*, whereby the "breaking and remaking" of performance is made clear.[36] Time moves at various speeds, like gushing water, or a glacier, with force and accretion. Productions are iterative, dynamic manifestations, gathering debris along the way, carving out gullies, and reshaping cartographies. At times, these performances made deposits, such as rubble from a flood, creating layered sediments or vast fertile terrains. The Black theater artists examined here invoked polytemporalities by citing historical moments to reorient O'Neill productions within racialized contexts, even those that they could not have possibly remembered, like Brutus Jones having a flashback of enduring the Middle Passage.[37] Or, to take other examples, Robeson incorporated slave work ballads into *The Emperor Jones* to underscore the importance of unpaid Black labor, while Gilpin referenced the legacy of anti-Black racism by wearing a Confederacy buckle for his Brutus Jones.

Finally, racing also has to do with spectatorship. As productions navigated away from the Great White Way, or altered Broadway's offerings, audiences at O'Neill plays critically viewed these productions against the grain, racing spectatorship to constitute counternarratives and epistemologies.[38] For example, Dora Cole Norman's portrayal of Hattie, Jim's outspoken sister in *All God's Chillun Got Wings*, incited white audiences when she challenged Jim's wife's racism.[39] Black spectators, on the other hand, applauded this scene, constructing oppositional spectatorship. In other O'Neill productions, African American spectators insisted that changes be made, thereby reconstituting new dramatic and filmic versions.

REMAPPING BROADWAY

The Great White Way has never been entirely great nor white. This is not news; and, yet, the myths persist. Traditional historical narratives of U.S. theater profoundly misunderstand its complexity. "Black expressive culture," E. Patrick Johnson observes, "has, until recently, been illegible and unintelligible to the undiscerning eyes and ears, and perhaps minds, of some scholars."[40] A look at the Internet Broadway Database or in conventional theater history books underscores this problem: many of the theater artists discussed in this project have Broadway credits for shows with white authors and directors, but their work in Harlem or on unconventional stages is often not recorded. This strange "critical amnesia" typifies the hegemonic critical treatment of works by theater artists of color: initially praising them, and then, by the end of the season or some years later, excluding them.[41] Such omissions present both a challenge and an opportunity for scholars of Black theater. Recent work has begun to unravel the tenacious hold of the Broadway narrative to interrogate which kinds of bodies, performance spaces, and, indeed, continents, count as legitimate parts of its history.[42] *Racing the Great White Way* builds upon these contributions to reshape our understanding of the rise of modern theater and performance practices while also attending to constructions of race and deployments of racial performativity.

Just as the Great White Way has never been a hermetically sealed cultural institution, so Broadway has never been a straight-and-narrow avenue. A creation of early nineteenth-century urban planning, Broadway was designed as a central artery cutting across Manhattan, significant not only for entertainment but also for transport and commerce. In her history of theater in New York City, Mary C. Henderson observes how "after 1850, Broadway was to become established as the center for New York's principal theatrical activity."[43] As a theater district Broadway was never defined literally as confined to the avenue itself, but was rather an ever-evolving district that included intersecting side streets. Fewer than a dozen of the eighty-five theaters had Broadway addresses and by the 1920s only "twelve of the Broadway district theatres were actually on Broadway," observes Brooks Atkinson.[44] Most theaters were, rather, situated on cross streets within two blocks of Broadway, beginning with 38th Street and continuing up to 63rd Street.[45] This distinction is both pragmatic and symbolic, for what we think "belongs" to Broadway is often attached to other spaces and performance practices. Harlem is literally off Henderson's map, a pattern in many historical narratives. Such conflations of Broadway as a theatrical institution with Broadway Avenue abound in historical narratives. Yet the stages on and near Broadway have always leaked out and into other venues, just as they have absorbed innovations near to it.

We need only look to the shape of Broadway to see what has been hidden in plain sight all along. Broadway stands out as the least straight line in Manhattan's meticulously planned grid. It juts diagonally across Manhattan, an emblem of connection to neighborhoods with different racial, gendered, classed, and sexual identities. From downtown immigrant theaters, to elite Upper West Side performance venues, to Gumby's queer salons in Harlem, Broadway is not straight in more way than one. The German verb *queren*, which means "to cross," aptly captures how Broadway crosses the topography of Manhattan. *Quer* can also be translated as something that is crosswise, diagonal, slant—not straight. The affinity of the word *quer* with "queer" designates a crossing of straight lines and heteronormative spaces. As Siobhan Somerville writes, "It was not merely a historical coincidence that the classification of bodies as either 'homosexual' or 'heterosexual' emerged at the same time that the United States was aggressively constructing and policing the boundary between 'black' and white' bodies."[46] Indeed, deployments of race and sexuality were deeply intertwined, and the surveillance—and, crucially, the *performance*—of racialized bodies were linked with hegemonic notions of homo-and hetero-sexuality. As cartographic metaphors, then, crossing and racing indicate an active cutting through Manhattan's theater district and beyond, to defy the straight and narrow contours, to show the intersections and mutually constitutive discourses of race and (homo)sexuality.

This kind of intersectional analysis is central to my dragging of the archive to account for performative interventions by Jules Bledsoe and Hemsley Winfield—two queer Black performers who invoked O'Neill's work to defy heteronormative notions of Black masculinity. It's important to note that "archival drag," as David Román characterizes this methodological approach, attunes not only to queer performances but also to embodied archival systems of those who are marginal or subcultural: "Performance lives not only in the memory of those who witness it," writes Román, "but also in the vestiges, artifacts, and performances that survive into a later cultural moment where they may be reembodied by other actors and received by other audiences."[47] In order to attend to this complexity, we must use an alternate cartography and performance methodology—one that interrogates and queers long-standing narratives of a straight Great White Way. Racing Broadway therefore means going off road. The case studies in this book demonstrate how performance crosses disciplines, cultures, topographical boundaries, and assumptions regarding what constitutes "legitimate" American theater and identities. Productions such as *The Emperor Jones* and *All God's Chillun Got Wings* traversed unusual coordinates along diverse theatrical grids over spans of time, extending the archive beyond traditional cartographies of power.

By traveling these routes, *Racing the Great White Way* unveils a new performative cartography of early twentieth-century American and transatlantic performance, revealing vibrant intersectional cultural scenes. Consider a 1907 headline in *Theatre Magazine*—"From Broadway to the Bowery"—that noted a geographically puzzling career move of an "actress of foreign birth," Yiddish actress Fernanda Eliscu. Instead of developing her acting chops "in obscure theatres of the East Side" and making her "debut in Broadway theatres with signal success," the actress "did it in reverse," starting on the Great White Way and descending into the working class, immigrant-rich Bowery.[48] The point of the *Theatre Magazine* story is that this trajectory was out of step with prevailing Broadway wisdom: "From Broadway to the Bowery, from English dramas to those in the Yiddish dialect. Usually it is the other way." And, indeed, usually the artistic movement usually *was* in the other direction. This unconventional shift signaled not only a racialized "slide" into Manhattan's unseemly cartography (the bowels of the Bowery) but also an aesthetic "downgrade," turning away from performances of classics with Fiske's Empire Theatre to perform Yiddish drama instead (in this case a translation of *Marta of the Lowlands*). A downtown relocation was inconceivable to Broadway logic, but that was precisely the point: the production was seeking Yiddish audiences beyond the Great White Way. The shift was also linguistic: from English to Yiddish. As the article put it, "After many successes on Broadway she has gone to the Bowery to act in a strange and uncouth tongue."[49] The Jewish actress was racing the Great White Way, but *Theatre Magazine* could only make sense of it by denigrating Yiddish as "strange" and "uncouth," implying that the Bowery was the grit to Broadway's pearls.

Movement *uptown* from Broadway to Harlem demonstrated other racialized patterns and entertainments. During the Harlem Renaissance, white audiences and actors often "raced up" to Black theaters and cabarets, where they saw, and sometimes poached, original work and performance practices. Black theater companies in the Harlem Little Theatre Movement—a brainchild of Alain Locke, Willis Richardson, and W. E. B. Du Bois—offered productions that signified upon, and raced, the harsh portraits on Broadway. During this time period, the Anita Bush Dramatic Stock Company (later renamed the Lafayette Players), the Lincoln Players, and the Krigwa Players hatched exciting work.[50] White audiences regularly traveled uptown to see the offerings, as the theater critic for the African American newspaper *New York Age*, Lester Walton, observed in 1920:

> It is beginning to dawn on the managers and actor[s] on Broadway that something worthy of more than passing consideration . . . is taking place weekly at the Lafayette Theatre further uptown. . . . Nowadays stage celebrities in goodly numbers are wending their way to Seventh Avenue and 131st Street by limousine to look upon the efforts of these colored thespians with [a] serious eye.[51]

Yet white Broadway actors were not only seeing Black productions—they were also stealing from them. This obsessive pattern of "borrowing" Black cultural materials for white consumption, or "love and theft," as Eric Lott has characterized it, was pervasive among white Americans within "the haunted realm of racial fantasy," which harkened back to minstrelsy entertainments and to slavery itself.[52] As an article from the *Pittsburgh Courier* warned, "White Actors Steal Your Art, Take Your Place and Your Job."[53]

> Every day one can see white stage aspirants from downtown wend-
> ing their way to Harlem to cabarets, night clubs, dance halls. They
> keep coming for weeks and months—these nervy white lads. They
> are determined to grab all they can from you, free. They finally do,
> then they stop coming. They fade right out of the picture. A month
> or so later you see them down Broadway—blackface and all—
> looking just like you. They even got your talk and do all your steps.
> Not just as good as you, certainly. But just good enough for the man-
> ager to hire him in your place.[54]

This cultural theft, recast in white-produced entertainments made up of
racist stereotypes, typified many offerings on the Great White Way.

By contrast, the poaching of Broadway standards by Black theater artists demonstrated a different pattern. With dramaturgical innovations and
radical casting, theater artists of color were able to race repertoires and
make them their own. The Lafayette Players, for instance, "sampled" and
revised Broadway productions with remixed productions. The Lafayette
Players performed "abbreviated versions of recent Broadway hits. . . . The
plays were not about black people, and, if the actors were not light enough
to pass for white, they would lighten their skins with make-up."[55] By revis-
ing the minstrel practice of "whiting up," Black performers "interrogate[d]
privileged or authoritative representations of whiteness."[56] They were in
effect dismantling the binary logic governing racial hierarchies, a practice
that Faedra C. Carpenter has described as "coloring whiteness," a process
by which "African American artists resist[ed] the presentation of whiteness
as normative and, in the process, expose[d] the fallacies associated with
racial designations."[57] At times, Broadway producers were unaware of
these borrowings. Anita Bush recounted with amusement: "No one on
Broadway, least of all David Belasco, knew that we had 'borrowed' his
play, *The Girl of the Golden West*. No matter to whom it had originally
belonged, for the week it belonged to The Anita Bush Stock Company and
they gave it to Harlem."[58] Unlike the predatory stealing of theatrical innovation of Black theater artists by white performers, Bush turned their
poaching of Broadway hits into a gift to the community.

Performers of color weren't only "whiting up" in Black theater companies; they were also appearing in Broadway shows, albeit in minor, and
often stereotypically racialized, roles. "For years the colored performer has
been sadly declaring that his field is limited," reported the *New York Age* in
1916, "given that his color permit[s] him to appear on the stage as a Negro
only, maybe occasionally as an Oriental."[59] Black performers were increas-

ingly populating Broadway stages.[60] The 1922 Ziegfeld Follies number, "It's Getting Dark on Broadway," playfully noted how "the Great White Way was white no more":

> We used to brag about the Broadway White Lights
> The very famous dazzling White Way nightlights
> They used to glare and glimmer
> But they are growing dimmer
> If you go out on a lark
> Just take a tip from me, take a trip you will see
> Broadway is getting quite dark.[61]

The lyrics lampoon the hypocrisy governing the Great White Way: even as "darktown entertainers hold the stage," they must "black up to be the latest rage." By 1927, the Great White Way was darker yet: "Race Stage Stars Are Numerous on Broadway," reported the *Pittsburgh Courier*.[62] "The American drama, if Broadway is to be taken as a criterion," continued the *Courier*, "will appear this year against a brown background."[63] The *Courier* not only questions Broadway as the epicenter of American drama but also shows how mainstream white theater achieved its success on the backs of actors of color.

While *Racing the Great White Way* is anchored in investigating Broadway productions of O'Neill, it also attends to the vibrant transnational exchange in early to mid-twentieth-century artistic production. The theater of Eugene O'Neill challenged racial boundaries well beyond Manhattan, across the Atlantic and within circum-Atlantic spheres. As Shannon Steen suggests, "Race is not a domestic, internally derived national formation, but is shaped by international dynamics as well, and shapes those dynamics in return."[64] *Racing the Great White Way* recovers not only vital lost performance histories but also the layered contexts for performing bodies across the Black Atlantic and the circum-Atlantic. The playbill for the 1924 New York revival of *The Emperor Jones*, for instance, included an illustration of the set design for the 1923 Paris production featuring Algerian actor Habib Benglia. Described as "decidedly African" in the Provincetown Players' playbill, this production reminded American audiences of the connections between O'Neill's Brutus Jones rule over an uncolonized West Indian island and colonial revolt within the Black diaspora.[65]

This is a crucial moment to dismantle the mythology of the Great White Way. As I write, many of us grieve the murders of George Floyd, Breonna Taylor, and countless other Black people who have died while in police custody or suffered from other forms of racism. Theater artists have recently responded to the call to enact antiracist practices, not only in reimagining artistic productions but also how we write about it. *Racing the Great White Way* speaks to the urgency of antiracist scholarly practice by critically reexamining racial hierarchies in the world of theater—and beyond. With a focus on Black performance nearly a century ago, *Racing the Great White Way* traces the through lines between breaking color lines in American theater and culture and the #BlackLivesMatter movement. Central to this story is not only the documentation of oppression of theater artists of color but also accounts of how Black performers resisted those forces to stage their craft.

CHAPTER OVERVIEWS

Racing the Great White Way contains an introduction, five chapters, and a conclusion. The first chapter, "The Emperor's Remains," demonstrates how Eugene O'Neill's expressionist drama *The Emperor Jones* (1920) dismantled racial barriers for decades on U.S. stages and, indeed, across the Atlantic. Hotly debated for decades, *The Emperor Jones* facilitated major breakthroughs in the theater and American culture more generally. As a central case study for this book, *The Emperor Jones*'s performance history demonstrates the kinetic force of racing American theater and film: it was a production constantly morphing, carrying the residue of racism while transforming the racial landscape of American theater through Black theater artists' performative interventions. This chapter examines multiple actors (from Charles Gilpin to Paul Robeson), sites of performance (from Greenwich Village to Broadway), racialized spheres (from Harlem theaters to the Metropolitan Opera), and genres (from independent theater to race cinema). Captured by Aaron Douglas's woodcut series, *The Emperor Jones* was an opportunity for Black actors to embody defiance, break color lines, and craft their own artistry. As the productions in this chapter show, *The Emperor Jones* was a play that theater artists of color embraced, but also adapted, while establishing repertory theaters throughout the world.

The second chapter, "An Algerian in Paris," takes up matters of the diaspora, transnational performance, and imperial representations. My analysis of an overlooked production of *L'Empereur Jones* in Paris in 1923 by French-speaking Algerian actor Habib Benglia notes his uncanny performance, as a colonized subject, of a despotic Emperor. Performed for French and American dignitaries at the Théâtre de l'Odéon, one of France's state theaters, Benglia's production literally staged what Homi K. Bhabha calls the "ambivalence of colonial discourse."[66] Benglia embodied the tension between empire and colonial subject, performing the spectacle of a failing Emperor (and failing empire). His portrayal of a tyrannical ruler who is destroyed by the Indigenous people of the island prefigured the Algerian struggle for freedom from France. Benglia's performance was, moreover, a theoretical intervention: the actor conducted a postcolonial critique through performance, inserting what Brent Hayes Edwards has called a "wedge" into previously conceived imperial exchange.[67] Benglia went on to perform the Witch-Doctor character from *The Emperor Jones* in his Paris nightclub at the same time as he developed a career in French cinema, signifying upon constructions of imperialism beyond the stage and screen.

My third chapter, "Broadway's First Interracial Kiss," examines the stakes of portraying miscegenation while crossing geographical, racial, and genre boundaries. The tumultuous 1924 premiere of *All God's Chillun Got Wings* ignited headlines predicting race riots if white actress Mary Blair kissed Black actor Paul Robeson's hand, leading one critic to call the play "the most radical" production of the 1920s. *All God's Chillun* also staged Broadway's first interracial kiss. The work of America's most famous "black Irish" playwright, *All God's Chillun Got Wings* lays bare the entanglements between Irish and Black minority cultures, as well as racial performativity. While some scholars have suggested that Robeson's portrayal of Jim in *All God's Chillun Got Wings* was a sellout to white theater, I situate Robeson's role alongside his invocation of diasporic rulers (especially Marcus Garvey and Toussaint Louverture), his work in Black theater (*Roseanne*), and his roles in race cinema (*Body and Soul*), which he was performing at the same time. This performative citation of Black diasporic identity yields moreover an uncanny foreshadowing of Robeson's increasing disenchantment with American politics and his civil rights activism.

Operatic adaptations of *The Emperor Jones* by both white and Black theater artists serve as the central case study of the fourth chapter, "Racing Operatic Emperors," which highlights the racialized performance history of opera within Black performance culture and white entertainment establishments. On the one hand, *Jones* featured white opera singer Lawrence Tibbett performing in blackface at the Metropolitan Opera, effectively reinstating the racial barriers that O'Neill had razed by casting Gilpin in 1920. On the other hand, the production broke the color line when African American dance pioneer Hemsley Winfield played the memorable Congo Witch-Doctor to great acclaim. My analysis of operatic adaptations of *The Emperor Jones* by both white and Black composers and performers documents their performative interventions at the Metropolitan Opera House, stages in Harlem, and beyond. I look particularly at two Black queer performers, Hemsley Winfield and Jules Bledsoe, who raced O'Neill's text in nonhegemonic venues. This chapter also reveals my discovery of Bledsoe's own adaptation of the opera that is not only Afro-centric but also portrays Jones with more strength and dignity.

Chapter 5, "Racing the Cut: Black to Ireland," shows how *Jones* was a film aimed at critiquing empire while also evoking the Black diaspora. The film was created by a team of Irish American artists (O'Neill, director Dudley Murphy, and actor Dudley Digges). Their work on *The Emperor Jones* came from a commitment to the idea that the colonization of Ireland shared synergies with the results of anti-Black racism, colonialism, and imperialism (although not similar), and as a way of negotiating their own contested relationship with legitimating structures in white, U.S. culture. The film's racial politics, which have been debated since its premiere, repeatedly interlinks a range of global and circum-Atlantic legacies of white imperialism. *The Emperor Jones* abounds with contradictions: it both shattered racial constraints in American film and articulated racial anxieties. The film's anti-imperialist, antiracist ambitions are visible in the director's attempt to overlay different cartographies, memories, and experiences of racial violation through a technique I call "circum-Atlantic double exposure." The film is also marked by what I call "race cuts," the imprint of state censors and local projectionists who spliced out potentially inflammatory material from the film. These two strikingly divergent and paradoxical features of the film—the director's accretions and the state's depletions—expose the problematics of representing imperial violence. I compare this version of the film to one cut for Black audiences—analyzed here for the first time in detail. This version of the film, I argue, "raced" the official cut, constituting a competing archive and a performative diptych with the Library of Congress restored version, which sought to replicate the original film.

ONE

The Emperor's Remains

The one thing that explains more than anything about me is
the fact that I'm Irish.[1]
   —Eugene O'Neill

I created that role of the Emperor. That role belongs to me.
That Irishman, he just wrote the play.[2]
   —Charles Gilpin

He's the Emperor.[3]
   —*New York Amsterdam News*, referring to actor
   Paul Robeson

When Paul Robeson stepped into the role of Brutus Jones in 1924, Eugene
O'Neill's famous drama had already played successfully for four years. *The
Emperor Jones* was one of the most widely performed and traveled cultural
artifacts of early twentieth-century America. It was also among the most
contested. It was through *The Emperor Jones* that major breakthroughs in the
theater and cinema were made, even as it was hotly debated for its racial
stereotypes. In spite of these contradictions, *The Emperor Jones* razed racial
barriers throughout American theater and, indeed, across the Atlantic. As a
central case study for *Racing the Great White Way*, *The Emperor Jones*'s performance history attests to the interracial artistic traffic among Harlem, Greenwich Village, and Broadway, and, especially, to the ways in which African
American actors transformed the racial landscape of American mainstream
theater through their performative interventions.

   Initially staged at the Provincetown Playhouse in 1920, *The Emperor
Jones* resonated with a variety of Black theater artists as a vehicle to challenge the Great White Way—a practice that I refer to as "racing" (see introduction). *The Emperor Jones* was the first Broadway commercial success in
which an African American actor was cast in a serious, leading role (Charles
Gilpin in 1920); it was also the first African American–directed play on
Broadway (Gilpin again, in 1926). In 1923, Algerian actor Habib Benglia

broke the color line in Paris by performing *L'Empereur Jones* at the Théâtre de l'Odéon for a nation that had colonized his own. An operatic adaptation of *The Emperor Jones* broke the color line at the Metropolitan Opera House in 1933 when Hemsley Winfield danced the role of the Congo Witch-Doctor. And the film version of *The Emperor Jones* was the first major studio-produced feature film with a Black leading actor—Paul Robeson—released for national distribution for white and Black audiences.[4] *The Emperor Jones* sparked breakthroughs in other cultural production, such as a race film adaptation by Oscar Micheaux, *Body and Soul* (1925, with Robeson); a satiric film, *The Black King* (1932); the first Black-authored play on a British stage with an all-Black cast, *Toussaint Louverture: The Story of the Only Successful Slave Revolt in History* by C. L. R. James (1936); and the feature film *Song of Freedom* (1936, also starring Robeson).[5] *The Emperor Jones* moreover extended beyond Manhattan, playing outdoors in Pennsylvania, in Black theaters in Southern California, at European national theaters, and in countless productions throughout America's heartland. By 1926, just six years after its premiere, *The Emperor Jones* had been performed in New York, Paris, Berlin, Prague, Vienna, and Tokyo, breaking color lines around the world.

The Emperor Jones was one of O'Neill's modernist experiments—an expressionistic play resembling a monologue more than a full-length drama. The action of the play pursues Brutus Jones, a former Pullman porter, who lands in prison after a gambling fight turns deadly. The action of the play takes place after Jones escapes to an uncolonized island in the West Indies and convinces the inhabitants that he possesses immortal powers. He quickly assumes the role of Emperor, presiding over a cockney British sidekick named Smithers and an island of Indigenous people led by a Witch-Doctor. Ultimately the native people revolt against Jones's greed and exploitation. They pursue him, to the beat of an ever-increasing tom-tom drum, into the jungle, where Jones encounters memories, visions, and, ultimately, death by his own silver bullet.[6]

While *The Emperor Jones* is a drama that scholars have long critiqued for its stereotypes, derision of Black empire, and use of offensive racial epithets (the n-word appears thirty-four times), it nonetheless broke with previous writing about African Americans, especially by white playwrights. In spite of its contradictions, *The Emperor Jones* was one of the first American dramas that portrayed a Black character of strength and complexity. As W. E. B. Du Bois wrote, "it was not until Eugene O'Neill's *The Emperor Jones* (1920), that the Negro became the central protagonist of a drama."[7] Montgomery Gregory (activist, critic, and founder of the Howard Players) concurred, having himself played the role of Brutus Jones at Howard University. He wrote in the 1925 playbill for *The Emperor Jones*:

Fig. 1. *Defiance* (sometimes called *The Fugitive*), one of four wood block prints from Aaron Douglas's *Emperor Jones Series* that appeared in Alain Locke's *Plays of Negro Life*. Set of 4 Prints (series title), 1926 (printed 1972). Detroit Institute of Arts, Museum Purchase, General Art Purchase Fund.

> In any further development of Negro drama, *The Emperor Jones*, written by O'Neill, interpreted by Gilpin and produced by the Provincetown Players, will tower as a beacon-light of inspiration. It marks the breakwater plunge of Negro drama into the stream of American drama.[8]

Gregory makes two points that are central to my argument: first, *The Emperor Jones* broke color lines, not unlike a rupture in a levee, as he says, to usher in new dramas about Black experience; and second, actors such as Gilpin and Robeson were crucial makers of theater—essential partners in interpreting, if not creating, O'Neill's works—as well as architects of American performance culture.

Even as it signified as problematic, *The Emperor Jones* became a symbol of defying what Cedric J. Robinson calls "regimes of race" on the Great White Way.[9] Its disruptive force was captured in *Defiance* (sometimes called *The Fugitive*), one of four woodcuts from Aaron Douglas's *Emperor Jones Series* that appeared in Alain Locke's *Plays of Negro Life* (1925).[10] A play that is fraught with contradictions, *The Emperor Jones* nonetheless became a vehicle for Black theater artists to defy not only the Great White Way but also stages throughout the circum-Atlantic.[11] This dichotomy is crucial to understanding its importance: on the one hand, *The Emperor Jones* conjured primitivistic (if not fatal) notions of Black sovereignty. Yet, on the other hand, the play showcased Black male actors portraying an emperor, a significant departure from the menial roles previously scripted in white theater and minstrelsy entertainments. As Charles Musser observes, "Although a controversial work from the outset, and one the African American community found particularly problematic, *The Emperor Jones* did possess significant progressive attributes, if not as an isolated text, then as a piece performed in 1920s America."[12] The play was an opportunity for Black actors to embody defiance, break color lines, and craft their own artistry.

The *Emperor Jones* productions highlighted in the pages to follow demonstrate the kinetic force of racing American theater: it was a production *on the move*, ever changing, while defying (to reference Aaron Douglas's woodcuts) racial barriers. Subsequent productions reinstated the color line, only for future productions to break it again. "This double movement of memory forward and backward is repetition's time signature," observe Soyica Diggs Colbert, Douglas A. Jones Jr., and Shane Vogel.[13] This is somewhat akin to the metered time of racing the Great White Way, which is not unlike the time signature of a musical score, where measures of regular beats are often followed by rests. You must wait. And count. You begin again but then are directed to return to the very beginning of the stanza only to repeat the verse again (but, crucially, with different words). After some repetition, you can move on again. Carving out new terrain, *Emperor Jones* productions raced forward along the Great White Way only to be slowed down by towing the rubble of racism. To take one example, in the original Provincetown Players production in which Charles Gilpin famously broke the color line, the part of Lem, the "Native Chief," was performed in blackface by white actor Charles Ellis.[14] Similarly, the 1924 revival with Robeson as Brutus Jones featured white actor William Stahl as Lem darkened with burnt cork. A 1925 production headlined by Robeson jettisoned blackface performance for the role of Lem (now portrayed by Black actor Frank Wilson), but also included white actors in blackface for minor roles (for example, James Meighan as the Congo Witch-Doctor). In 1927, an Abbey Theatre production in Dublin featured Irish actor Rutherford Mayne in blackface who earned the dubious distinction of being "the first white actor to play Brutus Jones."[15] When Hemsley Winfield and his New Negro Art Theatre Dance Group were the first Black performers on the Metropolitan Opera House stage in 1933, the leading role was performed by white baritone Lawrence Tibbett in blackface. And one year after Robeson broke into feature films, Al Jolson appeared in *The Emperor Jones* on the radio (in what we might call sonic blackface).[16] Such performative contradictions in the performance history of O'Neill's works attest to the irregular time signature of racial progress in the theater, as within society: racing forward, returning back.

The *Emperor Jones* was also a play that theater artists of color embraced to establish repertory theaters throughout the Black diaspora. Some all-Black companies played all of the roles, even those portraying white characters, and in so doing "colored whiteness," to use Faedra Chatard Carpenter's term, to "expose the fallacies associated with racial designations."[17] For example, in the 1938 Federal Theatre Project's *Emperor Jones* staged in Salem, Massachusetts, the white role of Cockney Smithers was "colored" by Jamaican American actor Frank Silvera.[18] Billed as an "all-Negro production," this staging featured Ralf Coleman, the director of the Massachusetts "Negro Unit" Federal Theatre, as Brutus Jones, who also directed *Jones*. Similar breakthroughs occurred abroad. In Brazil, *The Emperor Jones* was "most influential in motivating Black theatre" there; and, in 1945, the inaugural production for Brazil's Negro Experimental Theatre was *The Emperor Jones*.[19] In Paris, the "troupe noir," Compagnie des Argonautes, produced a "voodoo" *L'Empereur Jones* in 1950 to launch its season.[20] In sum, as this chapter demonstrates, the performance history of *The Emperor*

Fig. 2. Poster for the all-Black Federal Theatre Project's 1938 production of *The Emperor Jones* in Salem, Massachusetts. Library of Congress, Music Division, Federal Theatre Project Collection

Jones reveals the uneven tug and pull of the Emperor's remains, providing a snapshot of the contested terrain of performing race in U.S. culture.

BLACKFACE, BLACK IRISH

If functioning as a "beacon light of inspiration" in breaking color lines, as Gregory put it in 1920, *The Emperor Jones* also unveils the problematic, yet

common, use of blackface performance in early twentieth-century theater—as well as the cultural stakes of dismantling it. "There is no doubt,"
writes Johan Callens, "that *The Emperor Jones* did much to alter the racial
politics of the theater by helping to oust blackface."[21] As has been amply
documented, blackface minstrelsy had been a widely accepted performance practice on transatlantic stages since the nineteenth century, often
with Irish performers.[22] The connections and tensions between Irishness
and Blackness, as Robinson notes, were complex in the new American
republic, especially with Irish minstrelsy, where many "would have
thought that an Irishman masquerading as Black was redundant."[23] Indeed,
O'Neill's investment in Black performance culture can be understood
through his identity as "that Irishman," as Gilpin famously called him.[24]
Irish scholar Aoife Monks observes: "O'Neill's engagement with race in
The Emperor Jones can be read through the legacy of the minstrel tradition
that he both rejected, and—unconsciously—maintained in his play and
through the lens of his own Irish American ethnicity."[25] While it is true that
O'Neill "was both an heir of the Irish-American Blackface tradition and a
participant [in it]," as Robinson claims, it is also correct that *The Emperor
Jones* was the vehicle by which performers broke away from the blackface
tradition and raced the American theater.[26]

O'Neill had a track record of creating works that featured Black life as a
way of negotiating his own Irish American identity, which was often at
odds with legitimating structures in white culture. Early in his career,
O'Neill penned unforgettable Irish American characters, just as he was
sketching iconic African American figures. The son of a famous Irish American actor, James O'Neill, Eugene experienced "anti-Irish bigotry of his
day,"[27] in spite of his family's rise to white, middle-class privilege—a shift
that exemplifies "how the Irish became white," to use Noel Ignatiev's formation.[28] "O'Neill knew from background and experience," writes biographer Edward Shaughnessy, "that both black and Irish-Americans had been
hated and alienated, even if he saw differences in the nature of their
estrangements."[29] The O'Neills were known as "shanty Irish," recounted
one of the residents from his childhood town of New London, "and we
associated the Irish with the servant class."[30] O'Neill understood himself as
Irish, although he never traveled to Ireland. The stamp of Ireland was not
only on his characters' faces but also at the very center of O'Neill's identity.
His biographers, Arthur Gelb and Barbara Gelb, have written that O'Neill
was obsessed with his Irish heritage.[31] Not only did O'Neill claim Ireland,
but Ireland claimed him. The great Irish playwright Sean O'Casey said to
O'Neill, "You write like an Irishman, you don't write like an American."[32]
Later in life, O'Neill remarked to his friend Sophus Winther, "Straight

across the Atlantic, right over there, is Ireland. . . . My critics have never recognized how much my work is indebted to the Irish in me."[33] Indeed, O'Neill's writing near the end of his career shifted "Black to Ireland" (my title for chapter 5), and these masterpieces focused on his Irish family.

O'Neill was understood not only as Irish but also as "Black Irish" during his life—signaling another through line between the racialization of Irishness and Blackness. As Shannon Steen has observed, "O'Neill plays out his feelings of freedom and loss on the body of Brutus Jones," a character who embodied "a racialized vision of O'Neill's own psychic and social alienation."[34] O'Neill's sense of estrangement from legitimating structures was tied to his acknowledgment that he derived from the marginalized "original Black Irish" stock.[35] The connections between the Black and green Atlantics were evident not only in O'Neill's own psyche. Croswell Bowen characterized O'Neill as "Black Irish" in his essay of the same title.[36] And O'Neill's third wife, Carlotta Monterey O'Neill, referred to him as "Black Irish" (even right after he died), as did his biographers Arthur and Barbara Gelb.[37] In writing about *The Emperor Jones*, George Bernard Shaw described O'Neill as "a Fantee Shakespeare, who peoples his isles with Calibans."[38] Derived from "fanti," which describes African people from Ghana, "fantee" means "primitive" and is used in British English in the phrase "go fantee" (or, we might have once said, "going native").[39] In using a Ghanaian word to pejoratively label O'Neill as "fantee," Bernard Shaw not only cast his fellow Irishman as "Black Irish" but also invoked the circum-Atlantic by triangulating Europe with Africa and the Americas. His quote furthermore highlights the dichotomous nature of *The Emperor Jones*, as well as the connection between Shakespeare's Caliban and O'Neill as a "Celtic Caliban," to use Anne McClintock's phrase to describe the precariously raced Irish in the early twentieth century.[40] On the one hand, Bernard Shaw had a point in referencing Shakespeare's Caliban, a character who has been central in debates about imperialism and colonized subjects. Like Caliban, who was rendered as a primitivized Other in need of a master to "civilize" and govern him, Jones is a casualty of the racist imaginary that ultimately destroys him, and thus, Black empire. On the other hand, as Bernard Shaw well knew, Jones is the emperor of the island, something that cannot be said of Caliban, who is enslaved to Prospero in spite of the fact that the island was his before colonial contact. Moreover, as embodied by powerful actors like Gilpin and Robeson, the remains of previous rulers throughout the Black diaspora were summoned forth on stage as potent diasporic performatives.

THE EMPEROR (JONES) IS DEAD. LONG LIVE THE EMPEROR!

In order to attend to the traces of the Emperor across time and among multiple bodies, Joseph Roach's notion of surrogation seems an apt line of critical inquiry. We might say that the *Emperor*'s remains were summoned forth, recalling circum-Atlantic memories that had been long forgotten in a process of surrogation, where one thing stands in for another and the antecedent is forgotten. Roach's famous example of surrogation—"the King is dead, long live the King"—could well be replaced with "The Emperor is dead. Long live the Emperor."[41] And yet, because surrogation requires an absenting of the former thing (or Emperor) for another, it does not quite account for multiple citational threads. Diana Taylor's notion of "doubling" more accurately accounts for performative complexity. By attending to doubling, the predecessors—in this case, former actors as Brutus Jones and their historical contexts—can be preserved, offering "a form of multiplication and simultaneity rather than surrogation and absenting."[42] This doubling—or, more accurately, *performative layering*—reveals multiple Emperors on the move, as co-terminus productions. Given these layered productions, with multiple Brutus Joneses as surrogated Black sovereigns, it is productive to refer to them citationally in the plural—as "The *Emperors Jones*"—as Gwendolyn Bennett's 1930 article in the African American periodical *Opportunity* named them.[43] This chapter digs up various productions' past lives to excavate previous meanings and contexts. I am exhuming, in other words, the Emperors' remains.[44] In searching for the *Emperor*'s relics in this chapter, two iconic actors who raced the Great White Way while wearing the Emperor's coat take center stage: Charles Gilpin and Paul Robeson. Each actor altered O'Neill's script with performative interventions, creating their own resistant repertoires.

Gilpin's story not only serves as a quintessential example of racing the Great White Way but also complicates our understanding of theatrical authorship and unacknowledged contributions from Black theater artists.[45] Gilpin once famously declared, "I created the role of the Emperor. That role belongs to me. That Irishman, he just wrote the play."[46] His well-known hailing of O'Neill as "that Irishman" is telling, for it shows the entanglements with, and clashes among, Irish and Black culture. Indeed, it could be argued that Gilpin created the play as much as O'Neill (this is precisely Montgomery's point in the quote earlier in the chapter). Gilpin famously revised (or, *raced*) O'Neill's play, especially on tour, by taking out the problematic use of the n-word, which appears thirty-four times in *The Emperor*

Fig. 3. Charles Gilpin in the 1920 production of *The Emperor Jones*. A closer look reveals a belt buckle with the initials CSA (Confederate States of America), a performative citation of regimes of race. Eugene O'Neill Papers. The Beinecke Rare Book and Manuscript Library, Yale University.

Jones. As David Krasner observes, Gilpin "balked at what appeared to him to be an excessive and repetitive use of the term '*n— —r*', preferring instead to use the less offensive terms *Black-baby*, *Negro*, or *colored man*" (italics in the original).[47] Biographers offer differing accounts of O'Neill's displeasure with Gilpin's revisions, but, as Louis Sheaffer tells it, O'Neill warned: "If you change the lines again, I'll beat the hell out of you!"[48] But Gilpin *did* change the lines, and not only for the two years while he was on tour, but also for several years in revivals of the role and a production that he directed—on Broadway.

In addition to altering the offensive language in *The Emperor Jones*, Gilpin highlighted circum-Caribbean connections between Brutus Jones's despotic rule in the West Indies and the legacy of slavery in the U.S. As part of his Brutus Jones costume, Gilpin wore a large belt buckle with the initials CSA (Confederate States of America). Masquerading as a member of the Confederacy—and literally wearing the cloak of racism—Gilpin embodied the connections among oppressive regimes of race. By blatantly donning the symbol of the CSA, Gilpin was also pointing to the connective tissue between historical practices of slavery throughout the diaspora and racism on Broadway. Rather than seeing these choices as contradictory elements with a Brechtian alienation effect as Ronald H. Wainscott claims, I interpret Gilpin's performative interventions as showing the complementary citationality between these oppressive discourses.[49] Even in the final scenes when Gilpin (as Jones) confronts the Congo Witch-Doctor shirtless and in tattered pants, the CSA buckle stands out prominently. Though a despotic ruler, who learns exploitation from white businessmen while a Pullman porter, Jones is ultimately a casualty of racism—buckled in, we could say, by oppressive racial hierarchies.

On tour, *The Emperor Jones* raced spectatorship at a time when segregated audiences were the norm. When *The Emperor Jones* went on the road for almost two years from 1920 to 1922, both Black and white spectators came to see Gilpin. It was hardly a royal tour, but there was something regal about the audiences Gilpin commanded throughout the United States, in both highbrow and lowbrow spaces—from Los Angeles to Des Moines to El Paso—until he was threatened by the Ku Klux Klan.[50] Gilpin was inventive in bringing *The Emperor Jones* to unlikely places. Perhaps one of the most unusual venues was an early manifestation of what we now call prison theater: Gilpin performed O'Neill's play in Sing Sing prison in 1923.[51] Speaking about his extensive performances in a *New York Amsterdam News* interview, Gilpin recounted: "Oh, I guess I've played Jones about 2,500 times, from coast to coast, from beyond border to beyond border. In New York, on the road, at benefit performances and whatnot. And it hasn't played out its string yet."[52] Gilpin's choice of words—"from beyond border to beyond border"—is striking. It demonstrates not only the incredible mileage he logged while racing beyond Broadway, but also how his performances facilitated interracial border crossings. *The Emperor Jones* played to mixed houses in the South, as recounted by one Virginian reporter: "When the theatre was filled, by one of those unwritten laws that prevail in the South, the balcony was filled with Negroes and the orchestra with white people. Gilpin appeared on the stage, and a roar of applause greeted him from the galleries."[53] As with casting, *The Emperor Jones* raced spectatorship barriers.

Gilpin loved a good comeback and so in 1926 he not only revived *The Emperor Jones* for the Provincetown Players but also directed his own production on Broadway—and another color line was broken.[54] By breaking "The Color Line in Art," as the African American newspaper the *Chicago Defender* characterized it, Gilpin proved that "the color of a man's skin was [not] the deciding factor as to the success of his esthetic endeavors."[55] The revival received glowing reviews in both Black and white papers. Gilpin was back. "The return of 'The Emperor Jones' to New York discloses to those who might have entertained any doubts of the ability of Charles S. Gilpin's latent dramatic power," the *New York Amsterdam News* reported.[56] And, reminding its readership how the white press was often ignorant of Gilpin's roots in Black theater, the article continued, "we took pride in pointing [his talent] out to our readers years before his opportunity came to appear before exacting audiences in a sphere far removed from that of 135th street." Gilpin's dramatic powers ensured his success as one of the leading Black actors during his day. Gilpin made *The Emperor Jones*—just as O'Neill's drama made Gilpin. "They say there will never be another 'Emperor Jones,'" hinted the *Amsterdam News* apocryphally. "They say that it made Charles Gilpin and that it will break him."[57] If Gilpin broke the color line with *The Emperor Jones*, it may be equally true that the play broke him—but not before he made his imprint forever on American theater and culture.

One bitter reality of racing the Great White Way was that even as actors broke color lines with O'Neill's plays, Broadway, as an engine of American culture, was governed by entrenched racial hierarchies. This reality was articulated by a piece in the *World* in 1923: "The story of Gilpin of Emperor Jones who found that a Negro had freer opportunities as a Pullman porter than as a gifted actor, is the common experience of every Negro who aspires to a place in the theatre—certainly in the dramatic theatre."[58] When he was interviewed in 1921 for *American Magazine*, Gilpin reflected on the opportunity that *Jones* had afforded him, while also acknowledging the tenacious hold of Broadway's racism:

> I *am* pleased; especially with the generous praise of the critics. But I don't fool myself about the stone walls that are in my way. Mr. O'Neill made a breach in those walls by writing a play that had in it a serious dramatic role for a negro. The Provincetown Players gave me the chance to do the part. But—what next? If I were white, a dozen opportunities would come to me at once as a result of a success like this. But I'm black. It is no joke when I ask myself, "Where do I go from here?"[59]

Where did Gilpin go? One place was to the White House where he had a private audience with President Warren Harding in 1921.[60] He also received the New York Drama League Award that same year for his work in *The Emperor Jones*, breaking the color line again, in not only being selected as outstanding actor but also in attending, and integrating, the banquet after initially being excluded (O'Neill had a hand in this as well, threatening to boycott the event unless Gilpin was invited).[61] O'Neill remarked that Gilpin was one of "only three actors in my plays who managed to realize the characters . . . as I originally saw them."[62] But given these accolades, what was Gilpin to do once "The Emperor Jones has run its course," as the *New York Amsterdam News* put it?[63] There were so few roles for African American actors, Gilpin needed a new play "with a great Negro part, and even the casual observer knows how rare these plays are."[64] The plays were indeed rare. And so, *The Emperor Jones* continued to be revived.

In spite of paying his dues on the road for years, Gilpin was not asked to revive *The Emperor Jones* in 1924. Instead, the role was handed to Paul Robeson while he was rehearsing *All God's Chillun Got Wings*. Gilpin's legacy of racing Broadway became intertwined with Robeson's: the two actors performed the role of Brutus Jones in tandem for over a decade, each in different productions, but always moving along intersecting cartographies. Gilpin on Broadway, Robeson in Harlem. Gilpin on tour, Robeson in the Village. Gilpin touring again, Robeson in England. Gilpin directing his own production, Robeson performing spiritual recitals. Gilpin dead at an early age, Robeson filming *The Emperor Jones*.[65] Step by step, year by year, the two artists performed the role his own way. Again and again, *The Emperor Jones* became the vehicle for African American actors to race Broadway during the 1920s, 1930s, and 1940s.

Robeson's encounter with *The Emperor Jones* forever changed the history of American theater. His collaborations with O'Neill and the Provincetown Players, uneasy as they may have been, as Glenda E. Gill points out, sutured his rise to fame.[66] These roles "positioned Robeson not only as a new celebrity, but also as firmly located within the avant-garde of American theatre," observes Tony Perucci.[67] Robeson's long-standing performance of Brutus Jones prepared him to perform other Black emperors throughout his career, constituting what we might call a polyptych of Black diasporic performance culture constituted by two plays (*The Emperor Jones* and *Toussaint Louverture*) and two films (*The Emperor Jones*, 1933, directed by Dudley Murphy; and *Song of Freedom*, 1936, directed by J. Elder Wills).

When Robeson took over the portrayal of Brutus Jones in 1924, he was extensively compared to Gilpin.[68] The headline for John Corbin's 1924 *New York Times* review made this clear: "Paul Robeson Triumphs in Role Made Famous by Gilpin."[69] Comparisons were often made between the two actors, for, as Marvin Carlson reminds us, former actors and productions often haunt the stage.[70] Gilpin not only haunted the role of Brutus Jones but also stalked it, for he was in the audience on the opening night for Robeson's revival. Strangely, only the *New York Post* mentioned this fact: "The chief interest in the present production lies, of course, in a comparison of the skill of the new 'Emperor' and the creator of the title part, Charles Gilpin, who was in the audience to witness the debut of his successor."[71] Robeson's wife, Eslanda (Essie), made the following note in her diary from opening night: "Performance really fine. Gilpin was there and he and O'Neill quarreled . . . after play."[72] The *New York Post* declared Robeson "the New Emperor," but Gilpin was plotting his directorial debut.[73]

Such judgments of the two actors often focused on their physicality. While many reviews pointed out Gilpin's small stature and even baldness, many more obsessed on Robeson's "vigor" and "virility."[74] Just as Gilpin faded away into obscurity, so Robeson was blown out of proportion. This discourse about Robeson's embodiment can be seen as a manifestation of racializing projections and anxieties regarding Black masculinity. "The black body," Harvey Young writes, is "an abstracted and imagined figure" that "shadows or doubles the real one. It is the Black body and not a particular, flesh-and-blood body that is the target of a racializing projection."[75] Such projections infused the reviews for *The Emperor Jones*, which almost obsessively described Robeson's "Black body," overshadowing not only white characters in the play but also whiteness itself. For example, the *New York Morning World* noted in 1924 that Robeson was "a fine figure of a man, possessor of an extraordinary and enviable physique and a deep, resonant voice."[76] The review goes on to remark upon Robeson's boxer-like build:

"Mr. Robeson was thrice called before the curtain to receive the cheers and applause of the house. He presented such a figure in a checkered bathrobe, that one might have been pardoned for wondering just what he'd do to [boxer] Harry Willis."[77] The peculiar reference to what lurked underneath Robeson's bathrobe reveals the reviewer's desire in more way than one. Robeson was not only bursting out of his bathrobe; he could not be contained by prevailing discourse either. "Big and robust" is what the *New York World* called Robeson.[78] A London reviewer referred to Robeson as "a negro actor of immense height and capability."[79] As another London review put it, "This actor has been dowered with a physique which fills the eye like a bronze of noble period."[80] Still another critic praised Robeson, "whose physique is as magnificent as his acting."[81] Most illustrations overemphasized Robeson's magnitude, making him appear like a goliath, dwarfing a cowering Smithers, the pathetic white colonizer of the play. Several headlines referred to Robeson literally as a giant (for example, "Giant Negro Actor" and "Giant Negro-Actor and His Ambition to Sing").[82] Another headline was all about numbers: "6 ft. 4 in. Negro Actor's Triumph."[83] Lloyd L. Brown sums it up well: "There was always a largeness about Paul Robeson."[84]

Of course, Robeson was large, but hardly a giant. The point was not just that Robeson was tall and muscular—but rather that there was a largeness about his Blackness. As the caption to one illustration put it ("Oh, the Black and White of It"), Robeson's performance of Brutus Jones subverted racialized dichotomies underpinning regimes of race. In other words, these examples demonstrate not the enormity of Robeson's physicality, but rather the immense power of racializing fantasies projected onto Robeson's Black body, which seemed larger than life itself. Such projections were not new, however. As Jeffrey C. Stewart points out, "the racial coding of Robeson's body size had begun long before he played Emperor Jones in 1924."[85] In fact, as a Rutgers' football star, Robeson was billed as a "Colored Giant" on a game flier. Whereas on the football field Robeson's "largeness" was seen as beneficial, in American public spheres it was another matter. "Throughout the plays that Robeson acts in during the 1920s," Stewart continues, "his particular body comes to signify the gargantuan threat of the Black body to civilization."[86] Robeson was, moreover, conscious of his physicality, which he understood as both an asset and a limitation.

Although Robeson was sometimes depicted in his Emperor's coat in the role of Brutus Jones, on stage and in film he ended up shirtless by the end of the story. As Callens has shown, "the racial coding of Robeson's naked (upper) body" while playing Brutus Jones was inscribed "within a racialized representational practice" that played upon numerous primitivist discourses.[87] The charge of primitivism in *The Emperor Jones* (and other O'Neill works) is a well-articulated critique, one that I examine in more detail in chapter 5. What is important for my argument here is how Robeson negotiated the signifying force of racializing projections. Stewart writes:

> That Robeson could play both the primitive and the dangerous Negro, embody the fantasy and the fear of the Negro, suggests one reason for his enormous popularity with white audiences of the period. He, wittingly or not, became a site for the doubleness of white consciousness about the Black male body in the 1920s—that it was both a site of rejection and identification, both completely Other and one's Self.[88]

Robeson had his array of admirers, including the arts patron and white slummer Carl Van Vechten and the raconteur of Harlem, Alexander Gumby, both of whom devoted pages in their scrapbooks to Robeson with their own sort of queer fandom.

Put another way, Robeson embodied the modernist tensions inscribed onto Black men that Hazel V. Carby discusses in *Race Men*. Insofar as being "a Black national symbol of masculinity," Carby writes, "Robeson combined, in uneasy stasis and for a brief period of time, the historically contradictory elements of race, nation, and masculinity."[89] I would argue that *The Emperor Jones* was central to Robeson embodying these modernist contradictions, and moreover that the theater allowed him the opportunity to literally perform them. Within the context of Black internationalism and representations of Black empire, Robeson's Brutus Jones embodied these contradictions across the circum-Atlantic. In many ways his performative interventions worked against O'Neill's portrait of a Black failed despot, "inspir[ing] just the right type of fear of masculine savagery and repression that civilization hopefully tamed and ensured against," as Michelle Ann Stephens has put it.[90] These dichotomous tensions become visible in some of the publicity images. In a 1924 production photo from *The Emperor Jones*, Robeson is "still standing," to use Harvey Young's formation, returning the gaze back at the viewer, challenging efforts to interpolate or contain him.[91] In such publicity photos, Robeson is in character as both the belligerent Brutus Jones and a radicalized citizen. The glaring stare challenges the spectator, anticipating the iconic Edward Steichen photo of the filmic Brutus Jones (see chapter 5).

Robeson's assumption of the Emperor's throne was not planned as a

Fig. 4. Photograph of Paul Robeson in the title role of Eugene O'Neill's *The Emperor Jones*, a play in eight scenes. White Key-sheet from February 11, 1925. ©NYPL. Billy Rose Theatre Division, New York Public Library for the Performing Arts, New York City.

full-fledged revival, and it occurred after he had already turned the role down in 1920. The 1924 staging of *The Emperor Jones* was, rather, a last-minute strategy to deal with the crisis brought on by *All God's Chillun Got Wings*, O'Neill's semi-expressionistic portrait of interracial desire. For nearly two decades, Robeson performed the part of Brutus Jones. As Robeson said in 1924, "This is undoubtedly one of '*the* great American plays'—a true classic of drama, American or otherwise. . . . And what a great part is 'Brutus Jones'."[92] In fact, *The Emperor Jones* was a performative anchor to Robeson's career, a play he repeatedly revived throughout the U.S. and Europe in various iterations for years.

While much has been written about how Gilpin edited the script by excising offensive language, little has been noted about how Robeson made his editorial (which is to say dramaturgical) mark on *The Emperor Jones*. From the very beginning, Robeson added spirituals and work songs to the play, part of his larger vision of promoting Black music throughout U.S. culture. O'Neill reflected upon Robeson's contributions in a letter to his lawyer, Harry Weinberger: "In the last production of 'Jones' at P. P. we introduced music. Robeson sang parts of John Henry, chain gang song, also (I think) a swatch of spiritual."[93] O'Neill's memory about this is not only inaccurate, but also revisionist—"we" didn't add the songs, but rather Robeson did. Robeson's contributions were far from musical ornamentation; his inclusions of spirituals and work songs shaped the very contours of O'Neill's play by performatively referencing slavery and Black performance culture.[94] Robeson was racing *The Emperor Jones*. After the Provincetown Playhouse production in 1924, *The Emperor Jones* was revived and transferred to Broadway at the Punch and Judy Theatre with Robeson in the title role. One critic remarked, "'The Emperor Jones' still has not exhausted its appeal"; nor would it, for dozens of years to come.[95]

In transatlantic productions, Robeson's *Emperor Jones* continued to disrupt racial hierarchies on stage. Robeson brought Londoners their first production of *The Emperor Jones* in 1925 at the Ambassadors Theatre, which "held a large audience spellbound."[96] As Robeson "towered over the egregious Smithers," observed one London review, "it was hard to formulate any theory of white supremacy."[97] The accolades belonged to Robeson, who "received a great ovation at the close."[98] Another review agreed: "The acting of Mr. Paul Robeson was superb. . . . His voice is one of the finest I have ever heard."[99] While generally positively reviewed, the British coverage of *The Emperor Jones* was also plagued by primitivism, as was the case in the U.S. The *London Observer* lamented, for instance, that Robeson's portrayal "was too intellectual." What they wanted instead, as they blatantly put it, was "a more primitive performance."[100] Other critics perceived Robeson's Brutus Jones as a regal monarch, calling him the "king of a 'Black' island."[101] Such accounts offer a different set of reactions to Stephens's dismissal of *The Emperor Jones* as "making fun of the idea of black self-determination," by instead perceiving Robeson's Brutus Jones as an intellectual sovereign.[102] As the London production was ending its run, one headline blamed "Gloomy O'Neill" for its closure, but London audiences were looking forward to seeing Robeson's proposed recitals of Black spirituals.[103]

Increasingly, Robeson reshaped *The Emperor Jones* to showcase Black agency as well as the legacy of slavery. For a 1930 London production, Robeson essentially rewrote the script by focusing on the songs and performing just the first part of the play—in effect focusing on Jones's *ascent*, not his demise.[104] Next, Robeson traveled to Berlin's Künstlertheater with a 1930 production that reviewers called "an achievement for American theatre" and a "*succès d'estime*."[105] Publicity photos from the German production included the rarely shown Middle Passage slave ship scene—a seg-

Fig. 5. American actor Paul Robeson in the play *The Emperor Jones* (Eugene O'Neill). Berlin. German Art Theatre. About 1930. Photograph. Mary Evans/Imagno.

ment that would be cut in the 1933 feature film, also starring Robeson. Robeson's transatlantic Brutus Jones thus performatively summoned circum-Atlantic history and Black internationalism.

With later productions stateside, Robeson added other innovations, molding his Brutus Jones to fit the cultural political moment and to speak back to white power. After being absent from the American stage for seven years, the role he chose for his comeback was Brutus Jones. In this 1939 revival, Robeson made a significant change, observes Paul Robeson Jr.: "Paul eliminated the word '*n — —r*' throughout after having announced in several interviews that he intended to do so."[106] Robeson's important excision of the n-word has not received the scholarly attention it deserves. And yet it belongs to a long history of Robeson racing American theater and culture through O'Neill's plays. This well-received production in 1939 once again opened the doors to future work, including the musical *John Henry* and the lead in *Othello*. Photos for this production reveal another intervention: Robeson is wearing a cowboy hat and a studded holster. Performed mostly in summer stock theater, Robeson retooled this Brutus Jones for

Fig. 6. Paul Robeson in the 1939 tour revival of *The Emperor Jones* retooled for Depression era audiences. Photo by Vandamm Studio. © Billy Rose Theatre Division, The New York Public Library for the Performing Arts.

Depression era audiences. Gone are visual references to Haitian revolutionaries (Toussaint Louverture, Guillaume Sam, Henri Christophe) or Black nationalists (Marcus Garvey). Brutus Jones had been remade as a quintessential American icon.

From 1939 to 1941, Robeson performed several summer stock productions of *The Emperor Jones* on the East Coast, experimenting with sound and adding Black diasporic performance practices. But first, Robeson needed O'Neill's permission for the changes. In a 1940 telegram to his agent Richard (Dick) Madden, O'Neill wrote: "TELL PAUL ROBESON IT IS ALL RIGHT EXPERIMENT SOUND EFFECTS EMPEROR JONES BUT TO WATCH IT CAREFULLY. TOO MUCH OF THAT STUFF CAN ATTRACT TOO MUCH ATTENTION AND RUIN BOTH HIS ACTING AND THE PLAY."[107] What O'Neill misunderstood is that Robeson's musical experimentation (or "that stuff," as O'Neill put it) did not "ruin" the play, but rather augmented it—just as Robeson's changes had added complexity in the film version. That same summer Robeson performed *The Emperor Jones* in the McCarter Theatre in Princeton, New Jersey; at Bucks County Playhouse in New Hope, Pennsylvania; and in the Theatre Guild's production at Country Playhouse in Westport, Connecticut.[108] The Guild production is especially intriguing, for it offered a circum-Atlantic perspective by incorporating music from Africa, Bali, and Martinique.[109] Robeson concluded the year by performing excerpts of the operatic version of *The Emperor Jones* with the Philadelphia Orchestra.[110] The summer of 1941 found Robeson yet again performing his "old role," as the *New York Times* put it, appearing at the Cape Playhouse in Dennis, Massachusetts; the Ivoryton Playhouse in Essex, Connecticut; the Spa Theatre in Saratoga Springs, New York; and at Marblehead's North Shore Players.[111] Toggling between concert tours and summer stock with *The Emperor Jones*, Robeson was crafting a political repertoire built upon the Emperor's remains.

ROBESON'S PERFORMATIVE DIPTYCH

Another emperor that rose from the ashes of *The Emperor Jones*—and that Robeson performed—was the title figure from C. L. R. James's play *Toussaint Louverture: The Story of the Only Successful Slave Revolt in History*, staged in London in 1936. Indeed, the roles of Brutus Jones and Toussaint Louverture constitute a diptych of Black diasporic performances that were central to Robeson's repertoire. As a Haitian revolutionary, Toussaint Louverture remains one of the most significant Black heroes to be represented on the stage. Robeson easily stepped into the role as Louverture, having performed Brutus Jones for over a decade, thus tracing a performative trajectory from O'Neill to James.

While *The Emperor Jones* portrayed a despotic ruler who is overthrown by the Indigenous people over whom he briefly ruled, *Toussaint Louverture* dramatized a Black diasporic icon who spearheaded the Haitian Revolution. The 1936 production sought to "tell the whole history of the Haitian Revolution, of international imperial rivalry, of the emergence of a revolutionary consciousness, and of the creation of both a nation and a people," observes Laurent Dubois in his foreword to the play.[112] As Christian Høgsbjerg notes in his introduction, *Toussaint Louverture* marked "the first time Black professional actors starred on the British stage in a play written by a Black playwright," and it was "the only play in which Robeson appeared that was written by a writer of African heritage."[113] Written by Trinidadian-born British playwright James in 1934 (building upon his work in *The Black Jacobins*) and rediscovered in 2012, *Toussaint Louverture* was performed on March 15 and 16 in 1936 at Westminster Theatre, under the aegis of the London Stage Society.

Robeson as Toussaint Louverture was haunted by Robeson as Brutus Jones, summoning ghostly traces from theater's "memory machine," as Marvin Carlson has put it.[114] (Indeed, I came upon Robeson's performance of Toussaint Louverture because the Museum of the City of New York mislabeled the publicity photograph as being from *The Emperor Jones*.) Increasingly, Brutus Jones and Toussaint Louverture blurred into one another, demonstrating the performative citationality between representations of Black diasporic power and what Roach has called genealogies of performance throughout the circum-Atlantic.[115]

Robeson's emperors cemented his authority as a cultural regnant, opening up a circum-Atlantic critique of imperial power. Much of this impression was achieved by the magnitude of Robeson himself, as a "thinking, fighting body engaged in the world," as Shana L. Redmond characterizes him, as well as onstage.[116] From the start, Robeson's Brutus Jones had flash, citing Black diasporic power. In 1924, when he assumed the role, Robeson wore a light-colored, military style tailor-made jacket with gilded epaulettes and fringe, gold braiding, chevrons, brass buttons, and embroidered details on the sleeves. This was a departure from the heavy, dark mid-thigh-length coat that Gilpin had worn, which had almost no trim or medals (with the exception of the CSA buckle). Robeson's costumes became increasingly ornamental and militaristic, citing emperors across the Black diaspora. Later, as Toussaint Louverture, the "Negro Napoleon," as one

Fig. 7. Paul Robeson dressed as a revolutionary. This could be a 1925 production of *The Emperor Jones* but is most likely a 1936 production of *Toussaint Louverture*. Photographer unknown. Museum of the City of New York. 51.116.146.

caption described him, Robeson wore a French blue emperor jacket, plus a Napoleonic hat.[117] Production photos no longer show Brutus Jones's gun, but rather now Louverture's sword, substituting early twentieth-century technology with that of the early nineteenth.

In addition to both productions featuring magnetic Robeson portraying powerful rulers, there were other similarities that evoked diasporic performance culture. To begin, both plays take place on Caribbean isles.[118] For O'Neill, the island has not yet been colonized by Americans, whereas for James, the plot centers on the colonization — and enslavement — of Black people, as well as fighting back against that oppression. Furthermore, both plays were created during the time of the ill-fated U.S. occupation of Haiti from 1915 to 1934. There are, moreover, citations of *The Emperor Jones's* West Indian forested setting in *Toussaint Louverture*.[119] Whereas in *The Emperor Jones*, the forest is the space in which Jones encounters hallucinations of his past misdeeds, as well as collective re-memories of slavery and the Middle Passage, in *Toussaint Louverture* the forest ignites the revolution. Rather than the site of repentance and ultimate demise (as with *The Emperor Jones*), the forest in *Toussaint Louverture* fosters a successful revolt. Moreover, and, importantly, both plays incorporated African drums for dramatic effect. Drumming was a signature element in *The Emperor Jones*, set to the tempo of the human heartbeat once the islanders pursue Jones in the jungle.[120] Yet, drumming signifies differently in each play: whereas in *The Emperor Jones* it underscores the islanders' hunting their deposed emperor, in *Toussaint Louverture* it signifies power, rebellion, and revolution. Given this use of drumming, it seems likely that James was citing iconic elements of O'Neill's play with Robeson at the helm.[121] One important distinction had to do with casting: while *The Emperor Jones* utilized blackface for some of the minor roles (depending on the production), *Toussaint Louverture* employed a remarkable cast of professional Black actors "drawn from across the African diaspora."[122]

In addition, both plays included scenes with Robeson singing spirituals. It seems likely that Robeson was the one who added these songs, for the scripts do not mention them, and he had altered scripts before by inserting African American music. Robeson had incorporated the work ballads "John Henry" and "Water Boy" in both the stage and film versions of *The Emperor Jones* to anchor the text within the context of forced Black labor and the music that resisted such captivity. In *Toussaint Louverture*, Robeson incorporated at least one spiritual during the emotional scene before Louverture dies. As one newspaper put it, "A little 'spiritual,' beautifully sung by Mr. Robeson in the prison scene, gave a refreshing touch of naturalness."[123]

Fig. 8. Movie still from *Song of Freedom* (1936). Robeson's costume looks very similar to the one worn for his stage roles of Brutus Jones and Toussaint Louverture. Courtesy The Stephen Bourne Collection/Mary Evans.

As a performer of the Emperor's remains, Robeson embodied what we might call a diasporic stature. As with the coverage of *The Emperor Jones*, the British press once again emphasized Robeson's size. The *Times* in London observed, for instance, Robeson's "gigantic vitality."[124] Robeson was repeatedly referred to as a ruler, general, or king, shattering previous conceptions of Black masculinity and leadership. Collapsing the difference between the roles he played on and off stage, one headline called Robeson a "negro leader."[125] Another review observed the synergies between Robeson's activism and the roles he played on stage: "The play must have been a great pleasure for Paul Robeson to act, for Toussaint's opinion on the necessity of Black people being educated has always been a plank in his platform."[126] Still another noted, "It is a noble character nobly played with all the actor's resonance and dignity."[127]

Moreover, while he was staging *Toussaint Louverture* in London, Robeson was gearing up to film *Song of Freedom* (directed by J. Elder Wills), in which Robeson portrayed Zinga, a British opera singer who returns to an island off the west coast of Africa to eventually become king. Tellingly, one of the musical numbers from *Song of Freedom* is called "The Black Emperor," yet another performative citation of *The Emperor Jones*.[128]

Crucially, Robeson had planned to include *Toussaint Louverture*—along with *The Emperor Jones*—as part of his anticipated repertory theater in London.[129] The *Negro Star* reported that Robeson "declared he wants particularly Negro plays by Negro playwrights as previously such drama has been written almost exclusively by whites."[130] In a piece called "I Want Negro Culture," Robeson wrote that the theater should be "the first step" in "winning freedom" over oppression. Through theater, he maintained, "we aim to win world recognition for negro productions and so help the negro back to self-respect. I intend shortly to launch this theatre in the West End."[131] Robeson did not propose to limit the repertoire only to Black theater (hence O'Neill is included in his plan), but he did have his sights on a mix of European classics, "plays calling for a mixed cast," along with "purely African plays."[132] Robeson never formed the theater, likely due to the financial pressures of the Depression.

And what of his Emperor's remains? In Robeson's front-page obituary in the *New York Times* in 1976, his roles as Brutus Jones and Toussaint Louverture were both mentioned as standout performances.[133] The *Chicago Defender* wrote, "It is easy to understand why Paul Robeson is the most beloved and greatest of [the] artists we have produced. Robeson is an artist-fighter for Negro America. Robeson is more than an ambassador for his people. He sings for freedom."[134] Robeson's embodiment of both "artist-fighter" was co-terminus with performing Brutus Jones.

WHAT IS IT WORTH NOW? "ALL I KNOW: IT MEANS A LOT TO ME"

Though in many ways a drama beset by contradictions, *The Emperor Jones* meant a lot not only to actors who performed in it but also to Eugene O'Neill. When O'Neill was nominated to the First Comprehensive Exhibition of the American Academy of Arts and Letters of the American Institute in 1942, he was asked to send a text to be put on display. What play did he choose? *The Emperor Jones*. It's a surprising choice. A more expected selection would have been one of the three Pulitzer Prize–winning plays he had garnered thus far (*Beyond the Horizon*, "*Anna Christie*," *Strange Interlude*), or one of his critical successes that paved the way for him to win the Nobel Prize in Literature (*Mourning Becomes Electra* or *Desire Under the Elms*). But instead, O'Neill sent a play that was "worth a lot" to him—even two decades later. The original script for *The Emperor Jones* was just three back-to-back pages in O'Neill's very small handwriting. In a letter to the Academy's secretary, Martin Birnbaum, O'Neill clarified:

> It sounds impossible but it's all there on these few pages, and when you see the handwriting, you will believe it. I chose the script because "Jones" is one of my most widely known plays and the script has interest as a novelty. . . . What it is worth now, who knows? All I know, it is worth a lot to me.[135]

O'Neill's statement uncannily (and perhaps unknowingly) cited lines that one of his characters, Jim Harris, says at the conclusion of *All God's Chillun Got Wings*: "A lot—to me—what it means."[136] Two decades later, O'Neill was still thinking about the value of his writing through Blackness.

The question of *The Emperor Jones*'s worth still remains. It was worth a lot not only to O'Neill but also to Gilpin and Robeson (among countless others) who launched their careers through this play. While it is true that O'Neill profited from his portrait of Black people, so did the actors who portrayed Brutus Jones and the theater companies who incorporated the play into their repertoires around the world. Ultimately, *Jones*'s worth needs to be considered within the dichotomous history of negotiating racial hierarchies while racing the Great White Way.

TWO | An Algerian in Paris

In 1923 the Algerian actor Habib Benglia played an uncanny *Emperor Jones* for the nation that colonized his own.[1] On the stage of Paris's Théâtre de l'Odéon, one of France's most esteemed national performance venues, the French-speaking Benglia—a colonized subject—assumed the role of a colonizer (Brutus Jones) in a play that has been central in discussions of racial performativity, empire, and diaspora. This *L'Empereur Jones* enacted the ambivalence of colonial discourse, to borrow Homi Bhabha's formulation; it cited, distorted, and reconstructed the image of the Emperor.[2] Benglia performed the tensions between empire and colonial subject, embodying the spectacle of a failing Emperor, a despotic ruler who is destroyed by the Indigenous people of the island. This North African actor's momentary assumption of imperial power onstage tellingly anticipated revolutionary struggles against colonial forces, like the Algerian fight for freedom from France, and the challenge to colonialist theater-making advanced by the Négritude movement, in which Benglia would later take part.

Widely covered at the time by the international press, Benglia's performance of Brutus Jones on French soil has received little notice in theater scholarship, critical race studies, and American studies. Equally forgotten is its performative afterlife nearly a decade later in which Benglia performed another character from O'Neill's *Emperor Jones*, the Congo Witch-Doctor, in his own Montparnasse nightclub, conjuring a counterperformance to the 1931 Colonial Exposition. And lost almost entirely is the revival of *L'Empereur Jones* twenty-seven years later with Benglia's all-Black theater company in Paris. In spite of this "racial amnesia," Benglia was known throughout Algeria and France for his classical stage repertoire;[3] he was the first North African actor to appear on a French national stage—tellingly while wearing the Emperor's coat. Throughout these pages I aim to show how this theater artist deployed and subverted tropes of empire while performing characters from *The Emperor Jones*. These performative iterations of *Jones* mark not only a vital lost performance history of O'Neill's groundbreaking drama but also the layered contexts and performative valences for performing bodies across the circum-Atlantic.

Important scholarly work has traced the significance of performing Black bodies in relation to empire, diaspora, and imperial representation. For example, Depression era productions such as *Haiti* and the Federal Theatre Project's "voodoo" *Macbeth* featured seminaked performers on U.S. stages, which produced both an exotic aesthetic "and a masked threat of rebellion," as Stephanie Leigh Batiste has shown.[4] Benglia's performance in Paris occurred almost a decade before such productions and on different transnational coordinates (Algeria and France), thus offering fresh insights on transnational Black identities, racial performativity, and diasporic (specifically Franco-African) performance. What is particularly instructive about Benglia's performances on French stages and in his Parisian club is how this actor was tracing, indeed constituting, alternate cartographies of Black internationalism and artistic expression while performing O'Neill's *Emperor Jones*.

AN UNCANNY EMPEROR

It is hard to imagine a performance of *The Emperor Jones* more densely saturated with colonial resonances than the Benglia production—or, indeed, any other American play of this era. The Algerian-French *L'Empereur Jones* staged the Black Atlantic as a counterculture of modernity, to invoke Paul Gilroy's formation. More specifically, Benglia's performance troubled what Gilroy calls the "nationalist or ethnically absolute approaches" seeking to reductively categorize him and instead brought his ambivalence, or hybridity, to light: he signified as both North African and French; as ruler and colonized; as subject and fetish.[5] Benglia's Algerian-Paris 1923 production built on Gilpin's 1920 premiere stateside just as it cited and resignified "Africana chic" in Paris and complicated colonial exchange between France and North Africa. From the 1923 Théâtre de l'Odéon performance of *L'Empereur Jones*, to its 1950 Parisian revival, to re-performances of the Congo Witch-Doctor in his Montparnasse nightclub, Benglia was undoing empire while performing roles from O'Neill's drama about imperfect imperial rule.

Benglia's assumption of the Emperor's role in 1923 was extraordinary not only because he performed as an Algerian in Paris but also because the venues, as well as the audiences, reflected the legacy of colonialism. He first performed the role at the home of the president of the French Chamber of Duties for a Franco-American fête in June 1923.[6] It was billed as an international, if not diplomatic, engagement. Five months after the Franco-

American fête, *L'Empereur Jones* opened in Paris's Théâtre de l'Odéon, one of France's most revered national theaters. With Habib Benglia in the starring role, it premiered on October 31 and was performed several times between November 1923 and early January 1924.[7] As the *New York Times* reported, "Everything was done to make the début a gala affair. It was put under the patronage of the Minister of Public Instruction and Fine Arts and was marked as a celebration of international artistic concord, advertised widely as a '*Soirée de Gala Franco-Americaine*.'"[8] The production at the Odéon, "on the eve of 'Toussaint,'" auspiciously drew upon hallowed saints (Toussaint is the name used for All Saints' Day in France), just as it conjured Black diasporic revolutionaries like Toussaint Louverture.[9] O'Neill's semi-expressionistic one acter yoked diplomacy together with modernism, colonial power, and Black diasporic performance.

As a North African hailing from the French province of Oran (on the northern tip of Algeria), Benglia's very presence onstage as Brutus Jones invoked all three axes of circum-Atlantic flow (Africa, Europe, and the Americas). And yet, given that the premiere was commemorating war-hero athletes, Benglia embodied a different kind of hero and anticipated a different kind of war, positioning what Brent Hayes Edwards has called a "wedge" into previously conceived imperial exchange. Key aspects of diaspora, Edwards shows, are the wedges, fissures, gaps, and *décalage*. He writes that "*décalage* is the kernel of precisely that which cannot be transferred or exchanged, the received biases that refuse to pass over when one crosses the water . . . [the] 'differences within unity,' an unidentifiable point that is incessantly touched and fingered and pressed."[10] Benglia serves as a case study of an artist who embodied this diasporic *décalage*, all while performing a unique iteration of imperialness: a commanding Emperor (Brutus Jones) embodied by a colonial subject on a colonial nationalist stage.

Benglia's powerful stance and self-assurance captivated me when I located a publicity photo at the Beinecke Rare Book and Manuscript Library of Yale University (not filed among the O'Neill Papers, but rather somewhat puzzlingly in an African American collection).[11] The photo reveals an *unheimlich* (uncanny) image, where the familiar is seen as strange: the actor is immediately recognizable as Brutus Jones, the oversized epaulets extending off the jacket's shoulders like armor.[12] As always, a gun is strapped to the Emperor's side, signaling imminent danger, if not the mythical silver bullet that will be his undoing. And yet something is unfamiliar about him as well, compared to other depictions of Brutus Jones, especially to the American actors Charles Gilpin and Paul Robeson. Benglia's suit is slim-fitting, with a short European cut that is composed of light fabric with matching white pants—hardly the

Fig. 9. Publicity photo of Habib Benglia, Black Algerian actor, while performing title role in *The Emperor Jones* at the Odéon, Paris, 1923. Photo by Underwood & Underwood. Randolph Linsly Simpson African-American Collection. James Weldon Johnson Memorial Collection in the Yale Collection of American Literature, Beinecke Rare Book and Manuscript Library.

bulky, looser fitting jackets worn by Gilpin and Robeson. The photo's uncanniness, together with its theatricality, highlights the intertwined, and deceptive, ontology of imperial representation as performed by this colonial subject, thus unsettling the boundaries between the two; it also reveals the power of Benglia embodying these contradictions, for he is armed. Benglia's holster is cinched high around the waist (not around the hips, where Gilpin and Robeson hung theirs), like a French gendarme. Armed African soldiers were familiar in the French colonial imaginary, as the *New York Evening Mail* noted in its review of *L'Empereur Jones*: "The French, on the other hand, are used to African Colonial troupes [*sic*], who carry themselves proudly and with a gravity of demeanor that is impressive."[13] The Freudian slip of using troupes (instead of troops) underscores my argument about the theatricality and performativity of imperial representations both onstage and off, as well as their unsettling effects. Benglia's intense glance to the side reveals the tension of what lurks outside the frame, piercing the photo with the force of what Roland Barthes calls the "punctum"—that "element which rises from the scene"—the rare detail that grabs a viewer and causes her to see the image anew.[14] Benglia's sideward gaze also alerts us to what cannot be captured in official publicity or archives, suggesting a productive space outside the dominant discourse for that which has not been entirely overridden by imperial power.

The background in Benglia's publicity photo also highlights its theatrical artifice as if to suggest the fraudulent ontology of empire: the lush curtain spilling onto the floor behind Benglia gives way to walls and everyday furniture in the room, visually interrupting the photographic containment. The shimmering curtain also emphasizes the constructed nature not only of Brutus Jones but also imperial qualities themselves. Benglia's photo moreover reveals how a performer's identity is unstable, with contradictory and ambiguous qualities. Publicity stills have frequently been vehicles for actors to craft their identities, and the curtain has surfaced as a playful prop in these photos. For instance, Paige McGinley has observed in her work on female blues performers that "the curtain emerges as a central image, a theatrical tool manipulated by both photographer and subject to produce" the performer's identity.[15] Similarly, Benglia positions himself stiffly in front of the fabric: it is not a proscenium curtain, but rather a drape in front of a large window or French door. Not quite a theatrical set, but also *not* not a theatrical set (to use Richard Schechner's phrase), the background hovers in a liminal space between O'Neill's scripted mise en scène and the photographer's studio, simultaneously revealing role and actor, emperor and subject, colonizer and colonized.[16] At a moment when North

African actors inhabited only one side of those binaries in European theater, typically performing demeaning roles, Benglia's simultaneous embodiment of both emperor and colonized subject unsettled the imperial project both onstage and off.

In wearing the Emperor's grand regalia in Paris and performing in French, Benglia subverted his appellation as mere colonial subject, challenging "the narcissistic demand of colonial authority," as Bhabha puts it.[17] Benglia reversed colonial appropriations by portraying the familiar story of Brutus Jones, but with a difference: by performing an Emperor as a North African in the very country that colonized his own. "The menace of mimicry," Bhabha writes, "is its double vision, which in disclosing the ambivalence of colonial discourse also disrupts its colonial authority."[18] In the publicity photo, Benglia's figure threatens to burst forth at any minute, providing resistance, even in the still moment. Caught between his Emperor role and colonial subjectivity, Benglia commands attention while barely disguising his discomfort.

The photo moreover provides an insight into its futurity, because Benglia would reprise this role in Paris twenty-seven years later on the cusp of the Algerian War. His posing for this publicity photo can be seen as a way of anticipating his "*futured* look," to borrow Harvey Young's work on enslaved people who posed for daguerreotypes. Performing stillness for the camera invites recognition of Benglia's own "*futured* body," not only as a photographic subject anticipating its documentation but also as a performing artist who would reprise the role of Brutus Jones.[19] As an artifact misplaced in the archive, the photo thus serves as a dissonant imperial representation and points to its unsettled colonial epistemology, jumping from its incorrect indexing (it does not belong to African American photography, as cataloged in the Beinecke) and improper cartographic placement (Benglia was North African, not African American). His photo also jumps temporality with its paradoxical liveness. Time can jump, Rebecca Schneider has argued, becoming syncopated and doubled so that the "still" photo is never still: "It jumps medial boundaries, from theatre to photography and back," she writes. "It travels *and* returns. It passes *and* recurs. Syncopation troubles ephemerality. It troubles medial specificity."[20] Benglia's publicity photo thus looks both back in time to pre-French rule in Algeria and forward to the Battle of Algiers; from the 1920 premiere of *The Emperor Jones* in the United States to the 1923 French dignitary soirée; from a Parisian national theater to Benglia's own Montparnasse club; and it jumps again to the 1950 Parisian revival with Benglia's "troupe noir", suggesting connections among these temporal, racial, and cartographic coordinates.

This performance of dissonant imperial representation created carto-graphic confusion in the press. Many headlines reductively referred to Benglia's nationality in trying to locate his identity. The caption for the Paris publicity photo, for example, labeled him as an "Algerian Negro." Many other critics simply got lost in the map. The *New York Times*, for instance, erroneously identified the "New Emperor Jones" as hailing from Bengal.[21] This conflation of Benglia's last name with a part of India is at the very least bad reporting, if not ethnocentric. The African American *New York Amsterdam News* mistakenly referred to Benglia as "Soudanese," at least getting the continent correct if not the country or spelling.[22] Back in the States, the African American *Cleveland Gazette* mistakenly called him "Senegalese," while the *Forum* bungled his name as "Negro Genglia."[23] Such misidentifications signaled Benglia's indecipherability within the coordinates of imperial representation; commentators literally could not locate him on the map. He was actually known as "Beng" to his friends, according to a feature story in the French periodical *La Rampe*.[24]

In addition, some critics declared they had "discovered" the actor as if he were an ethnographic specimen and not a seasoned artist. This faulty reasoning was epitomized by the *New York Times*, which (inaccurately) boasted the headline "A Bengali 'Discovery.'" Such phrases played on the familiar, and problematic, colonial trope of capturing something primitive, like a Bengal tiger on safari. As the *Times* put it, there was a quasi-ethnographic thrill in finding, but also *displaying*, the actor: "It is predicted that the 'discovery' will be one of the biggest sensations of the theatrical year."[25] By contrast, the *New York Amsterdam News* not only contextualized how Benglia had been a working actor years before the Paris engagement but also how his career had been characterized by typecasting, having been cast in "minor parts in various plays of Oriental coloring."[26] In spite of already having performed on Paris stages, Benglia was incorrectly referred to as a novice actor whom critics and audiences repeatedly "discovered," only to put him in stereotypical roles. A discovery narrative, or scenario, as Diana Taylor calls it, is deliberately simplistic and banal and "simultane-ously constructs the wild object and the viewing subject—producing a 'we' and an 'our' as it produces a 'them.'"[27] Such crude formations rely upon power dynamics within distinct racialized optics, rendering certain sub-jects visible and others unseen. Crucially, discovery scenarios require embodiment, finding extraordinary articulation through performance. Benglia's embodiment of Brutus Jones—as a North African commanding a role on his colonizer's national stage—disrupted familiar discovery narra-tives, if not the ontology of empire itself.

Black bodies within French colonial contexts have long been viewed through the prism of primitivism. Theater and film representations of colonial subjects were no different, recycling long-standing discourses of discovery and display. Not surprisingly, performance played a vital role in disseminating such tropes. As Christophe Konkobo demonstrates, Africans were often transported to France and exhibited along with animals in simulated African villages as part of ethnographic displays. These not only drew on zoo discourse as models but also were, in effect, human zoos. As a performative justification of colonialism, "human zoos carefully designed popular spectacles to focus entirely on the physicality of the so-called savage."[28] Primitivism found its way from ethnographic displays to the stage, whether it was in the form of staged savagery or with "ethnographic primitivism," to use Kurt Eisen's formation, in O'Neill's plays.[29] In her book *Black Paris*, Bennetta Jules-Rosette documents the powerful ways in which anthropology shaped desire for Black American and African performers in France. "The role played by French anthropology in creating this receptive atmosphere," she writes, "was fraught with contradictions that other French intellectuals and artists were quick to recognize."[30] The anthropological legacy for Africans in France seems clear in the misrecognition of Benglia as Senegalese, Sudanese, or Bengali.

In addition to resisting familiar discovery narratives and ethnographic paradigms, Benglia's *L'Empereur Jones* was difficult to locate within a performance history comprised exclusively of African American performers in the role. If the white press deployed discovery narratives regarding Benglia, some U.S. Black newspapers that covered the Paris performance narrated a different kind of encounter, one that flipped the rhetoric of Empire and conquest. For example, in an article entitled "Negro Theatrical Invasion of Europe," Benglia's *L'Empereur Jones* was listed as a significant incursion into European stages. Moreover, Benglia (or "Bengelia," as they mistakenly referred to him) "is the only serious Negro actor in Europe," adding in conclusion: "We hope that this invasion of Europe will be as successful as it has been in New York."[31] Some of the revised discovery narratives harkened back to Gilpin, the actor who originated the role of Brutus Jones. The *Chicago Defender*'s headline "Algerian Star Thrills Paris in Gilpin Role" foregrounded Benglia as a star, but tellingly absented O'Neill entirely. Gilpin, however, was credited as the de facto creator of the piece—which he always claimed he was.[32] Baltimore's *Afro-American* was decidedly blunt, running the headline "He's No Charles Gilpin" and faulting Bengalia (as it misspelled his name) for failing to make the Paris production a success.[33] The *New York Amsterdam News* likewise inserted Gilpin in the headline, but characterized the play as distinctly African American and seemingly unproducible without "our own" Gilpin.[34] "From now on," it wrote, "'The Emperor Jones' without Charlie Gilpin will be as empty as a graveyard in the early morning hours."[35] But one actor's graveyard was another artist's kingdom, for Benglia's supposed flop guaranteed Gilpin's reign. The *Amsterdam News* continued: "We might add in conclusion that this [failure] is the greatest tribute that could be paid to Gilpin."[36] As this newspaper saw it, no other actor, especially an Algerian one, could occupy the role that Gilpin originated. And yet, Benglia not only tore away the iconic role of Brutus Jones but also reinscribed it with new meaning with diasporic performatives.

UNTIDY DIASPORIC TRANSLATION

While there were several problems in mounting *L'Empereur Jones* at the Théâtre de l'Odéon, this production nonetheless produced a diasporic performative that unsettled the imperial imaginary. As the *New York Times* observed bluntly, "Of flaws there were sufficient."[37] It would be tempting to analyze the Paris performance as an "unhappy performative": on one level it misfired (or as the *New York Transcript* put it, "missed fire") for not having the proper conditions to allow it to succeed. J. L. Austin has characterized this aspect of speech acts as an unhappy performative, which occurs when something "*goes wrong* and . . . the utterance is then, we may say, not indeed false but in general unhappy."[38] While many aspects of *L'Empereur Jones* adhered to Austin's "doctrine of the Infelicities," as he called them, what is striking about this production is not how it failed or "missed fire," but rather how these infelicities produced an altogether different kind of diasporic performative—one that succeeded in critiquing colonialism.

Although *L'Empereur Jones* was not an entirely accurate translation, it demonstrates that tidy translations are not always possible—or desirable. Translation, as Edwards has noted, is a central concern of diasporic identity, and is particularly so in diasporic performance, as this instance of *L'Empereur Jones* makes clear. Indeed, "points of misunderstanding, bad faith, unhappy translation" can reveal important ideological assumptions about racialized identities.[39] One French critic raised the issue by bluntly asking: "Is *The Emperor Jones* a masterpiece? By that we mean: Does it merit the honor of a translation?" (*L'Empereur Jones est-il un chef-d'œuvre? Nous entendons là: méritait-il l'honneur d'une traduction?*).[40] If O'Neill's play was worthy of a translation, it was indeed untidy. Translated by Maurice Bourgeois, the French version noticeably lacked the American "Negro dialect," as it was called, found in O'Neill's script. As originally written, Jones's first lines read: "Who dare whistle dat way in my palace? Who dare wake up de Emperor? I'll git de hide frayled off some o' you 'n— —r's sho'!"[41] With dialogue such as this, O'Neill sought to capture the Black vernacular in the same way that he had scripted Swedish American or Irish American voices in other works. (In the case of *The Emperor Jones*, O'Neill was critiqued for his primitivistic portrait and use of racial epithets—see chapter 1). The Paris production engaged with O'Neill's portrayal of Black identity differently, invoking diasporic resonances between France and her colonial subjects. Instead of African American or Cockney dialects, both Brutus Jones and Smithers are scripted with French slang.[42] Maurice Bourgeois created this patois by dropping vowels at the end of words, as can be seen in Jones's opening lines: "*Qui os' siffler comm' ça dons mon palais? Qui os' éveiller l'Empereur? Sûr que j'frai écorcher quéq's-uns d'entre vous, sal's nègres!*"[43] With the exception of a dropped 'e,' from words like '*ose*,' '*je*,' '*comme*,' and '*sales*', or an 'l' and 'u' from *quelques-uns*, the language is otherwise proper French. Gone in this version are O'Neill's attempts to capture the African American vernacular, which harken back to minstrelsy utterances (i.e., "I'se" for "I am" and "heah" for "here"). Yet, paradoxically, the more grammatically correct version was seen as lacking when performed in Paris. While the *New York Times* reported that "the translation was good," another paper stateside reported that "some of the atmosphere was lost by the translator using full French words," which made for disgruntled audiences.[44]

Most significantly, "n— —r" was missing in this French translation. In its place, Bourgeois used "*nègre*," a word that translates more closely with "Negro," and which was considered less offensive in the 1920s. It is still used today to signify "Black" (for example, Achille Mbembe's book *Critique de la Raison Nègre* [2013] is translated as *Critique of Black Reason*).[45] To take one example from *L'Empereur Jones*, Bourgeois translated Jones's line "fool bush n— —r's" as "*ces imbéciles de nègr's de la brousse.*"[46] While Jones directs his rage at those whom he perceives to be his imbecilic underlings, he does not hurl racialized epithets at them in this French version, as in O'Neill's script. In sum, in the French translation Brutus Jones's language is clipped, colloquial, and distinctly not bourgeois—an ironic effect from Bourgeois, the translator.

In addition to a French translation that cut the racialized dialect, this production also "mercilessly" excised some sections, such as the important Middle Passage slave ship scene, an essential moment in representing Jones's collective unconscious (this was also tragically removed from the

Fig. 10. Design of the throne room by Walter René Fuerst for the 1923 Paris production of *L'Empereur Jones*. Eugene O'Neill Papers. Yale Collection of American Literature, Beinecke Rare Book and Manuscript Library.

1933 film version).[47] Thinking that the Middle Passage context was too American for French audiences, the director chose unwisely to eliminate it, although they did feature the slave auction scene. Such excisions led one newspaper to claim that the production had "committed atrocities difficult to believe, even if reported by eye-witnesses."[48]

Not everything was cut, however. Some things were embellished. First, the set design by Walter René Fuerst, according to the *Forum*'s columnist, "was more expressionistic, in movement and interpretation it was more stylized than in the New York production."[49] The set was also "decidedly African in its highly developed architecture, rather than West Indian," noted a short article in the playbill for *The Emperor Jones* stateside.[50] French critic René Wisner observed that "*L'Empereur Jones* has remarkable scenery. A forest by simple means and precise, is evoked rather than shown" ("*L'Empereur Jones est remarquablement mis en scène. Une forêt, par des moyen simples et précis, est plutôt évoquée que montrée*").[51] He called the first tableau "one of lucid, rippling intelligence" ("*Ce premier tableau est d'une intelligence lucide et ondoyante*").[52] In addition to the augmented expressionism, the staging was critiqued for adding pantomime elements during scene changes, according to a *New York Times* critic:

In order to sustain the intensity from scene to scene the French producer decided that the tom-tom and the darkened house were not enough. He knew the restlessness of a French audience, and to counteract it he added the ingenious device of sending detachments of the natives across in front of the curtain, groping on hands and knees, as a reminder that the pursuit continued; sometimes the Emperor himself would cross and recross, or the cockney Smithers would shamble out and utter his cynical laugh. All this in darkened pantomime—and the result was too much like a chapter out of Fennimore Cooper, as the French (who know that author well) themselves recognized.[53]

This bizarre staging led to the audience's confusion, sparking "uneasy applause from time to time."[54]

Reviews in both the Black and white U.S. press repeatedly pointed out how the French did not grasp, or like, the American context. "Paris," observed the African American periodical *Afro-American*, "received the production coldly."[55] The *New York Times* reported, "For the French, there was some scorn, much bewilderment and very little honest admiration" of the production.[56] The French, "suspicious of anything calculated to give comfort to foreign invaders," shied away from the event, leaving an unusual mix of spectators.[57] "The resulting audience," the *New York Transcript* observed, "consisted of a few American students and artists, several tourists of all nationalities, a handful of curious French, and a greater number of empty seats than a Parisian theatre had probably ever seen on the eve of a holiday."[58] Those who came to the production had a limited understanding of French, let alone O'Neill's expressionism: "Paris-American high society does not concern itself with art, or else does not know enough French to enjoy an evening of French dialogue," continued the newspaper. The confusion was augmented by the fact that there was no free playbill, and the program that was offered (for three francs) failed to summarize the story. Therefore "some of the audience, who did not follow the exposition too closely, came away with the idea that Jones, after leaving the penitentiary, went to some negro colony in the South, and possibly believed that there were districts in the United States where aboriginal superstitions and customs are still practiced by the native blacks."[59] The transnational resonances of the play had been profoundly misunderstood; and yet the infelicities provided insights into diasporic cultural practices in the American South.

The *New York Evening Mail* attributed this puzzlement to France's different colonial history:

Although it had been turned into French with a real French colonial Negro in the title role, the critics found themselves unable to grasp the point—the change from a Pullman car flunky to a savage tyrant who at last succumbs to his instinctive fear of the jungle. To the Frenchman color prejudice is practically unknown. Racial mixtures in the French colonies have not been viewed seriously as dangerous to the purity of the white blood.[60]

Putting aside the debatable claim that France had scant racial prejudice, what is intriguing is the assertion that what made the play "French" was a "real French colonial Negro in the title role." *Frenchness*, to pursue this logic, requires colonial Black subjects; it also requires performance. Yet this production did not offer a familiar imperial representation or recognizable imperial actor. A review in the African American publication *The Crisis* put it succinctly, saying that Paris had "found a puzzling ethnological problem that her own experience with black colonials did not help solve."[61] In other words, France's vexed colonial history did not prepare audiences for an actor like Benglia portraying an emperor. The *New York Times* miscalculated those resonances, writing that "the Emperor Jones is not an international drama."[62] In fact, the opposite was true: the North African-French *Emperor Jones* was an intensely international drama. Rudolf Kommer, covering Parisian theater for the *New York Times*, summarized the problem concisely: "It isn't easy to produce an American play in Europe. The misunderstanding of 'Emperor Jones' in Paris was grotesque."[63] Rather than interpreting the misunderstandings as misfires, however, I see these disjunctures as productive performative wedges within the imperial imaginary—and Benglia's embodied practices were central to this critique.

In addition to the "puzzling ethnological problems" mentioned in the Paris production, French reviews commented upon Benglia's physicality (something that also befell Robeson and Bledsoe when they performed Brutus Jones, as I argue in other chapters). The French press frequently mentioned Benglia's physical attractiveness, particularly his muscular body. French scholar Nathalie Coutelet has called Benglia the "'nègrérotique' du spectacle français," or the eroticized Black performer of French entertainment. She provides several examples in relation to Benglia's *L'Empereur Jones*, including this 1923 French review: "Mr. Benglia, he acts with his muscles. It can be said of Mr. Benglia that his chest speaks, and his shoulder blades are screaming. Sweat bathes him, brightening his tanned chest." Benglia's sculptural "bronze torso," the review continued, "is a triumph of anatomy."[64] Another critic referred to him as an "admirable athlete" ("*un admirable athlete*"); another gushed over "muscles like that!" ("*muscles comme ça!*").[65] This "magnificent bronze" ("*un bronze magnifique*") actor, as he was called, also appeared to have a following among French women, referred to as "the ladies in the colorful Academy of Mr. Benglia," who would erupt with "little cries of admiration" during performances.[66] Coutelet has argued that the characterization of Benglia's performances during the 1920s and '30s are plagued by exoticization: "The characters he plays are always linked to sexuality. . . . The artist is deleted in favor of a mere physique—an erotic body. Admired for his flawless, almost plastic body, Benglia was compared to ancient statues. . . . These clichés reflect the fears and fantasies of a public fascinated by blacks."[67]

While Coutelet's analysis indisputably reveals the ways in which Benglia became exoticized in French theater and film, it would be a mistake to disregard his performances as merely fetishistic. Rather, the contradictory discourse about Benglia's body was a manifestation of racial projections and anxieties regarding Black masculinity during the 1920s that was seen on many national stages. Benglia's Brutus Jones subverted racialized discourse projected onto him by citing, and redeploying, imperialness within and beyond *The Emperor Jones*. Thus, while Benglia may have been admired for his "magnificent bronze" body, he put a wedge into such primitivistic fantasies with performance choices that refused his appellation as mere fetish, as I explain in more detail below. He had, after all, a gun strapped to his waist and a fan base composed of colonial dignitaries. Benglia commanded the stage. As the weekly Parisian arts periodical *La Rampe* reminded its readers: "he carries himself like a conqueror" ("*Il se redresse comme un vainqueur*").[68]

Benglia moreover made calculated performance choices that unsettled some of the problematic aspects of O'Neill's play. In spite of the slang scripted in Bourgeois's translation, Benglia, who "speaks French fluently," as the *Crisis* observed, did not add an African or African American dialect.[69] As a classically trained actor, he approached the text with precision and craft—and was roundly praised for his excellence. Yet, rather than understanding Benglia's lack of "negro" dialect as a choice, the *New York Times* saw it as a flaw: "M. Habib Benglia, a French Colonial negro of great talent, was handicapped by the lack of the dialect which made Gilpin's task easier—for there is no French patois that matches our darky lingo."[70] The racist backhanded compliment continues: "But his facial and body technique were so good that his inappropriate language could be forgiven."[71] Perversely, Benglia's proper French was described as "inappropriate" because he declined to incorporate O'Neill's dialect into some form of

Franco-African patois. Much like Gilpin, who notoriously crafted O'Neill's text to his liking by expunging racial epithets and dialect, so too Benglia made the text his own. These speech acts, as I wish to see them (and unhappy ones at that), led to confusion for those audiences expecting a less articulate Emperor, which supposedly Gilpin delivered: "[Gilpin] laid less stress on the intellectual side of his character," a French newspaper reported, "portraying him rather as a heavy-witted, uncouth savage. And in this he was right."[72] Benglia, the article suggests, got it wrong by being quick-witted, by undoing primitivistic projections, and by resisting his colonial interpellation. He put a wedge into the existing imperial imaginary, featuring his acting talent, intellect, and command of language. One French critic from the newspaper *L'Avenir* noted Benglia's commanding performance: "He breathes authority and incisiveness. He has the grace of an animal in his movements and shows himself to be a person of rare intelligence. He is handsome in appearance, and his gestures, attitude and dancing show admirable harmony and grace. His diction is clear, his enunciation distinct."[73] Enmeshed with primitivism, the French review nonetheless credits the actor for his talents, pointing out his distinct diction and intelligence, revealing stereotypes even in the compliments. Benglia's training caught the *New York Amsterdam News*'s attention back in the States: "He has a good education and speaks refined French," it wrote.[74] The French newspaper *L'Eclair* went further with its praise: "Monsieur Benglia as *Emperor Jones* was magnificent. All admired him, all praised him."[75]

While Benglia sidestepped Brutus Jones's dialect, Smithers (Jones's Cockney sidekick and, tellingly, the only white character in the play) became strangely racialized in the Paris production: he was "transformed conveniently into a Paris 'apache,' the French equivalent," reported the *New York Transcript*.[76] In a French context, "apaches" were working-class Parisians; they were not, however, a subculture equivalent to London's Cockneys, as the *Transcript* claimed, but rather violent gang members whose "savagery" was likened stereotypically to Apache Indians from the American frontier.[77] Thus, another paradoxical aspect of diasporic (mis)translation emerged in this production: Smithers, the white character, became racialized as an apache just as Benglia steered away from racialized dialect.

It should come as no surprise that O'Neill's play, a drama that has been pivotal in discussions of racial performativity and empire, evoked such rich contradictions when staged in Paris. Benglia's *L'Empereur Jones* refused to gloss over the unhappy translations of imperial performance, and indeed underscored the discomfort of those conflicting discourses. Like the publicity photograph that could hardly contain his uneasy glance outside the frame, Benglia's performance literally embodied the ambivalence of colonial discourse, suggesting a rich repertoire that exists beyond official archives and performance spaces. Hardly a subject of discovery narratives or ethnographic primitivism, Benglia instead deployed and subverted tropes of empire, demonstrating the force of dissonant imperial representation.

PERFORMATIVE TRACES: THE CONGO WITCH-DOCTOR AT LE TRAIN BLEU

Benglia performed subsequent iterations of *The Emperor Jones* in Paris, where he lived for the rest of his life. He would become part of Black Paris, traversing performance venues and nightlife with other performers of color before opening his own nightclub in Montparnasse called Le Train Bleu (The Blue Train) in 1931 that was hailed as the toast of Paris. Here, Benglia utilized dance and performance to challenge racial hierarchies, and the Emperor's remains were once again unearthed, invoked, and deployed. In this unexpected venue, empire and its subversion collided with an iteration of *The Emperor Jones*. At his club Benglia was especially known for performing the Congo Witch-Doctor, a character that appears near the end of *The Emperor Jones* in a hallucinatory scene and demands a sacrifice.[78] Jones refuses and shoots the last of his bullets at the vision. Although the character has a short scene with no lines, the Congo Witch-Doctor often captured the audience's attention, depending on the performer.

On one level, we might say that Benglia's reperformance of O'Neill's Congo Witch-Doctor was in the service of empire. Yet, on another level, Black performers sometimes wielded primitivism even in the act of asserting their agency against imperial cultural production.[79] Benglia's performances of the Witch-Doctor expressed a form of modernist dance that incorporated primitivism that was already familiar to the French. Just a month before Benglia took the stage as Brutus Jones in Paris in 1923, the Ballets Suédois presented its *ballet nègre*, called *La création du monde*, created by "some of the most sophisticated French artists" seeking to produce "primitive" work as a vehicle of modern dance.[80] As dance scholar Richard Brender has written, "the image of Africa that had come down to Frenchmen of the twenties" had a long history, harkening back to stereotypes originating as early as the sixteenth century.[81] There were a number of dancers who cashed in on this "Africana chic," as one critic called it, performing to full houses; Benglia was one such performer who "reinvented

Fig. 11. Albert Rudomine, "Habib Benglia, Folies Bergère," 1921. Gelatin silver print, 29.9 × 19.9 cm (11 3/4 × 7 13/16 in.). J. Paul Getty Museum, Los Angeles.

Fig. 12. Habib Benglia wearing a costume that recalls the Congo Witch-Doctor role from *L'Empereur Jones*, 1931. Photo by Studio Henri Manuel. Screenshot by Katie N. Johnson.

Fig. 13. Habib Benglia holding a North African instrument while bending in a ballet first-position plié. Photo by Studio Henri Manuel. Screenshot by Katie N. Johnson.

Africa in their own image."[82] Indeed, in spite of his extensive stage and film work, Benglia considered himself primarily a dancer.[83] One publicity photo from 1921 for the Folies-Bergère shows him in a triumphant dance pose, wearing a waistcloth and looking upward, smiling. The high-key lighting emphasizes his strong form and graceful arms. A closer look reveals that he is creating a bird-like shadow behind his body, suggesting that there is more behind this dancer than meets the eye. Moreover, several African masks are carefully placed at his feet. The headline accompanying a review in the *Baltimore Afro-American* boasted that he "electrifie[d the] French Capital."[84] His African dance at Folies-Bergère bears an uncanny likeness to the famous photograph of Josephine Baker in her 1925 *danse sauvage* at the Théâtre des Champs-Élysées in 1925.[85] It is significant to note that Benglia preceded by two years "the Black Pearl," as Baker was known in Paris, with his *L'Empereur Jones*. Parisian audiences therefore already knew him when he took the stage as Brutus Jones in 1923. Given Benglia's desire to break into modernist dancing (just as he had done with O'Neill's modernist theater), it is therefore not surprising that dance was so vital to Benglia's Montparnasse club a decade later. While Benglia's dancing of the Congo

Witch-Doctor may appear to reinscribe colonial performances of *l'exposition coloniale*, Benglia subverted the colonial imaginary—and this is where the traces of *The Emperor Jones* leave their mark once again.

In shifting his performance from imperial tyrant (Jones) to formidable witch doctor and from the national stage to a Montparnasse club, Benglia deployed diasporic performatives as a counterperformance to the Paris Colonial Exposition. *La Rampe* observed that Benglia, whom they donned *"Le grand acteur noir,"* danced every night at his Montparnasse club.[86] As the *Chicago Defender* reported, "dressed as an African witch-doctor" Benglia gave "a thrill with his dancing."[87] Publicity photos accompanying a 1931 *La Rampe* feature story show Benglia costumed in this role. He is shirtless, with white symbols painted over his entire body, wearing numerous necklaces with beads and shells that cover much of his torso. Strapped around his arms, knees, and ankles are beaded bracelets with dangling shells. He wears a kind of kilt composed of an assortment of feathers and possibly a rabbit's tail. One curved feather arcs erectly to the side, a possible playful citation of Baker's famous banana skirt. He strikes a pose of intensity, as if in mid action. By contrast, in the next photograph he appears relaxed while holding a stringed instrument (likely an Algerian quwaytara).[88] Given the elaborate ornamentation of this costume, it might be easy to miss that Benglia's feet are turned out in first-position ballet, combining aesthetics of empire with African diaspora. In contrast to the intense first photo, he calmly looks downward, bending into a deep plié. His turnout is impressive. Only a trained dancer would be able to perform this classical ballet position. Ballet, as Susan Foster has argued, disciplines the body toward a "phallic pointe," a patriarchal (and, I would add, a white European) ideal.[89] But not so with Benglia. He places a performative wedge by juxtaposing a foundational European classical dance pose with Black diasporic performance practices.

The opening of Benglia's Le Train Bleu also coincided with the 1931 Colonial Exposition in Paris—a prime example of "colonial myth-making," as historian Jennifer Anne Boittin observes.[90] Indeed, *"L'Exposition Coloniale Internationale de Paris* feted the accomplishments of colonialism," and it was the last world's fair to celebrate colonialism (at least explicitly).[91] Performance was crucial for commemorating empire in the form of ethnographic villages, dance, and theatrical spectacles. By contrast, Benglia's club presented another mapping of colonial subjectivity, reshaping the contours of what Boittin has called the "urban topography of race" in Paris during the 1930s.[92] Rather than perpetuating the ethnographic gaze of the Exposition, Benglia turned empire on its head with his dancing—and he did so by

Fig. 14. Le Train Bleu restaurant in the Gare de Lyon train station, Paris. Select patrons can dine in rooms named after former French colonies, including one called Salon Algerien. Habib Benglia named his Montparnasse club Le Train Bleu after this posh restaurant as well as after the opera-ballet of the same title. Photo by Katie N. Johnson.

invoking *The Emperor Jones*. Benglia's reperformances of the Witch-Doctor in his Montparnasse club made headlines in U.S. Black newspapers. By all accounts Benglia's Le Train Bleu was hailed as "the liveliest spot in Paris," known for its diverse and artistic clientele (including members of royalty and Charlie Chaplin).[93] One of the few integrated establishments at that time, the club was a space where "whites and blacks of all social grades may be seen in close embrace on the tightly packed dance floor."[94] Le Train Bleu was so popular that just three weeks after it opened the management had to turn crowds away.[95] With his counterperformance of colonial subjectivity, Benglia articulated the very early beginnings of what would become the Négritude movement, something he developed in his later body of work in film, theater, and dance.[96]

The name for Benglia's club connotes additional performative valence, for *Le train bleu* was also the name of a famous 1924 *opérette dansée*, a modern ballet that poked fun at the leisure class.[97] Long before it was satirized onstage, Le Train Bleu was the nickname of an express train that wealthy "blue bloods" took from Paris to the Côte d'Azur. Benglia's ironic reclamation of the Blue Train symbolically inverted tropes of wealth, spectacle, travel, and color (here, blue becomes black) while retaining the glam nod to Chanel fashion, dandyism, and modernism's hipsters.[98] Rather than traveling to the moneyed Riviera, however, Benglia's patrons trekked to the bohemian and artistic district of Montparnasse, "the center of Paris's black colonial population."[99] Benglia had divined his own blue train and routed the track back to Black Paris. Le Train Bleu was also (and still is) the name of an exquisite belle époque restaurant built in 1900 within Paris's Gare de Lyon train station, adorned with neo-baroque gilded trim, paintings of theater icons, and, tellingly, "ethnically themed" rooms, including a beautifully adorned Algerian chamber (indeed, rooms are named for most of the former French colonies and the main room has murals depicting colonial contact). Benglia's blue train was another cheeky pun, a rebuke to the Orientalized interiors of a posh restaurant, a campy upending of elitist patronage.[100] In renaming his club audaciously after a blue-blood train route, a belle époque restaurant, and a modernist ballet, Benglia inserted Blackness (and specifically North Africanness) into otherwise white French spaces. Moreover, he asserted himself into the all-white field of modern dance in reappropriating Jean Cocteau's 1924 dance opera *Le train bleu*. This was Benglia's blue train. With playful citation he positioned himself in relation to the pantheon of modernist greats, such as Cocteau and Bronislava Nijinksa.

Benglia kept his club while performing roles in cinema and on the stage. In 1947, he followed a path similar to Robeson, by portraying the "black Napoleon" (Toussaint Louverture) in the five-act play *Napoléon Noir* by Paul Haurigot.[101] He would keep the Emperor close to his side, preparing for a Parisian revival.

REVIVING DIASPORIC PERFORMATIVES

When Benglia revived the role of Brutus Jones in 1950, he again made history in Paris with a troupe of Black actors (or "*acteurs noirs*," as the French press characterized the performers) named "Segg," performing under the auspices of the Compagnie des Argonautes.[102] In Greek mythology, the argonauts were a band of heroic fighters who accompanied Jason on his quest for the golden fleece just before the Trojan War. It was prescient timing, given that France was wrestling with its own colonial unrest in Algeria. Benglia had his sights on creating a Black French theater—a kind of dramaturgical golden fleece—but for now, the Emperor would have to do.[103] Directed by Sylvain Dhomme, this iteration of *L'Empereur Jones* was chosen to inaugurate the opening of a new Parisian theater called Point 50; it was paired with another American one acter: Susan Glaspell's *Bagatelle* (*Trifles*) and ran for one month.[104] Even though O'Neill was hailed in the press as "a revolutionary playwright" (*"un révolutionnaire de l'art drama-tique"*), the true revolutionaries were the performers in the 1950 French production, comprised almost entirely of a Black cast (with the exception of the role of Smithers), and with Benglia at the helm.[105]

Staged only a few years before the Algerian War of Independence (1954–62), this version of *L'Empereur Jones* conjured diasporic performatives to interrogate the enduring legacy of colonialism. "Those who needed to bol-ster their cause," reported the French newspaper *Le Matin*, "wanted to see [the play] in a distinctly anticolonial light" (*"Certains, pour les besoins de leur cause, ont voulu y voir un esprit anticolonialiste déterminé"*).[106] Even though *Le Matin*'s critic believed an anticolonial reading was a stretch (*Je pense qu'ils se trompent*), other commentators readily perceived the production as a cri-tique of colonial power: "It's a satirical and cynical interpretation, that makes one think in this time of heartbreaking colonialism" (*"C'est une vision satirique et cynique qui fait songer, eu ce temps de colonialisme déchirant"*).[107] In addition to unveiling the heartbreaking aspects of colonialism, this produc-tion of *L'Empereur Jones* also conjured revolutionaries who overthrew their oppressors. One review, for instance, observed that Habib Benglia "strapped into his uniform in the manner of Toussaint Louverture" (*"san-glé dans son uniforme à la Toussaint Louverture"*).[108] If Benglia's Brutus Jones was buckled into his Emperor's jacket like one of the most legendary dia-sporic revolutionaries (Louverture), he also added another performative layer by donning a "fiery red uniform" (*"l'uniform rouge feu"*), instead of the blue jacket stipulated in O'Neill's stage directions. Benglia's blazing red regalia could have been citing Jean-Jacques Dessalines—often rendered in portraits wearing a red jacket—who declared Saint Domingue's indepen-dence from France in 1804 and became Haiti's first emperor.[109] Benglia was likened to another Black diasporic ruler: Fastin-Élie Soulouque, president of Haiti from 1847 to 1849, who declared the Second Haitian Empire and served as emperor (1849–59) before being ousted. Unlike the other com-parisons to Louverture, Dessalines, or Henri Christophe, this reference to Soulouque highlighted despotic and tyrannical rule: *L'Empereur Jones* "undoubtedly derives its origin from the bloody buffoonery of Soulouque, who once performed a carnivalesque upheaval in Haiti" (*"tire sans doute son*

*origine de la bouffonnerie sanglante de Soulouque qui jadis joua en Haïti aux Cés-
ars de carnaval*").[110] While it is true that Benglia's revived Brutus Jones
shared affinities with the despotic Soulouque, what is telling is the reviewer's anxiety about the upheaval in Haiti as a possible precursor to disrup-
tions of French empire elsewhere.

The French revival referenced not only "Black Jacobins," to use C. L. R.
James's phrase, but also Black diasporic performance practices.[111] Performing a mimicry of colonialism, Benglia took the tools of oppression literally
into his own hands, as the French newspaper *L'Aurore* reported: "Despotic,
brutal, cynical, imposing his will with the whip or the revolver, Jones, fac-
ing an uprising, must abdicate soon" ("*Despote, brutal, cynique, imposant sa
volonté par le fouet ou le revolver, Jones, devant un soulèvement, doit bientôt abdi-
quer*").[112] Yet, more than handling the implements of oppression (whip,
revolver, intimidation), Benglia inserted *décalage* into previously conceived
imperial exchange by simultaneously conjuring colonizer and colonized.
Critics observed Benglia's power—"*la force grandiose de Habib Benglia*"—a
force almost too large for the hall in which the play was staged.[113] Other
cast members likewise infused the production with Black internationalism.
Among the cast was Diouta (sometimes spelled Douta) Seck, who performed "*l'étonnant sorcier*" (the Congo Witch-Doctor). Seck was a well-
known Senegalese performer who would go on to appear in another drama
about a Haitian revolutionary: *The Tragedy of King Christophe* (*La tragédie du
roi Christophe*), written by one of the founders of the Négritude movement,
Aimé Césaire. Appearing in the role of Native Chief Lem was Alioune Diakité, who was singled out in the press as possessing "a great allure" ("*la
grande allure*").[114] Accompanying Seck and Diakité were "their comrades
from the black troupe Segg, who recreate the songs and dances of their race
for us with exceptionally brilliant power" ("*leurs camarades de la troupe noir
Segg, qui nous restituent les chant et les danses de leur race avec un pouvoir de
rayonnement exceptionnel*").[115] While this review doesn't specify which
songs and dances are being performed (or from which country), the reference to "*dans leur race*" almost certainly pointed to the Black diaspora. This
may explain why stateside the production was reported as incorporating
voodoo, as this headline made clear: "Paris Does 'Emperor Jones' with
African Voodoo Troupe."[116] At times the French press succumbed to primitivism (like their counterparts in the U.S.), calling Benglia "*sauvage,*"[117] or
referencing the exoticism of the Segg company ("*l'exotisme de leur jeu*").[118]
Some French critics captured the tension between primitivism and Black
diasporic performance, by observing the company's "primitive and skilled
development" ("*les évolutions primitives et savants de la troupe noir Segg*").[119]

By all accounts, this revival was a success: the public gave the production "a well-deserved standing ovation" ("*une ovation méritée*").[120] A decade later, theater historian Shelby McCloy hailed Benglia's 1950 *L'Empereur Jones* as one of the two most memorable performances by an actor of color in France.[121]

No other African actor made a greater impression in Francophone theater, film, and dance during the first half of the twentieth century than Benglia. Largely absent from the scholarly record, but not from the repertoire of Black imperial performance or circum-Atlantic memory, his embodied practices intervened in colonial authority and discovery narratives. Benglia's engagement with *The Emperor Jones* demonstrates a new way of viewing O'Neill's play, offering richly layered performances that disrupted the colonial imaginary with diasporic *décalage*, crossing diverse racial geometries and temporal framings. Benglia's reperformances of Brutus Jones and the Congo Witch-Doctor—at a soirée for dignitaries, in a state-sanctioned theater, and at Benglia's own nightclub in the heart of Paris's Black colonial district—reveal the force and efficacy of performative imperial citation.

THREE | Broadway's First Interracial Kiss

In 1936, when Jesse Owens won his third Olympic medal and James Albritton set a record for the high jump, a drawing in the African American newspaper *Pittsburgh Courier* showed both Owens and Albritton racing toward victory with wings attached to their bodies. The headline, "All God's Chillun Got Wings," referenced a well-known spiritual and one of Eugene O'Neill's most controversial plays about miscegenation.[1] Why, twelve years after *All God's Chillun Got Wings*'s premiere, did the *Pittsburgh Courier* allude to this iconic spiritual and drama to celebrate two Black athletes? And how was *All God's Chillun Got Wings* relevant to the 1936 Berlin Olympics, a competition defined by Nazi white supremacist hate speech? At its core, the drawing captures triumph over racism, with Black competitors soaring beyond oppressive racial regimes. Owens would ultimately capture four medals, disproving Hitler's false claims of the Aryan race's superiority. Yet it was not the first time that Black Olympian athletes were celebrated by referencing O'Neill's play. During the 1932 Olympics held in Los Angeles, when Eddie Tolan and Ralph Metcalfe won the gold and silver medals in the 100-meter race, the *New York American* reported: "With Tolan and Metcalfe finishing one-two, it would appear that Eugene O'Neill said a mouthful when he pointed out that all God's chillun got wings. What chance did that blond German have with two dark men coming into his life at the same time?"[2] In depicting African American athletes racing across the finish line, these cartoons literalized a key insight from this book: Black citizens raced against structures of racism by performing, or invoking, O'Neill's dramatic works.

While "All God's Chillun Got Wings" is a nineteenth-century spiritual about African Americans transcending oppressive structures, citations of it in the press were not as abundant until after the 1924 premiere of O'Neill's play by the same title.[3] The spiritual was reignited with meaning after Robeson appeared in O'Neill's drama, and its circulation in American popular culture continued to grow after Robeson recorded it.

O'Neill's reference to this iconic spiritual is both ironic and tragic: the lead characters of *All God's Chillun* do not soar above racism, as the lyrics indicate. But then again, none of O'Neill tragic figures do so. Yet in spite of this, as the following pages show, *All God's Chillun Got Wings* served as a vehicle for breaking color lines and championing integrated casts on Broadway—and beyond. As seen in the 1936 drawing of Owens and Albritton, O'Neill's drama was reiterated in various cultural contexts as a sign of resistance to white racism, even as it was critiqued for its problematic portrayals of Black characters.

This chapter examines the stakes of staging miscegenation from the 1920s to the 1940s while crossing geographical coordinates with O'Neill's *All God's Chillun Got Wings*. Portraying interracial couples in American theater has long been considered taboo, and, as Glenda Gill has observed, when miscegenation has been dramatized, it has been portrayed "as sordid and tragic."[4] Plays featuring miscegenation in early American drama often portrayed it as nonconsensual, and they were often written by white or Irish Americans, as in Dion Boucicault's *The Octoroon* (1859), Edward Sheldon's *The N——r: An American Play in Three Acts* (1909), and Ernest Culbertson's *Goat Alley: A Tragedy of Negro Life* (1921). Given this context, *All God's Chillun Got Wings* portrayed interracial unions in a new way because *Chillun* "broke the silence surrounding *consensual* black/white sexuality in the North," observes Kevin Mumford.[5] *All God's Chillun* moreover reveals the intersections between Irish and Black minority cultures by portraying a mixed-race marriage that is crushed by the encroaching pressures of racism within a segregated neighborhood—forces that lean in, like the walls of the expressionistic set, to squash their union. Of O'Neill's representations of damaged love (and there are many), *All God's Chillun Got Wings* is unique not only because it is the first U.S. drama to portray a consensual interracial marriage, or that it broke the color line with a mixed cast, but also because it featured the first interracial kiss on Broadway.

On many levels, *All God's Chillun Got Wings* is hardly the model drama for interrogating white supremacy. *Chillun* was—and remains—one of O'Neill's most widely debated, if rarely performed, plays. The drama is problematic on many fronts: it features Jim Harris, an African American character striving to be a lawyer, who is destroyed by a destructive interracial marriage, as well as by racist structures that deny him a foothold in society. While for some commentators, O'Neill was one of the first American playwrights to write a serious leading Black character with complexity, other scholars, such as Glenda Frank, have taken O'Neill to task for his inability to portray a Black perspective in *All God's Chillun*. "A romantic scene between an interracial couple," she writes, "was perceived by the black community as self-destructive, beyond sensible discussion. O'Neill knew nothing of these constraints."[6] The script is, moreover, plagued with racial epithets: "n——r" is used twenty-seven times by my count (slightly less than in *The Emperor Jones*).[7] And, even though *Chillun's* casting practices rejected blackface performance, its success was uneven: some productions prohibited integrating child actors. This uneven production history demonstrates the erratic progression of racing Broadway with O'Neill's dramas: some productions broke color lines while others reinscribed the racial hierarchies of Broadway; some did both. In spite of the problematic plot and the intermittent use of blackface, Black theater companies in the U.S. and abroad used *All God's Chillun* to launch their seasons and integrate casts. *Chillun* therefore not only raced the Great White Way; it also raced theatrical stages across the world in London, Berlin, Paris, Budapest, Prague, Rio de Janeiro, and Tokyo.

At the center of this discussion are performances by Paul Robeson in plays and films about mixed-race unions in stages on Broadway, in Harlem, across the Atlantic, and in race studios. Robeson's performances in *All God's Chillun Got Wings*, which he played together with *The Emperor Jones*, launched his career, constituting an important stepping stone to future roles. It was also a drama that he revived several times over decades.[8] While some scholars have suggested that Robeson's portrayal of Jim in *All God's Chillun* was a sellout to white theater, I situate Robeson's role alongside what might be called his performative triptych: his militant performance of Brutus Jones (*The Emperor Jones*), his work in Black theater (*Roseanne*), and his roles in race cinema (Oscar Micheaux's *Body and Soul*), a silent film that has been characterized as "a profound reworking and critique" of O'Neill's plays.[9] Robeson *raced* O'Neill's play by invoking citations of diasporic rulers, therefore situating his portrayal of Jim Harris within the context of Black nationalism. Some scholars dwell on Robeson's political activism in his later years, but I contend that Robeson strategically utilized performances of *All God's Chillun* early in his career to challenge regimes of race. Scholars are mostly invested in the older Robeson, the Robeson after the Second World War, the Robeson who was defined by his leftist politics and surveilled by the U.S. government.[10] However, there is a great deal of radicalism in the young Robeson, especially when he was performing O'Neill's plays.

RADICAL, DANGEROUS STAGING

> The most radical step on the stage in this generation.[11]
> —*Brooklyn Eagle*, 1924

Although miscegenated marriages were not unusual in the United States during the early twentieth century, and most cities had neighborhoods where people of different ethnicities and races socialized, no American drama had thus far captured urban interraciality without resorting to melodramatic formulas before *All God's Chillun Got Wings*. O'Neill's drama captured a previously underrepresented aspect of mixed-race marriage as well as the racialized geographies of U.S. urban centers. "In most of our cities there are slums like that which Mr. O'Neill depicts," observed John Corbin in 1924, "in which black and white children mingle from infancy, playing together and going to the same schools. Mixed marriages are by no means uncommon."[12] Yet, in spite of mixed-race marriages existing in the United States during this time period, representing it onstage was another matter. As one reviewer put it, *All God's Chillun* "has a tendency to break down social barriers which are better left untouched."[13] The *New York World* ran numerous articles objecting to this "ill-advised performance," noting that "an act which is illegal in more than half the Nation and is disapproved in the entire country" should not been seen in a public theater.[14] The *World* moreover raised "the question as to whether it is legal to enact upon the stage something which is 'illegal and punishable as a crime . . . in all Southern and border States.'"[15] In fact, such sentiments about *Chillun's* illegality—if not illegitimacy—underscored ensuing censorship debates.

As it raced the Great White Way, the 1924 production of *All God's Chillun Got Wings* threatened to provoke "racial disorder," as one paper put it.[16] Headlines predicted there would be "race strife" if white actress Mary Blair kissed Paul Robeson's hand.[17] The impassioned social response has been likened to the tumultuous Astor Place riots. Indeed, *All God's Chillun Got Wings*'s staging of miscegenation was so provocative that death threats were issued to Robeson, Blair, O'Neill, and his son.[18] An editorial in the *Chicago Defender*, an African American newspaper, cautioned: "They talk about *The Birth of a Nation* causing trouble; you watch this play that is coming out."[19] New York public officials such as Chief Magistrate William McAdoo, who had a history of condemning good plays, warned that pandemonium would ensue: "I should think that in a country where racial prejudice is so deep-seated any play of such character as is described might prove very dangerous."[20] This characterization of the play as a threat to racial hierarchies found its way to the Midwest. Chicago's Legislative League protested against *All God's Chillun Got Wings*, as the *Chicago Defender* noted: "The country is torn at this moment by sinister racial dissension to a greater degree than in generations." *Chillun*, the piece continued, might "intensify racial consciousness, to fan flames already much too high for the nation's good."[21] The *Defender* summarized by stating: "The only effect of the play can be to make matters worse." The repeated references to "danger" demonstrate the perceived performative force of *All God's Chillun Got Wings* to not only race the Great White Way but also to influence integration at a time when miscegenation was still illegal in thirty U.S. states.[22]

Apprehensions about staging *All God's Chillun Got Wings* began well in advance, with unprecedented hype in the press. Anticipating these anxieties, O'Neill decided to publish the play before its premiere in the February issue of the literary magazine *American Mercury*.[23] Like many playwrights before him, O'Neill had hoped that the published text would assuage anxieties.[24] However, it had the opposite effect, sparking months of protest. Reviewer Arthur Pollock wryly observed that *All God's Chillun Got Wings* had received "almost as much publicity as a murder" when it opened in the Provincetown Playhouse.[25] Kenneth Macgowan (part of the triumvirate team with O'Neill and Robert Edmond Jones) reflected upon the overwhelming press coverage: "*All God's Chillun* received more publicity before production than any play in the history of the American theatre, possibly of the world."[26] In his work diary, O'Neill mentioned the "sensational stuff" of the controversy with measured reserve.[27] But when the "stink" became overwhelming, O'Neill took to the press to defend his play, proclaiming that he "would stand by 'All God's Chillun Got Wings' to the end" and support the mixed cast "despite all opposition."[28]

The antagonism became ignited by white supremacist groups like the Ku Klux Klan. John Corbin of the *New York Times* noted: "From the moment the Provincetown Players announced the production of Eugene O'Neill's play, it was evident that we were in for a campaign of race hatred and bigotry differing in no essential way from the propaganda of the Klansmen."[29] Indeed, a Klansman left a calling card during one of the performances to intimidate the Players. As has often been recounted, O'Neill wrote "Go Fuck Yourself" on the card and returned it to its owner.[30] O'Neill tracked the event with little emotion in his diary on February 23, writing only: "Threatening letter from K.K.K."[31] The threat of the Klan was no small matter, however, for the KKK had an estimated membership of five million during this time period.[32] In 1924, as Frank observes, "in the presidential race both major parties were catering to the Klan."[33] In addition, other white supremacist groups mobilized to intimidate the actors, as Province-town historians Helen Deutsch and Stella Hanau have recounted:

> Ku Kluxers, Citizen Fixits and Southern Gentlewomen, most of whom did not trouble to read the play . . . were goaded into action. Facts were enlarged and distorted, and expressions of opinion from pastors in Mississippi, from Colonels of the Confederate Army, from champions of Nordic integrity in Iowa were printed and reprinted from one end of the country to another.[34]

The play was disturbing not only to white supremacists but also to some African Americans. Writing in *Black Manhattan*, James Weldon Johnson observed: "The play, as a play, did not please white people, and, on the other hand, it failed to please coloured people."[35] Theater historian Loften Mitchell put it bluntly: "The [white] critics disliked the work. They were many steps behind the Negroes, who hated it."[36] More than disliking the play, as Frank has written, "the black community, troubled by job discrimination, social restrictions, and retaliatory violence, believed that the 'wrong' image would endanger all its members."[37] The *Pittsburgh Courier* echoed the concern about *All God's Chillun Got Wings*'s potential harm to the Black community: "[It] remains the most damaging and insulting piece of propaganda against the Negro race that could possibly be written."[38]

In spite of the varied response to *All God's Chillun Got Wings*, "the support for the production was novel and ultimately historic," observes Mumford.[39] O'Neill rallied to defend his casting decision: "I chose Robeson," he said, "because I thought he could play Jim Harris better than any one else."[40] Paul Robeson publicly defended *All God's Chillun* (keeping his disagreements with O'Neill private), making what would be one of many measured statements that negotiated between white and Black communities. Robeson had an uneasy relationship with O'Neill, and his inroads into the Great White Way were just as calculated as his "sustained effort to become a part of the Provincetown Players," as Gill has shown.[41] In particular, Robeson refuted claims that the portrayal of Jim Harris was disparaging. In an essay called "Reflections on O'Neill's Plays" that appeared in *Opportunity* in December 1924, he wrote: "I honestly believe that perhaps never will I portray a nobler type than 'Jim Harris' or a more heroically tragic figure than 'Brutus Jones, Emperor,' not excepting 'Othello.'"[42] In this essay Robeson is the consummate diplomat, defending O'Neill: "If ever there was a broad, liberal-minded man, he is one. He has had Negro friends and appreciated them for their true worth. He would be the last to cast any slur on the colored people." At the end of the article, however, Robeson advocates for the development of Black drama by African American theater artists themselves: "What lies ahead I do not know. I am sure that there will come Negro playwrights of great power and I trust I shall have some part in interpreting that most interesting and much needed addition to the drama of America."[43] When touring with *All God's Chillun Got Wings* in London, Robeson said in an interview, "If I could not get a part such as I have created in two or three O'Neill's plays I should probably drift into vaudeville or cheap stock companies and no one would hear from me."[44] Robeson would have a large role in the development of Black drama—and O'Neill would remain in his repertory while he carved out that body of work.

Given predictions of riots and other threats, the Players were prepared for the worst on opening night. "At the premiere, police ringed the theater," observes Frank, "and steelworkers, hired by the Provincetown, guarded the dressing rooms and streets. Robeson said he half-expected to hear shots from the stalls."[45] In spite of the anticipated acrimony, however, there were no disturbances. Critic Burns Mantle summed it up: "Well, we were all set for a riot the night the Provincetown players presented Eugene O'Neill's *All God's Chillun Got Wings* in the Village. And nothing happened. Nothing resembling a riot, at least. Not even a good healthy protest."[46] O'Neill elaborated: "Nothing at all happened, not even a senile egg. It was a dreadful anticlimax for all concerned, particularly the critics, who seemed to feel cheated that there hadn't been at least one murder that first night."[47] While *All God's Chillun Got Wings* sparked no violence, the play continued to unravel some of the racist fabric of modern theater by challenging which bodies could cross the color line on stage.

IRISHNESS, BLACKNESS, AND RACIAL INNOCENCE

We might well ask, as did the *Pittsburgh Courier* in its 1924 headline: "Why Did Eugene O'Neill Write 'All God's Chillun' Got Wings'?"[48] In crafting this play O'Neill "had no occasion to smile," as biographer Louis Sheaffer observes, for the plot "evoked in him somber memories of his parents," whose dysfunctional relationship underwrites the play (the leads in *All God's Chillun* have the same names as his parents, Ella and James).[49] While *Chillun* traces in many ways the unhappy marriage of his parents, it was O'Neill's third play with central Black characters and part of his larger dramaturgical project of documenting diverse American voices. In

O'Neill's notebooks, he scribbled the initial idea for *All God's Chillun Got Wings* in 1922. He wrote, "Play of Johnny T.—negro who married white woman—base play on his experience as I have seen it intimately—but no reproduction, see it only as man's."[50] *All God's Chillun Got Wings* was also inspired by a tragedy that befell a well-known interracial couple: heavyweight champion Jack Johnson's wife, Etta, took her own life in 1912 (her name is also similar to Ella from *All God's Chillun*). O'Neill was a reporter covering the story at the time and never forgot how Johnson's wife felt ostracized by both the white and Black communities.[51] Growing up as "shanty Irish," O'Neill knew something about being an outcast and Jack Johnson's "unforgiveable blackness," as Ken Burns has put it, resonated with the playwright.[52]

As with *The Emperor Jones*, *All God's Chillun Got Wings* was produced by a team of Irish American theater artists who had investments in Black performance culture: playwright Eugene O'Neill; theater manager M. Eleanor Fitzgerald (known as Fitzi); stage manager Harold McGee; and the following actors: Clement O'Loghlen (Salvationist), James Meighan (Organ Grinder), Kathleen Roarke (Woman), and Helen McClure (Little Girl). Irishness was significant not only to the production team but also, crucially, to the interracial love story of the main characters, Ella Downey and Jim Harris. O'Neill was working through his own racialized Irish identity by dramatizing Blackness in *All God's Chillun Got Wings*, something not lost on the Klan. When the KKK sent their threatening letter to O'Neill, they insulted him with a racialized slur, calling him a "dirty Irish mick."[53]

The opening scene of *All God's Chillun Got Wings* unveils the interchanges between Irish and Black minority cultures, foregrounding the stakes of racial performativity and miscegenation. O'Neill's "anxiet[ies] of colour," as Irish scholar Aoife Monks puts it, become apparent in *All God's Chillun* by running them through the miscegenation of Irish American and African American characters.[54] Set "at the edge of a colored district" in lower New York City, as the stage directions describe it, the first scene (also called the prologue) takes place seventeen years before the main action of the play. The prologue unfolds at the interstices of Black and white space, on a corner where two neighborhoods intersect, rendered expressionistically with Cleon Throckmorton's set design. While the adults in this scene remain in their segregated spaces, listening to their own music and speaking their own discourses, the children cross over and integrate through childhood play. *All God's Chillun Got Wings* therefore begins with a site of interracial contact, a zone (or "interzone," as Mumford characterizes it) that takes place not only in a liminal racial sphere but also in a working-

Fig. 15. Frank Wilson as Joe and Paul Robeson as Jim Harris in the 1924 Provincetown Players' production of O'Neill's *All God's Chillun Got Wings*. Billy Rose Theatre Division, The New York Public Library for the Performing Arts.

class neighborhood. It is here where children of different races play together and where two of the kids—Ella, an Irish American girl, and Jim, an African American boy—meet and develop crushes on one another.

Tellingly, the first line delivered to Jim invokes minstrelsy—the very performance practice that the play's casting dismantled—and it is spoken by a young Irish boy named Mickey: "You's de winner, Jim Crow," he says.[55] In the opening scene alone, Jim is called "Jim Crow" three times (and eight times in total throughout the play). In earlier drafts of *All God's Chillun*, Mickey calls him simply "Jim." As he revised the original typescript, however, O'Neill inserted "Crow" so that the character's name reads "Jim Crow."[56] In referencing Jim Crow, a character from mid-nineteenth-century minstrelsy that became synonymous with structures of racism, O'Neill directs our attention to racist utterances as well as to moments of *performing* racism. Significantly, the scene shows how racist hierarchies hinge upon enactment. Mickey's hailing of Jim through the lens of minstrelsy moreover highlights the synergies, as well as the tensions, between Irishness and Blackness. In spite of his Irish dialect, which is strikingly similar to Jim's, Mickey seeks to distance himself from Blackness, a process commonly pursued by Irish immigrants, as they positioned themselves closer to whiteness, as Noel Ignatiev observes in *How the Irish Became White*.[57] If Mickey strives to distinguish himself from Blackness, Ella pursues proximity.

Just as Jim is referred to as the quintessential minstrel performer, so Ella Downey is identified as someone whose race is performed: it is painted on (her nickname is Painty Face). Significantly, Ella is a lower-class Irish character who is situated between whiteness and Blackness. From her childhood perspective, Ella naïvely thinks she can change her racial identity, as a kind of game, saying: "I like black. Let's you and me swap. I'd like to be black."[58] Through the conceit of childhood play, O'Neill experiments with the concept of race as something that can be performed and not necessarily fixed or defined by supposed "authentic" measures. On one level, this scene illustrates what E. Patrick Johnson has called the appropriation of Blackness, where whites "reappropriate these stereotypes of affect as a fetishistic 'escape' into the Other to transcend the rigidity of their own whiteness."[59] On the other hand, Ella's desire to appropriate Blackness (and Jim's desire to whiten his skin by drinking chalk) unveils "the arbitrariness of authenticity" regarding race.[60] The children understand race, in other words, as something that can be performed, moved, and *crossed*, much like the casting practices of *All God's Chillun Got Wings*, which broke prevailing color lines. As an Irish American character, Ella's racial liminal-ity facilitates her desire for Jim, rendered as a childhood crush that borders on the forbidden. The children ridicule Jim and Ella's infatuation. Mickey taunts: "Mush-head! Jim Crow de Sissy! Stuck on Painty Face!"[61] According to this childhood logic, Jim's "mushy" reasoning leads him to believe he can cross the color line with romance. Mickey's comment interpolates Jim as both a minstrel caricature and a sissy. As Siobhan Somerville reminds us, the process of racialization and heterosexuality are intertwined as joint ideological projects.[62] This dual marking of racialization and feminization plague Jim tragically throughout the entire two acts of the play, even as he reaches manhood, culminating in the tragic final scene.

While *All God's Chillun Got Wings* staged the difficulties of miscegenation, the casting suggested the opposite: the production challenged the Broadway convention of blackface with a racially mixed cast. In the 1920s, blackface was still the normative performance practice governing the Great White Way, where "white actors play[ed] 'colored' roles in black face to avoid mixed casts."[63] Given that "non-traditional casting was extremely rare in the American theatre in the 1920s and early 1930s," as Gill has written, "Robeson and O'Neill were brave pioneers" by "selecting a cast composed equally of white people and colored people."[64] In fact, other theaters were not pursuing interracial casting during this time period. For example, in 1925 (a year after *All God's Chillun Got Wings* premiered) white actress Nedda Narrigan quit the Black-authored play *Appearances* "when she learned that the cast was of a mixed nature." [65] Much of the ensuing controversy with *All God's Chillun* dealt not only with the miscegenation of the *characters* but also of the *actors*.[66] A front-page story in the *Brooklyn Daily Eagle* clarified the stakes of *Chillun*'s mixed cast: "O'Neil [sic] and Macgowan are taking what is *the most radical step on the stage in this generation* in casting a play with half the actors and actresses negro, the other half white" (emphasis mine).[67] It is worth emphasizing this radical step: even as miscegenating domestic realms was illegal in most states, the Players were integrating the American stage by way of O'Neill.

Battles over *All God's Chillun Got Wings*'s integrated cast were especially focused on the child actors from the prologue. The issue was not "the fact that the color line does not cross childhood," as director James (Jimmy) Light maintained, but rather that childhood crossed the color line.[68] The prologue demonstrates an instance of what Robin Bernstein has called "racial innocence" whereby "innocence was raced white," especially during nineteenth-century entertainments, and cathected onto white children in order to preserve racialized hierarchies.[69] Because *All God's Chillun Got Wings*'s initial scene was perceived as threatening to "innocent" (which is to say, white) children, New York City's mayor, John F. Hylan, shut the play down by invoking a child labor law. Hylan claimed he was protecting the children's "tender ages" and not, supposedly, acting in response "to any protests that may have been received regarding the racial issue raised by the drama."[70] Hylan's defenses were transparently fabricated, however, as he had gone on record that he disliked *All God's Chillun*.[71] In Hylan's hands, the child labor law sought to safeguard racial purity by prohibiting an integrated cast of young actors, and also (and, especially) by prohibiting the implications of their intimacy.[72] Efforts to censor *All God's Chillun Got Wings* caught everyone at the Provincetown Playhouse by surprise. The production team was led to believe up until the afternoon of opening night that a license would be granted to allow the children to perform. License granting was a fairly routine procedure and permits were almost always approved.[73] Seemingly out of nowhere Hylan issued a "last-hour" injunction and pulled the permit just before opening.[74] The mayor's strategy to shut down *All God's Chillun Got Wings* did not work, however.

The stakes of embodiment in racing the Great White Way could not be clearer: an integrated cast of child actors was not allowed to perform, but their lines could be spoken—by a white surrogate. The evening of the premiere, director James Light took to the stage and informed the audience about the attempted censorship, suggesting that he might read the scene out loud in lieu of the child actors performing it. In response to this, "There were cries of 'Read!' from the audience and, accordingly, the scene was read."[75] When *All God's Chillun Got Wings* transferred to the Greenwich Village Theatre in August 1924, permission for the child actors was granted and "the first scene of O'Neill's play reache[d] public performance at last."[76] A reviewer for the *Messenger* noted the significance of this interracial casting: "White and colored actors can rehearse and play together without biting each other. It has made a manly effort to erase the color line from art, and in doing so has made the cultural life of America its debtor."[77] And yet, if American culture was somehow indebted to *All God's Chillun Got Wings*, as the *Messenger* characterized it, this victory was short-lived: with the exception of a few performances in late summer, subsequent performances in 1924 were unsuccessful in securing child permits.[78] Indeed, throughout its production history on various stages around the world, integration often stopped short of the child actors, demonstrating that childhood was a color line too volatile to cross. Given that the children utter lines about Jim Crow—the minstrel character that became synonymous with racism—while performing in blackface themselves, the censored productions highlight an uncanny return of racializing the Great

White Way. The production history of *All God's Chillun Got Wings* more-over provides a fascinating case study of how structures of racism enact ideological work through the bodies of child performers.

Drama critic Lester Walton proposed a casting idea that would elimi-nate the color-line controversy with a searing instance of what Tavia Nyong'o has called "critical shade" in other contexts.[79] Walton suggested casting light-skinned African American actress Evelyn Preer to play the part of Ella Downey—and perform in a kind of *whiteface*. Observing that "there are several talented Negro actresses whose services could be utilized in the new show in the leading part," he noted that Preer was not only a talented actress but also that she could pass as white.[80] Citing previous reviews by white critic John Corbin as evidence, Walton continued: "If, as Mr. Corbin says, because of the whiteness of her skin Miss Preer never sug-gests a Negro, it must follow that she suggests a Caucasian." Using Corbin's racist logic against itself, Walton argued that race was not fixed but rather could be performed. If white actors could perform in blackface, then the reverse could also be true in Black actors assuming white roles. Walton hit home with this point: "Casting Evelyn Preer in the principal female part would serve as a balm for those who would suffer untold anguish over the thought of a real white woman playing opposite a simon [*sic*] pure Negro."[81] Walton was suggesting something that was quite possible to imagine: the Lafayette Players regularly performed Broadway hits with all-Black casts. Yet neither Broadway nor the Village was ready for Walton's cross-racial casting suggestion.

AN INTERRACIAL MARRIAGE PERFORMATIVE AND BROADWAY'S FIRST INTERRACIAL KISS

The precarity of staging miscegenation in *All God's Chillun Got Wings* becomes especially visible in act 2, when adult actors stepped into the roles of Jim and Ella. Set seventeen years later, things have changed for the worse. Having been dumped by her working-class lover, lost her baby to illness, and barely making ends meet as a factory worker, Ella is desperate. She accepts Jim's offer to marry. Although O'Neill does not portray the marriage ceremony, he does script intriguing consequences of the nuptials. The challenge of portraying interracial marriage onstage intersects with one of the key, and long-debated, points in J. L. Austin's speech act theory. Austin analyzes the spoken phrase "I do" during a marriage ceremony as a central example of a performative utterance—words that "do things," to

Fig. 16. Robert Adams, left, in the British production of *All God's Chillun Got Wings*, 1944. © Victoria and Albert Museum, London.

paraphrase the title of his book.[82] At the same time, Austin considers theatrical performances as "parasitical," or inferior to those in "real" life, which is why he considers them insufficient examples of performatives. Even though Austin does not mention race as a factor in his analysis, there are two things relevant to my analysis here. First, O'Neill does not portray the wedding scene in *All God's Chillun Got Wings*: there are no "I do's" spoken on stage.[83] Rather, there is a gap in *All God's Chillun*'s plotline, which skips ahead to a scene featuring the couple *after* the nuptials, when they are greeted by their respective communities that are literally divided into racialized spheres. According to the stage directions, the couple is dwarfed by the imposing set, which has closed in around them, and flanked by "two racial lines on each side of the gate, rigid and unyielding, staring across at each other with bitter hostile eyes."[84] As Brenda Murphy writes, this expressionistic scene "performs the simultaneous function of calling the audience's attention to the racism of the community and externalizing the racism that exists in the characters' minds, whether they are conscious of it or not."[85]

Second, in spite of this hostility, Ella and Jim's marriage ceremony has not been undermined by possible "infelicities," as Austin calls them, or conditions that can cause a performative to "misfire" and thus undermine its efficacy. While miscegenation was illegal in three-quarters of the states in the 1920s, it was legal in New York. What's unusual in *All God's Chillun Got Wings* is that the wedding ceremony as a performative act *succeeded*—albeit offstage. Taking the legality of Ella and Jim's wedding as a given, O'Neill focuses on the aftermath of the nuptials. The performative portrayed here, in other words, is not the utterance of "I do," but rather the cultural consequences—or the "perlocutionary force," as Austin would say—of interracial marriage. Walking the gauntlet between the two groups, Ella is paralyzed by fear, unable to walk. Jim nervously compels Ella to ignore the crowd's threats: "We're all the same—equally just—under the sky—under the sun—under God—sailing over the sea—to the other side of the world—."[86] Jim's words ring hollow, for *All God's Chillun Got Wings* ultimately shows that they will not be treated equal by society. This is pure O'Neill: there will be no happy endings or triumphs. Yet we should not mistake the imminent failure of their marriage as O'Neill's commentary about miscegenation, but rather as his investment in crafting tragedy. The couple travels to the other side of the Atlantic, seeking refuge in France. But France is hardly the utopian space the couple imagined, and O'Neill withholds portraying their time there. They return, marked by defeat. Like all O'Neill lovers, the couple is doomed.

Fig. 17. Paul Robeson and Mary Blair in the final scene from *All God's Chillun Got Wings*, 1924. Billy Rose Theatre Division, The New York Public Library for the Performing Arts.

If *All God's Chillun Got Wings* indelibly raced the Great White Way by demonstrating the performative force of staging miscegenation, it also staged the first interracial kiss between Ella (Mary Blair) and Jim (Paul Robeson). *All God's Chillun's* concluding scene is among the most problematic of O'Neill's plays; it is a brutal depiction of the destructive power of racism. By the last act, Ella has gone crazy from her narcissistic desires and racism. She has all but destroyed Jim, hurling frequent racial epithets, making him repeatedly fail his bar exam, and even trying to stab him; she stabs instead an African mask in their apartment (the mask appeared on the publicity poster). Despite her abuse, Jim remains puzzlingly true to her. *All God's Chillun Got Wings* charts the tragic destruction of both characters, a common O'Neillian theme.

The tragedy is sealed with a kiss—Broadway's first interracial kiss. At the end of the play, Ella has become fully deranged and mentally retreats to the time of her childhood. After her violent outburst, according to the stage directions, "She kisses [Jim's] hand as a child might, tenderly, and gratefully."[87] Next, Ella is scripted to sit on the floor at Jim's feet. But this is not what we see in the publicity photo that was released and widely printed. Instead, the photograph shows Jim kneeling, with Ella standing and pulling away, capturing the final action of the play *after* Ella kisses Jim's hand when they swap positions. The fabled kiss—with Blair kneeling at Robeson's feet—was too controversial to capture. In its place, the image stages the chasm between their love (and races), underscored by the pronounced parting of the white Irish-lace curtains behind them. Visually, Irishness and Blackness share this doomed fate, while also being torn apart.

For some cultural commentators, this interracial intimacy was a line that should not be crossed: "The scene where Miss Blair is called upon to kiss and fondle a negro's hands is going too far," wrote the *New York American*.[88] Some critics faulted O'Neill for not showing more than a kiss. In his scathing two-part review of the play, Will Madden wrote that not only was the romantic relationship between Ella and Jim "laughable," but, in particular, "O'Neill fails to make his play ring true" during the kiss scene. Madden continues:

> Whoever heard of a wife continually kissing her husband's hand? How many wives in real life do this? Ella should be kissing her husband's lips, not his hand, and if the author lacked the nerve or moral courage to write and produce this play as it should have been written, then he should not have written it at all.[89]

As far as we know Blair never kissed Robeson's lips on stage. Given prohibitions about performing miscegenation in American theater, Broadway's first interracial kiss was placed on Robeson's hand, but this was controversial nonetheless.[90] According to one biographer, Blair defiantly kissed Robeson's hand "at every curtain call," fully aware she was pressing "the buttons of still-bigoted America."[91] Two years later, when Mary Blair acted in another play about miscegenation, *Beyond Evil* (a play written in response to *All God's Chillun Got Wings*), she was disparaged as being "infatuated with race men."[92] For years to come, Mary Blair's work to integrate the stage was reduced to the singular act of kissing Paul Robeson.

WHAT IS MARCUS GARVEY DOING IN THE LIVING ROOM?

The final scene of *All God's Chillun Got Wings* not only staged the epochal interracial kiss; it also invoked the Emperor's remains. In so doing, the 1924 production situated Jim's characterization within the context of Black nationalism and diasporic rulers. In the production photo of the concluding scene, hanging directly behind the kneeling Robeson is a painting, which, according to O'Neill's stage directions, should be a canvas of Jim's father. But instead, the portrait depicts a ruler in soldier regalia. Wearing a dark jacket with epaulets and a sash adorned with medals, the figure stares out to the audience with authority and power. The portrait bears a striking resemblance to Marcus Garvey, the controversial Jamaican-born Black nationalist and Pan-African leader, whose Universal Negro Improvement Association offices were located in Harlem.[93] The figure sprouts Garvey's trademark moustache, stout physique, and his penchant for donning military attire. Standing before the portrait, Ella observes the figure's performative excess: "It's his Old Man—all dolled up like a circus horse!"[94] Given that Garvey was frequently in the headlines during 1924, the visual reference would have been obvious to Village audience members. Thus, even though Robeson is shown kneeling in front of Blair, the deliberate positioning of the picture behind him suggests a citation of Garveyism and Black nationalist power. The painting functions as a militaristic doppelgänger to Jim's submissive posture, endowing Robeson with authority. The performative citation of Garvey (and other diasporic rulers) moreover suggests a future beyond American borders, evoking Black internationalism. Seen in this way, the portrait serves as an uncanny foreshadowing of Robeson's increasing disenchantment with American politics and his eventual expatriate existence beyond U.S. borders.

The portrait also could be a visual citation of *The Emperor Jones*, the title role that Robeson performed for two weeks in May 1924. It was, really, a twenty-one performance interlude, while he was rehearsing *All God's Chillun Got Wings*. The day after *The Emperor Jones* opened (to five curtain calls), Robeson began rehearsals for *All God's Chillun*.[95] *The Emperor Jones's* invocation of Haitian revolutionary figures like Henri Christophe and Jean Vilbrun Guillaume Sam (the Haitian president who was assassinated in 1915) provides other citations of Black diasporic power in Jim Harris's living room. While scholars have analyzed Robeson's portrayal of the submissive Jim in *All God's Chillun Got Wings* or the epithet-slinging, deluded (and denuded) ruler in *The Emperor Jones*, little has been said about examining these two works and their embodied meanings as intertwined. Robeson's embodiment of both roles can be seen as a performative palimpsest: as citational, interrelated performances. If we tease out the hauntology of these performances together, we can see why the Emperor is in the living room. The Emperor ghosts the supplicant.

There were other performative framings in the production. A key plot element of *All God's Chillun Got Wings* centers on Ella's efforts to prevent Jim from passing the bar exam. In act 1, after Jim learns he's failed the bar exam after five years of trying, Ella proposes: "Why don't you give it up?" Ella's inability to imagine Jim succeeding in law is constrained as much by her own racism as by her limited sense of class mobility. "After all, what's being a lawyer?" she asks Jim. Yet, Jim sees it otherwise, replying, "A lot—to me—what it means. (*intensely*) Why, if I was a Member of the Bar night now, Ella, I believe I'd almost have the courage to—."[96] Jim's interrupted speech reveals how structures of racism prevent him not only from success but also from expressing it verbally. It becomes clear that uplift is not enough. While Jim cannot even finish the sentence about achieving success, his sister, Hattie, does, in a powerful rebuttal to Ella: "Yes, he could! He can! He'll pass them now—if you'll give him a chance!"[97] According to actress Dora Cole Norman, who originated the role of Hattie, "a perceptible sway of uneasiness" was expressed by white audience members after she "had disclosed her opposition to the white sister-in-law."[98] Norman was well aware that talking back to a white woman, even on stage, was problematic for some white spectators, which she addressed in an essay she published in the *Messenger* in January 1925.[99] It's worth noting that "Hattie's Point of View" (the title of her *Messenger* article), and the perspectives by other female actors, were often eclipsed by their male counterparts. Norman's essay provides a rare and important insight into female actors of color in *All God's Chillun Got Wings*.

O'Neill closes the play just as he begins it: by returning to the figure of Jim Crow—but with a difference. In the final scene, Ella succumbs to her insanity, wielding a knife in her hand. The ensuing dialogue is the final blow to Jim, who has failed the bar exam yet again, and for the final time.

> ELLA: (*writhing out of her chair like some fierce animal, the knife held behind her—with fear and hatred*) You didn't—you didn't—you didn't pass, did you?
>
> JIM: (*looking at her wildly*) Pass? Pass? (*He begins to chuckle and laugh between sentences and phrases, rich, Negro laughter, but heart-breaking in its mocking grief.*) Good Lord, child, how come you can ever imagine such a crazy idea? Pass? Me? Jim Crow Harris?[100]

It may appear that Jim has accepted his interpolation as Jim Crow, but even as he raises the question of passing (in more sense than one), it is with a question mark. Ella next invokes the practice of minstrelsy by proposing that *she* becomes Jim Crow and that Jim whitens up to become Painty Face: "Be my little boy, Jim," she says. "Pretend you're Painty Face and I'm Jim Crow. Come and play!"[101] Yet O'Neill shows that ultimately minstrelsy will no longer work (if it ever did). Ella's childhood fantasy of donning black-face or of Jim lightening his skin color has lost its efficacy. Instead, the couple is left with the brutal reality of crossing the color line. If anything, this scene shows the vacuity of blackface minstrelsy. The couple is left to their tragic trajectory—like all of O'Neill's fated couples.

Jim's onstage failure was in tension with the well-known fact that Paul Robeson was a Columbia University law school graduate, having received his bachelor of laws (L.L.B.) degree in 1923.[102] Robeson's legal credentials offer a performative counterpoint to Jim's inability to pass the law exam, something not lost on the press. Reviews for *All God's Chillun Got Wings* repeatedly referenced Robeson's Ivy League pedigree and law degree.[103] Robeson's achievements, both as lawyer and actor, performatively framed (if not offset) Jim Harris's dramaturgical decline.

PERFORMATIVE AFTERLIVES OF *ALL GOD'S CHILLUN*

After its memorable 1924 premiere, *All God's Chillun Got Wings* had impor-tant performative afterlives in productions that continued to race the Great White Way and beyond. For Robeson, *All God's Chillun Got Wings* was part of a performative triptych resonating with Broadway, Black theater, and race cinema. When the controversy regarding *All God's Chillun* made the Players postpone its opening to May 1924, Robeson went back to the Lafayette Theatre in Harlem to perform in *Roseanne* (another part he took over from Gilpin).[104] According to critic Theophilus Lewis, *Roseanne* was a "significant" drama for Black theater. "Excepting two works by Eugene O'Neil [*sic*]," he wrote, *Roseanne* "is the most significant dramatic work about the life psyche of Negro yet revealed to the public."[105] Lewis's pairing of *Chillun* with *Roseanne* is telling, for both dramas involved Robeson, portrayed flawed Black protagonists, and were authored by white playwrights (Eugene O'Neill and Nan Baby Stephens). But there is one important difference: the premiere production of *Roseanne* (running from December 1923 to February 1924) was initially produced with an all-white cast in blackface.[106] When Gilpin entered the *Roseanne* production, he raced it by portraying the Black preacher Cicero Brown and the production transferred to Broadway.[107] Then, when the production was set to tour the "colored circuit" and not return to Broadway, "Gilpin Quits," and "Paul Robeson Takes His Place," as one headline put it.[108] Robeson's assumption of this role vacated by Gilpin was reminiscent of when he took over Brutus Jones in the 1924 revival of *The Emperor Jones*. The new *Roseanne* production (now with Robeson) raced back to Harlem with an all-Black cast, reopening on March 24, 1924 at the Lafayette Theatre.[109] Theater critic Lester A. Walton observed that "the present experiment has fully demonstrated the advisability of giving preference to a competent colored cast when Negro life is to be portrayed."[110]

Moreover, while performing both roles, Robeson also began shooting the race film *Body and Soul* (released in 1925) by African American director Oscar Micheaux, a silent film that reworks — or *races* — two key O'Neill dramas. This was Robeson's first film role and it was doubly important. To begin, he performed two characters: Jenkins and his evil brother Sylvester. In addition, as film historian Charles Musser observes, "These two brothers are linked to the Robeson characters in O'Neill's two race places. If Jenkins is [Brutus] Jones's alter ego, then Sylvester is the non-neurotic healthy counterpart to the tortured Jim Harris of *All God's Chillun*."[111] The similarities are clear: "There are many ways in which Micheaux draws parallels between characters in his film and those in O'Neill['s] play — often as a way to underscore differences — to create reversals or inversions."[112] For one, as Musser tells us, Sylvester dresses like Jim Harris from *All God's Chillun* in an almost identical suit. Moreover, the stagings share striking similarities, with Paul Robeson kneeling before women in

Fig. 18. Screenshot from the silent film *Body and Soul* (directed by Oscar Micheaux, 1925) with Paul Robeson kneeling. The blocking recalls the final scene in O'Neill's *All God's Chillun Got Wings*, 1924. Screenshot by Katie N. Johnson.

both. The pose "mirrors the moment of the kiss in *All God's Chillun*," — but, importantly, without the kiss.[113] There, the similarities end. Just as Micheaux reimagined the "white fantasies" in O'Neill's plays, so Robeson raced not only the Great White Way but also American cinema, while performing, or referencing, O'Neill's works.

BLACKFACE, JEWFACE

When *All God's Chillun Got Wings* was revived in 1927 in Los Angeles, a stunning thing occurred: Jewish actor Irving Pichel assumed the role of Jim Harris in blackface, accompanied by an all-white cast.[114] Paradoxically, Pichel's "whiteness" was repeatedly referenced in both the Black and white press, even though he was a Jew playing an African American character. Having previously performed ethnic roles in silent film, Pichel, like many Jewish actors during this time period, negotiated the space between whiteness and ethnic otherness through performance.[115] As scholars have amply documented, Jewish performers built successful careers around blackface in American entertainments. "The conjunction between blackface and Americanization," writes Mike Rogen in *Blackface, White Noise: Jewish Immigrants in the Hollywood Melting Pot*, was often negotiated by "Jewish male entertainers and producers."[116] Such performance practices had another benefit: blackface performance aligned Jewishness more closely to whiteness—a practice that Esther Romeyn calls "Jewface," and which can be understood as a "theater of whitening."[117] Yet, O'Neill's *All God's Chillun Got Wings* was not intended as a theater of whitening, but rather of interracial mixing, an objective that the racialized scaffolding of American theater did not always support.

Very few reviews mentioned blackface performance, but an illustration in the *Los Angeles Times* and its caption makes it clear: "Irving Pichel, the male lead, who does a blackface in taking the part of Jim, the colored boy."[118] Was blackface moreover used by the other white actors portraying Black characters in the play (such as Jim's sister Hattie, his mother, and the children in the prologue)? The archive is silent on this matter, but it is telling that Pichel's whiteness became visible precisely when he was performing a Black character from *All God's Chillun Got Wings*. By contrast, during the previous year when he performed in another O'Neill play, *Lazarus Laughed*, reviewers did not mention his ethnicity.

It can also not escape our attention that 1927 was the year that *The Jazz Singer*, the first talkie, hit major screens and featured Al Jolson in blackface, thereby suturing sound cinema with the problematic practice of minstrelsy. In spite of Jolson's blackface performance, *The Jazz Singer* — another story about miscegenation — nonetheless appealed to Black audiences, observes Musser, especially in how the emotional excess of this melodrama pulled on the heartstrings of Black women.[119] This may explain the attraction of *All God's Chillun Got Wings* to African American audiences in Los Angeles even if blackface was utilized. Jolson was performing in blackface not only in film but also on American stages during this time. Jolson's blackened-up image promoting the musical *Big Boy* was shown on billboards all over the country in 1927 (before he appeared in the film version). Blackface was so entrenched in American stages and cinema that the idea of Robeson venturing down south to perform *All God's Chillun Got Wings* in 1927 was unacceptable, observed American humorist Irving Cobb, with this not-so-veiled threat: "If Paul Robeson plays down here in my home (Paducah, Kentucky), he'll need 'em" (i.e., wings, presumably to make a quick exit).[120] Yet, an editorial by Chandler Owen in the *Messenger* challenged this racist logic by circling back to Jolson:

> One sees Al Jolson, face blacked and hair woolly, cuddled up amidst a veritable embankment of white girls. There is no objection, though, because it is known that Jolson is not a Negro, he is simply *playing* Negro. In other words, color is only an incident of distinction, the basic prejudice being race prejudice.[121]

Because he was "*playing* Negro" and perceived as "white" (although in fact Jewish), Jolson enjoyed the privileges of being intimate with white women onstage, as well as securing work in film and theater. Robeson, on the other hand, could not do so, without controversy or peril.

RACING, BLACKFACING TRANSNATIONAL *CHILLUN*

Various productions of *All God's Chillun Got Wings* were staged throughout Europe between 1924 and the 1940s, but blackface was sometimes still used. Heeding the irregular temporality of racing the Great White Way, the color line continued to be broken—racing forward—only to fall back. Often this meant that the role of Jim Harris was performed by a Black actor while the supporting characters were performed by white actors in blackface. It was a case of racing and blackfacing at the same time. As in the U.S., the uneven advancement for actors of color in British theater "is marked by stages, "the *New York Amsterdam News* observed.[122] This irregular pattern can especially be seen in the 1926–27 Gate Theatre production of *All God's Chillun Got Wings*, in which "the blacks were painted-up whites."[123] It took an African American company performing *Porgy* on tour in London in 1929 to break the color line by staging their own production of *All God's Chillun* (with Frank Wilson as Jim) at the Royal Court Theatre.[124] The way that the *New York Amsterdam News* tells it, the American *All God's Chillun* production facilitated integration of the London stage.[125] Taking its cue from the Royal Court Theatre, the Gate Theatre staged a 1929 production with British Black actor Harold Young portraying Jim Harris, thereby finally ditching blackface for the leading role.[126] Yet, in spite of that breakthrough, production photos reveal that the prologue featured children in blackface, as well as other actors in supporting roles.[127] Racing and blackfacing would continue to go hand in hand.

The Moscow Kamerny Theatre performed a unique transnational adaptation in 1930: a Russian version of *All God's Chillun* (retitled as *Negr*) was directed by Alexandre Tairov (spelled Tairoff in the U.S. press) and staged at the Théâtre Pigalle in Paris in May 1930.[128] The *New York Times* captured these transnational resonances in its headline, "Russians in Paris."[129] Writing from his home in France (Château du Plessis), O'Neill raved how Tairov's theater "is one of the most famous over here now."[130] Tairov called *All God's Chillun* "The N——r," but he misunderstood the translation from the Russian *Negr*, which was more equivalent to the use of "Negro" in the 1930s.[131] In his *Work Diary*, O'Neill noted that he traveled to Paris to see the Kamerny production, and he especially liked the expressionistic elements.[132] As Katherine Weinstein observes, there was a crucial change in the script: "After a scene in which the crazed Ella attacked an African mask displayed on a wall with a knife, she died in Jim's arms of a heart attack."[133] The *New York Times* reported that this was an outstanding scene performed by Alice Koonen (Tairov's wife) that created emotional intensity "in topping the terrific emotional intensity that has gone before by the use of a tragic and pitiful stylization of movement which lifts the play into realms of transcendent tragedy."[134] Tairov's radical change in having Ella die onstage decenters her vindictive hold on Jim. In some ways, then, the Kamerny production raced forward, and yet backwards as well. Production photos show that the Russian actors used blackface, though it was not mentioned in the press.[135] These examples demonstrate that the time signature of racing the Great White Way is not linear: it involves racing forward while also dragging along the vestiges of racism. The tug and pull can, at times, catapult one backwards. And yet, it can also move one forward as well.

Racing across the Atlantic, Robeson performed *All God's Chillun Got Wings* in London in 1933—the same year he broke the color line with the film version of *The Emperor Jones*—receiving rave reviews opposite white British actress Flora Robson.[136] The *New York Times* called this production "the biggest success at the moment" for the London stage.[137] The publicity photos were more daring in terms of interracial intimacy, showing Robeson embracing Ella closely.[138] This British production of *All God's Chillun* moreover became a vehicle for Robeson's political activism, when he agreed to perform in a benefit matinee to raise funds for Jewish refugees fleeing Nazi Germany.[139]

ALL GOD'S CHILLUN IN BLACK THEATER REPERTOIRES

"All God's Chillun" is a splendid play and a play distinctly in our favor.[140]
　—W. E. B. Du Bois, 1930

Black theater companies throughout the world embraced *All God's Chillun Got Wings* in their repertoires, often featuring all-Black casts. In 1931, *All God's Chillun* was performed by the Boston Players with "an all colored cast," as the *New York Herald* put it, featuring Ralf Coleman (Coleman would soon be appointed as the director of the Negro Federal Theatre in Massachusetts).[141] Modeled on the all-Black Lafayette Players in New York, the Boston Players was a group of amateur actors who produced leading works with all-Black performers. Did this mean that the white roles in their production were performed by Black actors in *whiteface*? There are few archival traces, but the "all-colored" billing suggests that it could have been true.

On the other side of the Atlantic, British actor Robert Adams, founder and director of London's Negro Repertory Arts Theatre—one of the first

Black theater companies in Britain—produced and starred in *All God's Chillun Got Wings* in December 1944.[142] With a "full cast of coloured Artistes," featuring Ida Shepley (Robeson's voice coach) and Earl Cameron (one of the first Black British film stars), the production was so successful that it was held over for a second week.[143] *All God's Chillun Got Wings* was revived again in 1946 by the British Unity Workers Theatre, featuring Ida Shepley again. Yet "Shepley was one of only two black actors in the company in this Unity production so . . . white actors playing black characters had to 'black up.'"[144] The pattern of racing and blackfacing continued.

In other parts of the world, the first Black Brazilian theater company, Black Experimental Theatre (Teatro experimental do negro, abbreviated as TEN) was created in 1944 with the mission of fighting racism. "How did black Brazilian companies confront this racism onstage?" asks Christine Douxami. "In the 1940s, the TEN looked to the U.S. staging of Eugene O'Neill's *The Emperor Jones* as no Brazilian play was suitable at this time."[145] Tellingly, TEN's 1946 production of *Todos os filhous de Deus têm asas* (*All God's Chillun Got Wings*) was their second play. Oscar Fernández writes that in "a spirit of cooperation," O'Neill waived the royalty rights for the Brazilian company.[146] The Teatro experimental do negro revived *All God's Chillun* in 1950, with Ruth de Souza as Hattie and Abias Nascimento, the founder of TEN, as Jim Harris. From Manhattan to Rio de Janeiro, *All God's Chillun Got Wings* was a vehicle by which actors of color throughout the world established repertoires featuring Black characters while breaking color lines and denouncing prohibitions against miscegenation.

Nearly a hundred years after the premiere and with the critical investigations from these pages to offer a fresh perspective, how does *All God's Chillun Got Wings* signify? It would be an exaggeration to proclaim that all productions of *All God's Chillun* soared beyond racist structures toward victory, like the triumphant figures portrayed in the 1936 Olympic cartoons with their enormous, if not epic, wings. Given the entrenched dominance of regimes of race within the Great White Way, there is only so much work a theater piece can accomplish. And yet, *All God's Chillun* was an important vehicle for Robeson for over two decades, just as it was for Black theater companies and actors in Boston, New York, London, and Rio de Janeiro. Whether invoked at the Olympic Games or on stages throughout the world, performative iterations of *All God's Chillun Got Wings* unraveled a bit of the fabric of miscegenation with theater artists of color defying racism and establishing Black repertory theaters around the world.

FOUR | Racing Operatic Emperors

In 1933 dueling Emperors emerged in major New York performance venues: the operatic adaptation of *The Emperor Jones* with white Metropolitan Opera star Lawrence Tibbett in blackface, and the film version starring the first Black leading actor in a studio-backed major motion picture, Paul Robeson. This dichotomy was captured by competing covers of two major periodicals that year: *Time Magazine* featured Tibbett as a blackened-up Brutus Jones while *The Crisis* (the official magazine of the NAACP) showcased Robeson in full emperor regalia. Their images provide literal snapshots of the contested terrain of performing *The Emperor Jones*—and, more specifically, the dialectical tensions between blackface performance and breaking color lines. Robeson commands the cover of the *Crisis* by wearing medals, chunky epaulets, and an impressive, plume-adorned military helmet.[1] He sits upon the throne, smiling with authority and self-assurance: a low-angle shot confirms his power. By contrast, Tibbett appears diminutive on the cover of *Time*, his half-naked body painted in black grease paint.[2] Tibbett's awkward pose jumps out from the flat scenery behind him, while a shadow cast behind him looms large, suggesting that something (perhaps another Emperor?) is ghosting him.

The 1933 Metropolitan Opera House production reveals the conflicted, and, racialized, performance history of *The Emperor Jones* within Black performance culture and white entertainment establishments: on the one hand, it featured Tibbett in blackface, effectively reinstating the racial barriers in theater that O'Neill had razed by casting African American actor Charles Gilpin in 1920. On the other hand, this production broke the color line when African American dance pioneer Hemsley Winfield played the memorable Congo Witch-Doctor: he and his company of dancers were the first Black artists to ever perform onstage at the Metropolitan Opera House. Another groundbreaking artistic achievement was Jules Bledsoe's own adaptation of the opera, which he called *L'Empereur Jones*. As I discuss in detail below, this previously lost manuscript is an important archival artifact not only because it sheds light on the struggle to break through on white mainstream venues like the Metropolitan Opera, but also because it reveals the means by which Bledsoe raced O'Neill's text by creating a score that is more Afro-centric and that endows Jones with enhanced authority and complexity. This varied performance history demonstrates how operatic versions of *The Emperor Jones* became a means for both breaking, and reinstating, regimes of race through O'Neill.

The two performers who form the centerpiece of this chapter, Winfield and Bledsoe, not only raced operatic Emperors but also queered the color line with their performances. It is no wonder that that the intersection of Blackness and queerness has remained largely invisible in historical accounts of *The Emperor Jones*, despite the fact that these two discourses were significantly intertwined in American culture during this time period. For as Siobhan Somerville has noted, "it was not merely a historical coincidence that the classification of bodies as either 'homosexual' or 'heterosexual' emerged at the same time that the United States was aggressively constructing and policing the boundary between 'black and 'white bodies.'"[3] Winfield was known for his drag performances of *Salomé* from 1927 to 1929 and was associated with the gay subculture in New York.[4] Bledsoe kept his relationship with his long-time Dutch partner Freddye Huygens closeted and yet the constraints on their interracial, same-sex partnership shaped the already limited contours of his career, as I clarify in more detail below. Rather than dwell upon personal histories, the point more relevant to my argument is that Bledsoe and Winfield were Black queer artists who were denied access to white, heteronormative venues and who nonetheless broke color lines with O'Neill's works. Their artistic production put pressure on normative expectations of Black masculinity, often while channeling performative aspects of *The Emperor Jones*.

While the 1933 operatic version of *The Emperor Jones* serves as my central case study of a production that both challenged and reinscribed racial hierarchies in white mainstream performance spaces like the Metropolitan Opera House, there were other important repertoires of Blackness in opera in different venues. To begin, Theodore Drury (c. 1867–1943) managed the first long-running Black opera troupe in America called Drury's Grand Opera Company from 1900 to 1907.[5] Drury's success was in spite of Jim Crow exclusions from mainstream opera houses and concomitant institutional resources. Soprano Sissieretta Jones (1869–1933) became the first African American singer to perform at Carnegie Hall in 1892, and her company, the Black Patti Troubadours, had success on many stages throughout the U.S. Another seminal figure in the Black opera scene was Harry Lawrence Freeman (1869–1954), who created fourteen operas in the late nineteenth and early twentieth centuries. Together with his wife, Carlotta, in 1920 he founded the Negro Grand Opera Company and the Salem School of Music (later renamed the Freeman School of Music) in Harlem. Unfortunately, many of these singers' contributions were sidelined from white performance venues. As Naomi André observes in *Black Opera: History, Power, Engagement,* "The history of black involvement with opera in the United States can be seen as a shadow culture to the all-white and segregated opera scene existent in the United States through the first half of the twentieth century."[6] Giuseppe Verdi's *Otello* (1887) and *Aida* (1871) are often cited as operas that broke out of "shadow culture" and into the white mainstream. Yet, even though these operas featured central Black characters, their performance histories have been plagued for more than a century by blackface—a problem that has vexed opera more broadly (and that figures in my discussion of *The Emperor Jones*).[7] In Verdi's *Otello*, Shakespeare's titular Black hero—a role played in early nineteenth-century theater by Ira Aldridge, we will recall—was so commonly performed in operatic blackface that the Metropolitan Opera House called their brown pancake makeup "Otello Brown" as late as 2015.[8] The rejection of "the enduring tradition" of blackface in a recent *Otello* production made headlines, for while blacking up had been eliminated, so too had Blackness. "'The Met breaks tradition, and I will be white,' Mr. Antonenko [the performer portraying *Otello*] shrugged."[9] As of this writing, no Black actor has performed the central role of *Otello* on the Metropolitan Opera stage. Moreover, as the following pages will make clear, the first Black performer on the Met stage was not Marian Anderson in 1955, as is often reported, but rather dancer Hemsley Winfield in *The Emperor Jones.*

A BLACKFACED EMPEROR JONES

> Incontestably . . . the finest American opera as yet
> produced anywhere.[10]
> —Olin Downes, *New York Times,* January 8, 1933

> The blackfaced Tibbett produced a pathetic burlesque.[11]
> —*New York Amsterdam News,* February 1, 1933

When the Metropolitan Opera House premiered Louis Gruenberg's adaptation of *The Emperor Jones* in 1933, it was seen as a triumph for American opera and a bold choice for the company, given its firmly entrenched European (and white) repertoire.[12] Gruenberg's version, raved *New York Times* critic Olin Downes, "is incontestably the finest American opera that the Metropolitan has produced, the finest American opera as yet produced anywhere."[13] And yet the operatic adaptation of Eugene O'Neill's *The Emperor Jones* was beset by several problems, demonstrating a larger problem of white artists engaging with African American culture only to plunder it. Even as *The Emperor Jones* was lauded as one of the best American operas of its time, it was also plagued by a number of problems. First, the score poached African American music while bleaching it for white audiences; second, the leading baritone, Irish American Lawrence Tibbett, performed the role of Brutus Jones in blackface; third, the libretto by Louis Gruenberg and Kathleen de Jaffa problematically changed Jones's murder by the Indigenous people of the island to a suicide by Jones; and, finally, Gruenberg's version eclipsed an original score by Jules Bledsoe. And yet, in spite of these predicaments, as I will clarify in what follows, it was a vehicle for racing the Metropolitan Opera and beyond.

If Gruenberg's score was perceived as a "triumph" for American opera, it incorporated distinctly African American music and idioms. Like other American composers (and especially Jewish American composers, as David Savran has shown), Gruenberg borrowed from jazz and spirituals in his scoring of *The Emperor Jones*.[14] Music historian David Metzer notes that even though Gruenberg incorporated Black music into the opera (inserting, for example the show-stopping spiritual "Standin' in the Need of a Prayer"), he effectively "bleach[ed] jazz" elements, as well as other African music:

> Gruenberg suffered from anxieties over cultural borrowing: by appropriating African-American music, he mixed races, albeit symbolically. In his discussions of African-American music, he tried to allay fears of miscegenation, his rhetoric giving the impression that he controls this cultural transaction and can prevent racial pollution. Gruenberg also underplayed the African-American origins of jazz.[15]

Seeking to avert "racial pollution," Gruenberg's bleached version was pitched to the white opera clientele, demonstrating the Met's complicity in (literally) producing racial hierarchies.

A second troubling aspect of the Metropolitan Opera House's *Emperor Jones* production was its use of blackface. As André observes, "The opera stage is perhaps the only space in American culture today where such overt racial imitation [i.e., blackface] is routinely performed without comment or query."[16] Indeed, blackface was a common performance practice in opera during the 1930s, and most accounts in mainstream white papers praised

Fig. 19. Lawrence Tibbett in blackface performing the title role in the operatic adaptation of *The Emperor Jones* in 1933. Photo: Carlo Edwards, Metropolitan Opera Archives.

Tibbett's minstrelsy. And, given Tibbett's Irish American identity,[17] his blackening up as Brutus Jones harkened back to long-standing practices of Irish Americans performing on minstrel stages. Given that the 1920 casting of Charles Gilpin in the lead role of *The Emperor Jones* broke with the tradition of blackface, the Metropolitan Opera House's return to it makes it all the more disheartening. Tibbett's embodiment of Brutus Jones was described in the mainstream press as "realistically brown," demonstrating how widely accepted and naturalized blackface performance was to white audiences.[18] Newspapers like the *New York Times* hailed the baritone's performance as "a masterpiece of dramatic interpretation."[19] *Time Magazine* was likewise enthusiastic, writing that for "Tibbett the moment was a career's fine crown."[20] By Tibbett's own count, he was given twenty-two curtain calls at the premiere.[21]

While the white press registered no criticism of Tibbett's blackface performance, Black critics were not pleased with the baritone "under cork."[22] As Susan Manning has noted, "the blackface version of . . . *The Emperor Jones* [was] roundly condemned in the pages of *The Crisis* and *Opportunity*."[23] Reviewing the opera for *Opportunity*, Harry Keelan observed: "Tibbett did not ring true as a Negro. Upon his entrance, with his slightly improved Al Jolson make-up, one wanted to laugh. . . . Why a white person thinks that Al Jolson can be more negroid than a Negro is one of the mysteries to contemplate whenever one thinks of the Anglo-Saxon mind."[24] The negative response by Black critics and theatergoers was epitomized by this editorial in the *New York Amsterdam News*: "My preference, obviously, would have been Jules Bledsoe or Paul Robeson for the title role. . . . The blackfaced Tibbett produced a pathetic burlesque."[25] Opera historian Paul Jackson has observed that the 1933 Met blackface production drew upon offensive caricatures from the graveyard of American performance culture: "O'Neill's language sounds decidedly odd now, with its profusion of 'dats' and 'derabouts' and unfortunately even so masterful an interpreter as Tibbett cannot help calling up the ghost of Mantan Moreland and other hapless Hollywood caricatures of blacks in the thirties."[26] Yet, in spite of being characterized as "pathetic burlesque," the role of Brutus Jones is still regarded as one of Tibbett's most memorable performances.

Even though *Time Magazine* referred to Tibbett's "strapping, coffee-colored" body, a discerning eye can see he is neither strapping nor Black. Rather than appearing larger than life (like the allegedly "gargantuan" Robeson or "mighty" Bledsoe), Tibbett strikes an indifferent, feminized pose on the cover of *Time Magazine*. With his hands on his hips, one gently resting on his holster, Tibbett's posture is decidedly lacking in familiar signifiers of virility. The shadow behind Tibbett accentuates another inadequacy of blackface mimesis, revealing the gap between body and the shadowy roles that actors assume. Such ghosting also raises the question of what lies behind the blackface role, drawing our attention to the artifice of burnt cork, the greasepaint, the pose. A second photo, taken presumably after a performance, shows Gruenberg and Tibbett together in his dressing room, a snapshot of Irish and Jewish American collaboration in plundering Black performance culture. Tibbett has clearly been sweating, and the body greasepaint is worn off in patches, signaling the vacuity and limited temporality of blackface.

In addition to Tibbett's "pathetic burlesque[d]" performance, another problematic aspect of the Metropolitan Opera's *Emperor Jones* was that Gruenberg changed the script to have Jones commit suicide. In O'Neill's version, Brutus Jones succumbs to a silver bullet delivered by Lem (the "Native Chief" of the island) and the islanders who pursue him. In Gruenberg's libretto, however, Jones takes his own life by firing the pistol with a silver bullet to his head.[27] "Gruenberg received permission from O'Neill to make a number of changes" to the script, observes John Perpener, which included Jones's suicide.[28] *New York Times* critic Olin Downes, the most enthusiastic champion of the opera, claimed the new ending didn't appear "to be in any way inferior to the original dénouement," observing, "and thus Jones dies, a savage, a victim of atavistic terrors."[29] Yet many observers in the Black community found it unbelievable that Jones would take his own life. As R. Vincent Ottley put it in the *New York Amsterdam News*, "I do not believe that the average Negro will destroy himself in a moment of desperation. His sweating slave heritage has sapped too much of that which goes to make up character to permit him to make so concrete a decision."[30] As imagined by Gruenberg, however, Jones would die by suicide night after night on the Met stage.

Throughout all of these changes at the Metropolitan Opera House, O'Neill had been displaced—literally written off the title page. The Met production had left his name off the playbill even though his contract stipulated otherwise. Expressing his displeasure with Gruenberg on more than one occasion, O'Neill wrote to his lawyer, Harry Weinberger: "Success certainly went to Gruenberg's head! I believe he thinks he wrote the play now!"[31] O'Neill called the ongoing battles about royalties and permissions "the Gruenberg mess."[32] As late as 1937, Carlotta Monterey O'Neill, O'Neill's third wife, grumbled in her diary: "That horrible Gruenberg had lied and taken money etc. We are always hearing unpleasant tales re Gruenberg and 'The Emperor Jones.'"[33] Gruenberg now became a problem for O'Neill to handle, and his score became another artifact within the repertoire of racing the Met.

"EPOCHAL" BREAKTHROUGH

In spite of Tibbett's critical acclaim as the blackfaced Brutus Jones, the unexpected star of the operatic *Emperor Jones* was modern dancer Hemsley

Winfield, another African American performer whose career wove in and out of Broadway and across O'Neill's dramaturgical landscape. In addition to being the first African American to perform at the Metropolitan Opera House, a color line not again broken until 1955 with Marian Anderson, Winfield choreographed the dances for *The Emperor Jones*—another pioneering breakthrough. Winfield was a growing star in African American concert dance; indeed, Nelson D. Neal calls him "the first black modern dancer."[34] He was known during his day not only as a dance visionary but also, as the *New York Amsterdam News* called him, a "Negro art leader."[35] The *Chicago Defender* lauded "the International and worthy recognition" that had "finally crowned the efforts of the young dancer and ballet master" and his company, the New Negro Art Theater.[36]

By many accounts, Winfield's dancing was the most captivating element of the Metropolitan Opera's production, even as some reviews were infused with primitivism. Bruce Gulden observed, for instance, that Winfield's dancing was "savage" and "frantic and violent." In spite of the so-called savagery (or perhaps because of it, from Gulden's perspective), Winfield "seemed to cast a spell upon the audience," Gulden continued, and "his scene was by far the most magnetic and pulsating scene in the entire work."[37] Writing for *Opportunity*, Harry Keelan noted, "when Winfield stepped upon the scene, everything became alive."[38] Winfield took a small role and stole the show, "receiv[ing] as much critical attention as Tibbett's performance."[39] Mary F. Watkins of the *New York Herald Tribune* agreed: "Mr. Winfield was, as a matter of fact after Mr. Tibbett, the hero of the occasion."[40] Keelan realized the groundbreaking stakes of Winfield racing the Metropolitan's stage:

> History was also made for Negro art on that day. For the first time a colored man, Hemsley Winfield, returned again and again to the stage and took curtain calls with Lawrence Tibbett, [conductor Giulio] Gatti-Cazzaza [Casazza] and the composer, Gruenberg.[41]

Noting how Black artists have often been erased from the historical record, Keelan observed with pride that Winfield's "name was also featured on the program" (while, tellingly, O'Neill's was not). Indeed, "the event," as Keelan characterized it, was "epochal."[42]

Winfield's breakthrough appearance at the Metropolitan Opera House stands in stark contrast to the problematic plot change in the Gruenberg/de Jaffa adaptation that culminates in Brutus Jones's suicide. Although Winfield's dance company broke the color line, little has been written

Fig. 20. Final scene from the Metropolitan Opera's production of *The Emperor Jones* in 1933, featuring Hemsley Winfield's New Negro Art Theatre Dance Group. Photo: Carlo Edwards, Metropolitan Opera Archives.

about these performers, in part because their names were never recorded in the playbill, by the press, or in any of the Metropolitan Opera archival materials. The dancers' contributions are not part of the official libretto or printed archive, but rather found in the ephemeral realm of performance. Yet the dance troupe upstaged other performers, including the barely mentioned "singing" Metropolitan chorus and other white leads.[43] *Opportunity* critic Keelan noted the significance of casting African Americans in these roles rather than using the conventional practice of blackface: "They have allowed some of the minor parts to be played actually by Negroes!"[44] In the prologue, these performers were intended to be "concealed among the musicians in the orchestra pit" and "chant vindictively."[45] As performed at the Metropolitan Opera House, however, a *double* chorus was used: one Black (that chanted and danced) and one white (that sang).[46] Winfield's dance company changed the action of the opera, thus blurring the lines between drama, dance, and opera—and shaping the future of modern dance.

Just as Winfield's company framed the action of the play, so they also moved center stage. Perpener notes: "As originally planned, Winfield and the chorus were to make their entrance by clambering onto the stage from the orchestra pit, but because there was no room, the plans had to be changed. Instead, Winfield entered alone, squeezing awkwardly onto the stage through the prompter's box."[47] The chorus began on stage, too, not in the orchestra pit. As Gulden tells it, "At the rise of the curtain, we see sinister faces, peering through tall grasses, artistically placed on either side of the stage. From these faces emit shouts, murmurs and moans, yelling vengeance upon Jones, who had robbed them of their all."[48] While Downes claimed the Black chorus functioned a bit like "scenic accessories," he also acknowledged the performers were dramaturgically essential as "active participants in the action. Their yells and chants, in conflicting rhythms and keys, always hurried forward the action."[49] The chanting was controversial within the world of opera, but Downes defended it: "Musically their presence has every justification," as it was a "moment of lyrical expansion."[50] This prompted several other articles in the *Times* to ruminate over "What Constitutes Opera," noting that *The Emperor Jones* raised questions about the relation between drama and music—another testimony to its performative work.

Winfield and his Art and Dance Group gave vibrant, threshold-breaking performances that functioned as a counterpoint to the overused death narrative for Black characters.[51] At the end of the opera, according to Gulden, "the painted witch-doctor stealthily appears and begins his death dance, while from all directions come the pursuing blacks, who dance wildly about the worn and prostrate body of their prey."[52] The final scene was stunning, observed Watkins: "When Hemsley Winfield's troupe of Negro dancers stormed on in the final scene, so much raw vitality and exuberance was a distinct shock."[53] A riveting production photo shows Tibbett as Jones cowering in front of the islanders who have finally captured their emperor. As the Witch-Doctor, Winfield captures the gaze at the center of the photo with his arms upraised. Blackface gives way to African American modern dance. If only for a moment before the deadly silver bullet, racial hierarchies were subverted through performance.

Winfield and his dance troupe broke the color line in terms of their compensation as well. According to the Metropolitan Opera's ledger, they were paid as a package deal. In total, for ten performances in January and March, Winfield and his company received $2,440.[54] Adjusted for inflation, this is

about $55,589—quite a large sum, especially for an African American per-
former breaking into elite venues such as the Metropolitan Opera House.[55]
Significantly, Winfield was the second highest paid performer in the show
(after Tibbett), earning more than the other two white performers—and
they were singers known to the Met.[56] In both critical acclaim and in remu-
neration, then, Winfield achieved more at the Metropolitan Opera than any
African American ever had—or would, for decades to come.

In spite of these innovations, the Black chorus almost didn't take the
stage at Lincoln Center. Given the prevailing use of blackface performance,
the Met wanted to darken the faces of white singers rather than use African
American performers. However, Tibbett threatened to quit the production
unless Winfield's group appeared. In a moment recalling O'Neill's objec-
tion to the Drama League's threat to exclude Gilpin from its awards dinner,
Tibbett insisted on integrating the Metropolitan stage (even, paradoxically,
as he appeared in blackface). The Metropolitan Opera conceded, but retali-
ated by not listing the dancers in the playbill. When the opera went on tour
in Chicago, Tibbett repeated this practice of enlisting local Black dancers in
the Windy City. The *Chicago Defender* praised Tibbett for hiring performers
of color:

> As in New York, Mr. Tibbett used a local ballet to support him. The
> honor came to the 'Negro Folk-Play group' under the direction of
> Bertha Mosely Lewis, which included Robert Dunmore who were
> listed upon the program. This recognition makes Lawrence Tibbett
> a person to be appreciated by our group, because of his evident
> belief and practice of fair play and opportunity for all.[57]

Tibbett's role in securing African American performers for the chorus while
at the same time donning blackface himself signals the contradictory performance practices in circulation at the time.

In addition to dancing in *The Emperor Jones*, Winfield performed in a
variety of Broadway shows, but he was always known as the founder and
artistic director of the New Negro Art Theatre. His career, like Robeson's,
emblematizes the artistic traffic that raced from Broadway to Harlem and
back down again. Manning writes, "Winfield spent his career moving
between the little theater movement in Harlem and the commercial and
subsidized theaters downtown."[58] Winfield would go on to become a pioneer of American modern dance. His untimely death at age twenty-six of
pneumonia was attributed in part to "overwork and to his devotion to
training other young Negroes in dancing at his own expense."[59] Or, we

might say that he was taxed by the difficult work of breaking color lines. His obituary proves the indelible stamp of *The Emperor Jones*, as it ran a picture of Winfield as the Witch-Doctor and credited him with "critical acclaim surpassed only by that given to Lawrence Tibbett."[60] Dance critic for the *New York Age*, Vere E. Johns, wrote in Winfield's obituary: "That he achieved the Metropolitan Opera Co. is a stirring example to all of our young artists and I am only sorry that the Fates did not permit him to achieve his dream of going abroad, for I fully believe that Hemsley Winfield would have made London, Paris, etc., sit up and take notice."[61] Sadly, the inroads blazed by Winfield were stopped short by his early death. His role in *The Emperor Jones* was one he literally took to his grave, but his legacy lives on. The *New York Amsterdam News* wrote apocryphally in July 1933: "Some day in the not too distant future Negroes will be called upon to take leading roles with the Metropolitan and with other grand opera companies. Color lines will be erased and Negroes will sing not only in operas depicting darker peoples, but also in . . . others."[62] Winfield had a large role in racing those color lines.

THE EMPEROR JULES BLEDSOE

> What would have meant the opera the Emperor Jones if
> there had not been The Emperor Jules Bledsoe![63]
>   —The Hague's *Residentie-Bode*

Like other actors, Jules Bledsoe launched his career through O'Neill. Yet he performed both the dramatic version of *The Emperor Jones* and the operatic adaptation—a feat not even Gilpin could boast. Bledsoe devoted his life to musical artistry and to challenging racial prejudice, both on and off the stage—often while wearing the Emperor's coat—until his untimely death at the age of forty-three. Moreover, Bledsoe composed his own operatic adaptation, a version that some critics thought was superior to Louis Gruenberg's adaptation, and which I have recently discovered and analyze in these pages. So meaningful was the Brutus Jones role to Bledsoe that he cut out a portion of the opera poster—tellingly, his name—to adorn the cover of his scrapbook containing clippings from his life's work.[64] With this simple act of textual manipulation, Bledsoe carefully deconstructed and reassembled language, cutting and pasting the letters on an angle so that they defied the straight line found in the poster—a gesture, perhaps, to his queering the (color) line. His reconstructed name, if not professional iden-

Fig. 21. Jules Bledsoe aboard a transatlantic ship, likely to Holland in 1934. Bledsoe Papers, The Texas Collection, Baylor University. Photographer unknown.

tity, was literally assembled from a remix of *The Emperor Jones*. As the following pages make clear, Bledsoe constantly negotiated Black and white social spheres as well as heteronormative and queer cultures.

As a closeted gay performer, Bledsoe likely understood the "the stakes of the emerging discourse of homosexuality/heterosexuality for African Americans," as Somerville has observed.[65] Bledsoe lived the last part of his life with Freddye Huygens, a well-to-do Dutch businessman, who was Bledsoe's manager and lifelong companion (he later accepted the American spelling, Freddy).[66] An undated photo, likely taken while returning from his 1934 tour of Holland, is emblematic of queer traces that can be found hidden in the archive. It features the rising star on a steamer, smiling in the foreground. Smartly dressed in a crisp suit and dapper hat, Bledsoe tilts his head back slightly and grins, confidently returning the camera's gaze. The world is his oyster. Yet unmistakably in the background, there is another man, a white individual, framed by the stairs to the upper deck. Likewise dressed in a fashionable summer suit, this man faces the camera and is positioned directly behind Bledsoe, seemingly to the side, but at the very center of the photo's vanishing point. His framing in the picture is not accidental, for now I recognize this is Freddy. Unlike Bledsoe's publicity images, this picture was tucked away among seemingly unimportant materials in the archive (tellingly labeled "Photographs: General"). The meaning of the photo—like the scenario for Bledsoe's opera, which was wedged between the empty pages of a travel diary—would go unread, at least for a while. With Freddy in the background, the mysterious man behind the great artist, this photograph functions as a literal snapshot of the bitter reality that faced interracial, same-sex unions of this era: intimate in private, they must appear apart in public. Their relationship not only crossed the color line but also queered it, only to remain closeted within the archive.

Bledsoe's career as a serious actor was launched with a "straight" play, as the *New York Amsterdam News* characterized it: *In Abraham's Bosom* by white playwright Paul Green (1926).[67] The *New York Amsterdam News*'s use of "straight" was meant to reference "serious" drama, but it also uncannily highlighted the white-authored, heteronormative work that typified the Great White Way. After *In Abraham's Bosom*, Bledsoe took a stab at the dramatic role of Brutus Jones in 1927 at Harlem's Lincoln Theatre. Seven years after its 1920 premiere, some Harlem audience members had grown tired of *The Emperor Jones*. In fact, the revival was met with a "hostile audience [that] in no unmistakable manner made it clear that the famous Emperor could not reign even for twenty-four hours in a domain largely inhabited by people of his own race."[68] The harsh reception indicated a split among

Fig. 22. Jules Bledsoe as Brutus Jones
(likely from 1927). Bledsoe papers, The
Texas Collection, Baylor University.

Black intellectuals and regular Harlemites, hinting at a division between
the emerging Black theater epitomized by the Krigwa Players (written
"about us," "by us," "for us," "near us," as W. E. B. Du Bois had outlined in
his 1926 essay) and depictions of Black experience by white dramatists
(Paul Green, Edward Sheldon, and O'Neill, to name a few).[69] "The intellectuals of sundown hue make believe they like [*The Emperor Jones*]," the
Amsterdam News article continued, "but crude Harlem hasn't learned the
art of walking out without voicing disapproval."[70] And disapprove they
did. The 1927 production of *The Emperor Jones*, with "the great Jules Bledsoe," as Loften Mitchell characterized him, was pulled after just one night.[71]

In his memoir *The Big Sea*, Langston Hughes famously recounted how
Bledsoe was booed off the Harlem stage, characterizing the production as
"a sincere but unfortunate attempt on Jules Bledsoe's part to bring 'Art' to
Harlem."[72] Hughes characterized the problem as a misguided attempt to
bring highbrow art to a lowbrow venue, which typically featured popular
entertainment. As Hughes tells it, *The Emperor Jones* failed in Harlem not
only because it was offensive or racist but also because the play's expressionism was not appreciated. It was, in other words, as much a problem of
aesthetics as of content. No American playwright emblematized the puta-
tively refined taste of modernist theater at this time more than Eugene
O'Neill, and *The Emperor Jones* was a prime example of his modernist

experimentation. Hence, when O'Neill's play featured figures of Jones's unconsciousness, such as the Little Formless Fears, "naturally they howled with laughter," Hughes recounted: "'Them ain't no ghosts, fool!' the spectators cried from the orchestra. 'Why don't you come on out o' that jungle— back to Harlem where you belong?'" The laughter was so disruptive that Bledsoe stopped the show and lectured the audience about viewing etiquette. "But the audience wanted none of *The Emperor Jones*," Hughes noted. "When Brutus continued his flight, the audience again howled with laughter."[73] A critic for the *New York Amsterdam News* reflected: "Today no amount of praise given Bledsoe can recompense him for the insults, slurs and mistreatment he received at the hands of his own people."[74] After just one night, "that was the end of *The Emperor Jones* on 135th Street," as Hughes put it.[75] But it was not the end of *The Emperor Jones* for one of Harlem's biggest stars, Jules Bledsoe.[76] The Harlem flop forever shaped Bledsoe's future engagement with *The Emperor Jones*.

Just a year after the Harlem incident, Bledsoe wrote an essay that appeared in *Opportunity* called "Has the Negro a Place in the Theatre?" In it, he responds to Du Bois, Alain Locke, and other Harlem Renaissance intellectuals about the necessity of Black theater artists, writing, "the Black Brother has his place and belongs in the Theatre." Referencing Paul Robeson's early success in another O'Neill vehicle, *All God's Chillun Got Wings*, Bledsoe makes the case for numerous Black artists to excel, not just the few stars: "We must prove, by the excellence of the many, rather than that of the few, that we as a race 'Got Wings' and expect to use them to fly to the heights of histrionic art."[77] Moreover, recognizing his own role in breaking the color line, he writes: "It is up to the few of us that have gotten past the sentinels at the gate, to fling the gates wide open for our successors."[78] Having blazed many trails in American theater, and landed the central role of Joe in *Showboat*, Bledsoe next set his sights on racing American opera— and, for that work, he again turned to Eugene O'Neill.

BLEDSOE'S SCORE

It could be said that Bledsoe had a score to settle with the operatic version of *The Emperor Jones*. As early as 1929, he was working with O'Neill's son, Eugene Jr., to obtain the opera rights from Gene. Yet, by March 1930, composer Louis Gruenberg had beaten him to the punch.[79] In a letter dated September 1930, Gene clarified to Eugene Jr. that he had already given Gruenberg the operatic rights, "signed and sealed."[80] In the letter, O'Neill treated Bledsoe as a literal postscript to the artistic production, writing: "P.S. I am sorry about Bledsoe but he was a damn fool to go ahead before he got a contract from Madden [O'Neill's agent]. I gave Gruenberg the composer the opera rights to Jones six months ago" (i.e., March 1930).[81] Far from being a "damn fool," Bledsoe was drafting his score as early as 1929, according to a *Chicago Defender* article from 1934:

> The irony . . . is that *five years ago* the son of Eugene O'Neill, the play-wright, encouraged by one of his classmates at Yale, worked hard with Bledsoe to obtain from his father the rights to the operatic version of "Emperor Jones" which Bledsoe had written. O'Neill Sr. was in France at the time. He cabled regrets, for at that time Gruenberg, the white San Franciscan, already held the operatic rights.[82]

Gruenberg's success in securing the rights illuminates his class and racial privilege; in this case, Gruenberg's Jewishness signified as "white," as the article characterized him. Whereas Gruenberg was pursuing his connections at the Metropolitan Opera, and even traveled to France to meet with O'Neill, Bledsoe was working the family angle by connecting with Eugene Jr., who had no official capacity in representing his father. While he would come to regret this, O'Neill went with Gruenberg, the composer more established with the Met and all its privileges.

In spite of not securing the rights from O'Neill, Bledsoe had raced O'Neill's text with his own operatic version of *The Emperor Jones*, crossing another color line as a composer. I found his scenario concealed in an undated travel journal, tucked away in his papers, which are housed at Baylor University's Texas Collection. The journal was empty with the exception of a few brief handwritten notes describing what he called *L'Empereur Jones*.[83] Given to Bledsoe in 1926, the small journal had "MY TRAVELS" printed in caps at the top of each page. The irony of a blank travel journal containing the goldmine of an idea—his own operatic *Emperor Jones* reimagined transnationally—could not be missed. It echoes the story of Brutus Jones's journey to a place where momentarily he shines only to be passed over, like Bledsoe himself. This rich trope of transnational travel aptly describes his artistic practice as well. Proficient not only in French but also Italian and German, Bledsoe transposed the Emperor across the Atlantic.[84] The scenario maps out some of Bledsoe's ideas, beginning with a scene with a chorus in the palace, where there is "great confusion and unrest." The chorus is "quarreling with his [Brutus Jones] portrait," thus setting the tension for the Emperor's entrance. Of particular interest is Bledsoe's notation that right after Jones appears, he sings a solo—"Invocation to Hoodoo God"—making his *Emperor* more Afrocentric than Gruenberg's (and O'Neill's). Next, there is a "danse [sic] of maidens," after which Jones "drives people from the palace."[85] Moreover, according to the scenario notes, Bledsoe intended to create an intermezzo out of "Swing Low Sweet Chariot," a spiritual that he arranged and subsequently recorded. The rough scenario also lists "Nobody Knows the Trouble I See" as a possible song.

There are also pages from the score among Bledsoe's papers at the Schomburg Center for Research in Black Culture, which I discuss here in detail for the first time.[86] Nearly thirty pages (and possibly more) of the operatic score, complete with orchestration in Bledsoe's telltale hand, are extant. The score is arranged as a concert staging for piano, three singers (Native Woman, Smithers, and Brutus Jones), as well as a chorus. In refashioning the opera as a concert piece, Bledsoe wisely made the opera more portable and performable. It is unclear from the surviving fragments whether Bledsoe incorporated all of his ideas from his scenario in his score, but what does survive is an adaptation that departs from O'Neill's text by amplifying Jones's power, highlighting his connections to the church, and removing racialized epithets from the script.

One of the most notable changes in Bledsoe's opera is his portrayal of Brutus Jones as more commanding over Smithers. During their first interaction, Bledsoe eliminates "Mister" when Jones greets his Cockney sidekick, scripting instead: "So it's you, Smithers."[87] In fact, Bledsoe amplifies Jones's power over Smithers throughout the scene. When Smithers relishes Jones's demise, Jones retorts, "I'm the Master here. Don't forget."[88] By contrast, O'Neill's version is less biting: "I'm the boss heah now, is you fergettin'?"[89] Bledsoe's shift from "boss" to "Master" is subtle, but significant. In his version, Jones articulates himself in the role of Master, thus citing the discourse of slavery while also reversing these racialized roles. In Bledsoe's libretto, Jones moreover reproaches Smithers for how the Cockney exploited him when Jones first landed on the island (this text is entirely Bledsoe's):

JONES: What I was den is one thing, and what I is now is another,
   Ain't no use'n you bringin' up dem ole times
   Trying to disturb me brother,
   Ain't no use'n you bringin' up em ole times,
   Tryin' to disturb me brother;
   Gimme credit for bringing things to pass,

> Gimme credit for sho' nuff travelling fast
> I done de dirty work for you dat season,
> I was wuth money to you dat's de reason,
> I was wuth money to you, dat's de reason.[90]

These rhymed lyrics highlight the enduring legacy of colonial power that has benefited from enslaved labor, only to discard workers after they perform the "dirty work." It's an astonishing narrative turn that provides sympathy for Jones by referencing who he was before he became the corrupt Emperor. The film version takes this tactic as well, but Bledsoe's version predates it. Bledsoe's Brutus Jones is fully aware of his worth to the oppressive regimes that use him.

Jones moreover rebuffs Smithers for "trying to disturb him," and turns the tables by reminding Smithers that he is "the Power":

> JONES: Dat's de reason, dat's de reason,
>   From stowaway to Emperor in
>   Just two years, hot dog dat's goin' some.
>   I makes 'em understand
>   That I'm de boss o' dis land,
>   And falls an bumps deir heads,
>   I makes em understand
>   Dat I'm de Power what am,
>   And dey stretches out for dead;
>   I cracks de whip and dey jumps through,
>   I cracks de whip and dey jumps thru,
>   Dat is all I ever has to do.[91]

Jones has learned from his Cockney oppressor how to be a despot, just as he acquired knowledge from white businessmen while working as a Pullman porter about embezzling money (a plot point also in O'Neill's script). What's striking about Bledsoe's libretto is not that Jones knows how to work the system to his advantage, but that he also embodies it. He *is* the Power. Jones also wields the power: he cracks the whip.

A second change in Bledsoe's version is that he highlights Jones's Baptist past, creating another dimension to Jones as a man of faith. When pondering the prospect of encountering ghosts in the forest, for example, Jones tells Smithers he's not afraid of the ghosts and that his church will protect him: "Cause I'm a Baptist bred and born / An' when I die dere'll be a Baptist gone."[92] This change makes sense, given that Bledsoe was a devout Baptist and his church in Waco, Texas was central to his upbringing and identity. Ultimately, Jones believes that the silver bullet will protect him, but another voice (possibly Smithers or an unattributed chorus) reminds him that his Christianity, symbolized by a cross, will be his salvation, not a secular bullet-charm: "The cross will speed you / Your charm won't help you, now / Won't help you to-day."[93] Bledsoe's inclusion of religion—and specifically his Baptist faith—is strikingly similar to the additional scenes added to the 1933 Dudley Murphy film version, starring Paul Robeson, which opens with an elaborate backstory with Jones in his Baptist church and offering an opportunity for Robeson to sing on film. Did Murphy and his producers see Bledsoe's operatic version and poach this idea for their film version? The archive is silent on this matter, but the similarities are worth noting.

A third change that Bledsoe made is that his score virtually eliminates the use of "n——r" (with just one exception) in the fragment that survives. In his duet with Smithers before he leaves the palace and heads into the jungle, Jones tells Smithers that he will be protected: "But de Baptist church will per- / Tect its own, an' lan dem odder 'n——r's' square in Hell."[94] This is the only time that Bledsoe's score uses the epithet, which he utilizes to describe the natives who have risen up against him. Like Gilpin and Robeson before him, Bledsoe "raced" the text to eliminate offensive language—and not only as a performer but also as a composer. By contrast, the Gruenberg/de Jaffa libretto had twenty-eight occurrences of the offensive term; O'Neill's play text had thirty-four instances; and the feature film with Paul Robeson had thirty-three. Just as he manipulated the poster text for his scrapbook, so Bledsoe rearranged O'Neill's language to suit his vision.

BLEDSOE'S EMPEROR ABROAD

His own opera version turned down by O'Neill, Bledsoe had no choice but to perform Gruenberg's version of *The Emperor Jones*. Europe would provide more possibilities than the racist structures of New York opera. Bledsoe clarified his choice to perform abroad:

By hanging around New York I would have been forced to accept terrible cuts in salary and work when and how they pleased. Well you can see I've gone too far to turn back now. I must maintain my dignity and that of my accomplishments and talents. [While abroad]

I expect to appear in concerts, opera and high class musical or theatrical productions.[95]

Bledsoe's expectations were fulfilled: he performed to great acclaim overseas. The reviews were stunning, pointing out his "magnificent voice and excellent acting qualities."[96] Once again, the *Emperor* was breaking a color line: in 1934 Bledsoe was the first African American to perform Brutus Jones. For a singer, it was the role of a lifetime, as he wrote to his Aunt Naomi ("Nace") Cobb:

This is one of the most difficult roles written for the voice[,] taxing and using all of one's acting ability to the utmost. I shall be very happy once I shall have done the role. And it will bring me great acclaim in the U.S.A. thereby making my path a little easier upon my return.[97]

Whereas Harlem rejected Bledsoe's performance of the dramatic version of *The Emperor Jones* and O'Neill had rejected his opera score, the Dutch were giddy. As one headline put it: "Holland Goes Drama Dizzy as Bledsoe Plays 'Emperor.'"[98] One reporter from The Hague noted, "This Beldsoe [*sic*] is great as a singer: great for his splendid timber, for his famous volume, for his noble delivery."[99] A special dispatch to the *New York Herald* from Amsterdam declared: "Bledsoe, already recognized here as a fine singer, won a new triumph in the role of Emperor Jones." Moreover, his dramatic talents were palpable to Dutch audiences, and the *Herald* noted that the "grandiose" Bledsoe "show[ed] himself as an artist and an actor."[100] Such praise must have felt like vindication after his past failure in the Harlem dramatic production. In another letter to his Aunt Naomi written from The Hague, Bledsoe conveyed the magnitude of this role: "Just a word to let you know I cleaned [up] in the opera 'Emperor Jones.' I have never had such wonderful things said of me in my life. And if I never do again, I shall not have lived in vain."[101]

In the Dutch poster for the opera (drawn by Jan Willem "Willy" Sluiter)—the same poster that Bledsoe used to adorn his personal scrapbook—the performer is portrayed as an imposing Emperor. Drawn with the focus from below, the poster's upward angle captures Bledsoe's corporeal command. The angle also expressionistically distorts the lower half of his body—the boots and red pants are disproportionately larger than his head. The trademark six-shooter is strapped to his side, but this rendering includes an additional sword, which is faintly outlined behind his hip. Surrounded by an orb of white, the figure's folded hands, wide stance, and menacing glance convey power and determination. Sluiter's poster did for Bledsoe what Steichen's photo did for Robeson in a famous publicity still for the 1933 film version (see chapter 5), and may be a conscious quotation of it. However, Sluiter uses a different aesthetic; his poster is more expressionistic than other publicity images for *The Emperor Jones*. Bledsoe's larger-than-life body—like his magnificent voice—mattered to his reception abroad.

Like Robeson before him, Bledsoe was perceived to be "a mighty figure" and "a figure of strength" in the Dutch press.[102] A review in the *Rotterdam Maasbode* reported: "His Herculean physique and his enormous voice help Bledsoe already to make an imposing performance in this role."[103] The *Haarlem Dagblad* relayed: "How impressive a moment, when, in despair, he threw off his uniform-coat, and bared his broad chest. And how small this athletically built man became in his fear and remorse."[104] Indeed, racialized projections about Bledsoe's commanding physique infused the reviews for *The Emperor Jones*. Just as Robeson was received as a "Giant Negro" when portraying Brutus Jones, so too Bledsoe was portrayed as having a "broad chest" and a "Herculean physique"—strong like Zeus's son. The reviewer evokes Greek mythology and primitivism to marvel at Bledsoe's "enormous" masculinity.

Moreover, Bledsoe's interpretation of Brutus Jones included the character fighting back against white oppressors. In his opera score that Bledsoe performed abroad (Gruenberg's version), Bledsoe wrote these handwritten notes: "Raise Whip against the guard."[105] Bledsoe's enactment of this scene is particularly dissenting, given that this action directly follows Jones being whipped by the prison guard. Like Robeson, who raised a shovel against the prison guard in the film version, Bledsoe fought back against the guard with a whip—appropriating an oppressive tool of slavery and turning it on his tormentor. But unlike the film, which censored out the actual striking of the guard, Bledsoe enacted resistance against his white oppressor. One Dutch paper captured the significance of Bledsoe's performances: "Bledsoe rose here and grew to such a height of humanity, until he stood, without denying his race, as a living link between that which God created white, and that which God created black."[106] Bledsoe was overwhelmed by the positive press abroad, saying, "I shall never have anything so grand written about me if I live a million years," reported the *New York Age* stateside.[107] With the wind in his sails from his triumphs abroad, Bledsoe returned to the United States with every intention of singing *The Emperor Jones*, even his own adaptation. Sadly, he would soon become an Emperor deposed on American soil.

The success that greeted Bledsoe's performances abroad could not mask the bitter reality that awaited him at home. The artist had raced performance venues in the Netherlands and other parts of Europe, but he would not have the same results at home. American opera houses during the 1930s, like most theaters and cinemas, were segregated. Given those constraints, Bledsoe was not destined to perform at the Met, but he would retain the Emperor's role in his repertoire for years to come. This pattern is constitutive of racing *The Emperor Jones* whether on the Great White Way or at the Metropolitan Opera House: progress in breaking the color line was accompanied by roadblocks, only to be broken yet again.

AN ALL-BLACK *EMPEROR JONES*

But there is another untold story. Bledsoe's adaptation of *The Emperor Jones* was performed, though how often or where is uncertain. The *Chicago Defender* recounted in July 1934: "Bledsoe's own version, according to those musicians who heard it . . . was far superior to the one Bledsoe sang at Mecca Temple and abroad" (i.e., Gruenberg's score).[108] While the *Defender* was certainly poised to rave about Bledsoe, its claim that his score was "superior" to the Metropolitan production is notable. Its headline, "N.Y. Raves over Bledsoe's Debut in Opera," signals not a debut of the role, for he had sung the role numerous times abroad, but rather a premiere of his own score. Given that Bledsoe's version was a concert arrangement, he could have easily performed it in a smaller setting with just a few voices. The *Defender* claimed that Bledsoe's version challenged Tibbett's blackface performance as the definitive one. "Jules Bledsoe . . . displayed the fact that Tibbett's portrayal was somewhat minstrel showish, and that it takes deep understanding and rare art to give all the thing demands."[109] It is unclear how often Bledsoe performed his version. The historical record—like Bledsoe's personal life—is plagued by omissions and near misses.

Later in the summer of 1934, in what can only be seen as the perverse logic of segregation, Bledsoe performed *The Emperor Jones* just a few blocks away from the Metropolitan Opera's revival with Lawrence Tibbett in blackface.[110] This production was the first *Emperor Jones* performed by an all-Black American cast, produced by the Aeolian Opera Association, a short-lived African American opera company. In development for seven months, the Aeolian Opera Association's production featured "Harlem's Finest Singers," and premiered in July 6, 1934 at the Mecca Auditorium on West 56th Street.[111] Tellingly, the piece that the Aeolian Opera Association chose in its "first of a repertoire of operas by colored casts" was Gruenberg's *The Emperor Jones* (in a double bill with *Cavalleria Rusticana*).[112] The *Chicago Defender* reported: "This will be the first time that a Race singer has taken the leading role since Lawrence Tibbett sang it first at the Metropolitan."[113] Significantly, this production eliminated "all objectionable parts," according to the *New York Amsterdam News*, "without impairing the dramatic value of the story," likely referring to the excision of the twenty-eight instances of "n——r" that plague Gruenberg's text.[114] The advertising for the Aeolian production did not credit O'Neill or Gruenberg; it simply highlighted Jules Bledsoe's name and *The Emperor Jones*, raising questions of authorship yet again.

The Black press heavily promoted the birth of the Aeolian Opera Association's production of *The Emperor Jones* "with an entire Race cast," and used Bledsoe's success abroad as a draw: "The booming, melodious voice of Jules Bledsoe, which wafted him to operatic triumphs in England and Holland, . . . [will] herald the birth of a Negro opera on a grand scale."[115] The producers also boasted that Bledsoe was bringing with him "special scenery and costumes . . . imported from Holland."[116] The all-Black *Emperor Jones* was billed as "the greatest conglomeration of modern artists ever brought together on a modern stage."[117] One critic from the *Chicago Defender* commended Bledsoe's "splendid voice and the artful use of it for stirring dramatic effects," which was greeted by "thunderous applause."[118] For this production, "Harlem turned out en mass[e] and the world of critics acclaimed the performance too," the review continued.[119] Bledsoe's performance was enthusiastically praised, even by the white press. The *New York Times* wrote: "Mr. Bledsoe's performance was received with salvos of applause. He used his brilliant and manly voice with prodigality and with telling dramatic effect."[120] Like the Metropolitan Opera star Lawrence Tibbett, Bledsoe regularly received ovations after singing the spiritual "Standin' in the Need of Prayer." Though the Aeolian Opera Association made its mark as an all-Black opera company, it was a short-lived victory, as audiences did not support this artistic endeavor beyond the first production and the company folded.[121] Nonetheless, as the *Chicago Defender* made clear, "Colored players made history here."[122]

In addition to his performance with the Aeolian Opera, Bledsoe also sang *The Emperor Jones* with the Cosmopolitan Opera Association at the Hippodrome in November and December 1934 to excellent reviews.[123] The Hall Johnson Choir sang spirituals before the opera (this same choir was featured in the 1933 film version of *The Emperor Jones*). Billed as "the Greatest Negro Play Ever Created" by Eugene O'Neill and adapted as "a Grand

Opera with Jules Bledsoe," an advertisement in the *New York Amsterdam News* boasted the all-Black opera production would be "a memorable performance not to be missed!"[124] According to Frances Moss Mann from the *Amsterdam News*, "an audience of more than 5,000 greeted" the choir and Bledsoe.[125] In spite of the initial enthusiastic response, the experiment by the Hippodrome to feature opera on the weekends to entice African American audiences waned after a few months.

As late as 1940, Bledsoe was reviving *The Emperor Jones*. Journalist Robert Darden noted that this year Bledsoe "also co-organized a grand opera caravan, The Bledsoe Grand Opera Company, to present [a] musical version of 'Emperor Jones,' together with the Negro Ballet."[126] Was this Bledsoe's version (the one O'Neill rejected)? It is impossible to know, but what is clear is that Bledsoe, like Robeson and other performers, performed Brutus Jones for years, if not decades, and revised the score to his liking.

CODA: OPERATIC EXCAVATIONS

Jules Bledsoe understood he did not properly fit into the pages of history. But neither did Hemsley Winfield. Both were Black, queer performers who died early (Winfield at age twenty-six of pneumonia and Bledsoe at forty-three from an aneurism). Both made their careers in operatic versions of *The Emperor Jones*, breaking and queering color lines on major stages through their performances. Bledsoe would keep *The Emperor Jones* in his repertoire, but he also began composing other works.[127] Winfield founded the New Negro Art Theatre and was a major figure in African American concert dance. If, at the end of his life, Bledsoe could have answered the question he posed in his essay ("Has the Negro a Place in the Theatre?"), he would have answered yes.[128] Had he not died so young, Bledsoe would have seen the day when great African American performers would take center stage at the Met and elsewhere. Bledsoe's lasting legacy is anticipated in this 1933 article in the *New York Amsterdam News*:

> Some day in the not-too-distant future, Negroes will be called upon to take leading roles with the Metropolitan and with other grand opera companies. Color lines will be erased and Negroes will sing not only in operas depicting darker peoples, but also in Wagner's 'Tristan und Isolde,' Alfano's 'Resurrection,' and many others. We hail [Caterina] Jarboro and Bledsoe as pioneers blazing a trail for others who are often asked to sing spirituals only.[129]

Hemsley Winfield's career was likewise defined by racing color lines. In July 1933, six months before he died, Winfield said at a forum before a dance concert: "All races, no matter what color, had fundamental human feelings and ideas to express in movement."[130] His obituary in the *Harlem Heights Daily Citizen* acknowledged his legacy: "Now that Hemsley Winfield is dead, Harlem will become more appreciative—more understanding—of him and give more encouragement to the group whom he sought to impart his art."[131] Both Winfield and Bledsoe had raced *The Emperor Jones* with great success only to perish far too soon after crossing the finish line.

FIVE

Racing the Cut: Black to Ireland

Everything about the 1933 film version of *The Emperor Jones* was unusual: it was a Depression-era, early Production Code picture made with independent financing by a maverick director and producers, and, importantly, featuring a Black star (Paul Robeson) and an almost all-Black supporting cast. It was, moreover, the first time that an African American performer was top billed in a white-produced, nationally distributed U.S. studio feature film. Furthermore, the producers of *The Emperor Jones*, John Krimsky and Gifford Cochran, were outsiders to the studio system, having presented the German film *Mädchen in Uniform* (1931), widely regarded as an anchor of early lesbian cinema, to the United States.[1] *The Emperor Jones* hovers between experimental, Hollywood, and race film, showing "surprising artistry for an early independent sound film, particularly in its realization of the various milieus of 1930s Black America through a building up of detail."[2] As film scholar Scott MacQueen notes, "It was also the kind of film that would have never been made in Hollywood."[3] Yet it was made by a major studio, although not in Hollywood.

At its core, *The Emperor Jones* was a film aimed at critiquing empire while also evoking the Black diaspora. Yet the film was created by a team of Irish American artists. While scholars have attended to Eugene O'Neill's investment in Black culture (both positively and negatively), less discussed are the ways in which Blackness and Irishness intersect in the film adaptation of *The Emperor Jones*, one of the most intriguing examples of early twentieth-century Black cinema created by Irish Americans. O'Neill, the most notable Irish American playwright at that time; director Dudley Murphy, known for his films about Black culture; and Irish-born actor Dudley Digges all devoted their creative energies to theatrical and filmic projects about, and featuring, Black people—or what we can call Black performance culture. Their work on *The Emperor Jones* came from a commitment to the idea that the colonization of Ireland and the Irish diaspora shared affinities with the results of anti-Black racism, colonialism, and imperialism— although certainly not identical. As we shall see, these Irish American theater and film artists had a track record of creating works that featured Black life as a way of negotiating their own contested relationship with legitimating structures in white, U.S. culture.

The film's racial politics, which have been hotly debated since its premiere, repeatedly interlink a range of global and circum-Atlantic legacies of white imperialism, demonstrating the "radical reciprocities" between minority cultures in the Black and green Atlantics.[4] The film aspires to make visible the connections between African and Irish diasporic experience, even as this analogy comes at the cost of eliding those important differences. One of the reasons *The Emperor Jones* makes such a fascinating case study is because it abounds with contradictions: it both shattered racial constraints in American film while also articulating racial anxieties. We can see this manifested in two ways. First, the film's anti-imperialist, antiracist ambitions are most visible in the director's attempt to overlay different cartographies, memories, and experiences of racial violation. This technique, which I call "circum-Atlantic double exposure," is a cinematic device aimed at developing a collective portrait of alienation and suffering caused by white racism and imperialism. The second characteristic, which I call a "race cut," is the mark of censors and local projectionists who spliced out potentially inflammatory material from the film. In so doing, the excisions can be seen as dichotomously marking sites of racial anxiety and opposition: on the one hand, those to white audiences who objected to Robeson's power, while on the other, cutting out material offensive to Black audiences. These forms of alteration resulted in several distinctive versions of the film (screened differently for white, Black, northern, and southern audiences). Central to my argument is that double exposure works *together* with race cuts in *The Emperor Jones*: the cuts point to the doubling; the dissolves highlight the (w)hole. These two strikingly divergent and paradoxical features of the film—the director's accretions and the censor's depletions—expose the problematics of representing imperial violence within white regimes of power.

The Emperor Jones co-inscribes the contested terrain of imperial representations in order to expose ways of performing back against the capaciousness of Empire, even in the role of the Emperor. Thus, while the film plumbs the Black diaspora to negotiate the Irish American creators' liminal positionality within white legitimating structures—and in so doing, breaks the color line and more—it also benefits from using Blackness. It is therefore important to take into account the larger cultural terrain of what Michael Gillespie calls "film blackness": a rethinking of Black film "as a practice that emanates from the conceptual field of black visual and expressive culture."[5] The film's production and distribution constitute an imprint of the ever-shifting manifestations of representing race and empire—as a *film-in-motion*—while highlighting doublings, ruptures, and reconstitutions. Crucially, this chapter concludes with an examination of a version cut for Black audiences, which I analyze in these pages for the first time in detail. This altered version of the film, I argue, "raced" the official cut, constituting a competing archive and a performative diptych with the Library of Congress restored version.

CIRCUM-ATLANTIC DOUBLE EXPOSURE

The Emperor Jones's use of what I am calling circum-Atlantic double exposure cinematically demonstrates Irish American notions of, and investments in, Blackness. There are productive cross-currents in examining the intersections of the Black and green Atlantics, as Peter D. O'Neill and David Lloyd have observed. The term the "'Black and Green Atlantic,'" they write, invokes a shift in Irish studies to consider

> the vexed question as to the relation between two historically oppressed peoples—the dispossessed and the colonized Irish, forced into emigration and often indenture from the late 16th century, and Africans captured and enslaved during the same period—whose experiences of racialization and citizenship not only differed utterly but were constituted differentially.[6]

Indeed, as Richard Rankin Russell points out, "we might even say that we are living in a 'Black and Green moment' in literary studies whereby the rich interactions of black and Irish cultures . . . are being mapped and elucidated."[7] Yet attention to these synergies and cross-currents cannot be at the expense of their differences, as critics of the film have noted. *The Emperor Jones* makes clear the tensions between, and differences among, the colonized Irish and peoples from the Black diaspora. Paul Gilroy's analysis of the Black Atlantic as a counterculture of modernity, one that rejects "nationalist or ethnically absolute approaches" to identity, is foundational to Joseph Roach's work on circum-Atlantic performance—and to my analysis.[8] "The concept of a circum-Atlantic world (as opposed to a transatlantic one)," Roach writes, "insists on the centrality of the diasporic and genocidal histories of Africa and the Americas, North and South, in the creation of modernity."[9] Indeed, the imperial networks that Roach maps along the Caribbean rim occupy the center of O'Neill's colonial drama, which is set somewhere in the West Indies not yet colonized by the United States. It is hard to imagine an American drama or film of the early twentieth century more densely saturated with circum-Atlantic resonances than *The Emperor Jones*.

Some of the distinctive qualities of the film adaptation derive from O'Neill's 1920 modernist masterpiece, which I have examined in detail in chapter 1. DuBose Heyward's screenplay, building on Murphy's film treatment and O'Neill's scenario,[10] added an elaborate prestory to Jones arriving on the island, constituting roughly two-thirds of the film (Heyward had also penned the 1925 novel about Black life, *Porgy*).[11] While primitivist tropes are at work in *The Emperor Jones*, the film diverges from some of the cinematic practices of the era, especially in using double exposures. During the beginning title sequence, one of the many scenes that Heyward added to flesh out Brutus Jones's backstory, there are intriguing dissolves and double exposures that literally overlay three axes of Roach's circum-Atlantic triad: the southern part of the United States, the Caribbean, and diasporic Ireland. The opening sequence layers not only images but also sounds, cartographies, and cultural memories within the circum-Atlantic.[12]

The title sequence constitutes a visual snapshot for the broader point of this chapter: Irish American dramatists and filmmakers used Black performance culture to negotiate their own racialized positionality. During this sequence, the names of what we might call the Irish triumvirate[13]—O'Neill, Murphy, and Digges—are projected onto Afro-Caribbean drums and bodies (portrayed by African American actors and musicians, providing another layer to its diasporic performativity). The film opens with a black screen, fading in to reveal a close-up shot of an Afro-Caribbean drummer and the sounds of chanting and drumming. The first credits appear: "John Krimsky and Gifford Cochran present Paul Robeson in *The Emperor Jones* with Dudley Digges." Robeson is prominently billed, but his name is not placed on the drum itself. Rather, Dudley Digges's name is. Next, the camera pans right and dissolves to reveal a medium shot of the drummers; then, it zooms out, tracks right, and dissolves into the next title card: "Based on the famous play by Eugene O'Neill." O'Neill's last name is projected onto a drummer's body, which then dissolves to a close-up shot of another drum (a djembe) with the text "directed by Dudley Murphy." Indeed, O'Neill and Murphy share a brief double exposure that, in effect, *doubles* their Irishness. Below this, another line, "Passed by National Board of Review," indicates that the film was approved by the regulatory organization known as NBR, an early iteration of the Production Code office that would come into full force in 1934 to regulate the film industry. Double

Fig. 23. The opening title credits for *The Emperor Jones* film project Dudley Digges's name onto an Afro-Caribbean drum. Screenshot by Katie N. Johnson.

exposure thus gives an uncanny meaning to the notion of passing (in both senses of the word), double consciousness, legitimation, and cinema's role in these enterprises. It facilitates a doubling of Irishness and the Black diaspora, and, importantly, this layering has been endorsed by the National Board of Review, a clearinghouse and censor for American film, exposing its role in producing film Blackness.

The sequence takes just twenty seconds, but it is striking how the camerawork creates a filmic space where Irish American and diasporic Black identity coincide—a cinematic moment that invokes historical precedent. New immigrants have long been perceived as nonwhite in antebellum U.S. culture. "The Irish who emigrated to America in the eighteenth and nineteenth centuries," writes Noel Ignatiev, "were fleeing caste oppression and a system of landlordism that made the material conditions of the Irish peasant comparable to those of an American slave."[14] Irish and African Americans shared not only urban centers but also "the scorn of the better situated."[15] However, as geopolitics and immigration legislation shifted, new immigrants such as the Irish "were gathered under the term 'Caucasian' in the twentieth century and thus unified as 'conclusively' white," explains

Fig. 24. Opening credits showing that the film passed the National Board of Review. O'Neill's name is projected onto drummers' bodies. Screenshot by Katie N. Johnson.

David R. Roediger in *Working Toward Whiteness*.[16] This messy realignment of whiteness was not without anxiety or confusion, as the historical residue of sharing the "common culture of the lowly" clung to this newly acquired, and always shifting, status of white privilege.[17] This helps explain why double exposure—a visual return to a sharing of precarious racial status—was so crucial to *The Emperor Jones*. The film's double exposure of Irish Americanness onto Black bodies (that is, African Americans *performing as* Afro-Caribbean drummers) is a visual metaphor not only for how the Irish creators were thinking through their own liminal whiteness in *The Emperor Jones*, or the performativity of race, but also more broadly for how the Black and green Atlantics collide in performance and cinema of the 1930s.

In looking "black to Ireland" and revisiting the controversial racial portraits in Murphy's film, we must begin with its creators: the Irish triumvirate. O'Neill's investment in Irish and Black performance culture mirrors Murphy's: both Irish American artists created works that featured Black life as a way of negotiating their own contested relationship with legitimating structures in white U.S. culture, while also benefiting from those structures. The son of America's most famous Irish American actor, James O'Neill, who never forgot the sting of the Irish famine, O'Neill witnessed his family's rise from poverty and bigotry ("no Irish need apply") to white, middle-class privilege—a shift that exemplifies "how the Irish became white," as Ignatiev has put it. Early in his career, O'Neill penned unforgettable Irish American characters, just as he was sketching iconic African American figures. As Irish scholar Aoife Monks has observed: "O'Neill, like Brutus Jones, was liminally and precariously 'coloured.'"[18] Although he never visited Ireland, O'Neill understood himself as Irish. "The one thing that explains more than anything about me is the fact that I'm Irish," O'Neill once said. "And, strangely enough, it is something that all the writers who have attempted to explain me and my work have overlooked."[19] If overlooked during his lifetime, O'Neill's place in Irish letters is indisputable today. Irish scholar Declan Kiberd has observed that O'Neill "is one of the very few truly great American writers who also casts a sharp light on the Irish condition."[20] O'Neill's sense of his connection to Ireland was clear. He wrote: "I am the last of this pure Irish branch of the O'NEILLS—my children are a weird mixture, racially speaking."[21] O'Neill's characterization of his Irishness in terms of race was in line with the racialized discourse of ethnicity in U.S. culture during that time period. Indeed, O'Neill was understood as "black Irish" during his day. As Robert M. Dowling observes, "Among the ranks of the 'black Irishmen' in American letters," O'Neill was characterized by journalist Croswell Bowen as "'the blackest one of all.'"[22] In *The Emperor Jones*, writes Monks, "O'Neill's deployment of blackness constituted him as a liminally white author, engaging with the anxiety of colour through a liminally/absolutely black figure."[23] O'Neill was not alone in expressing anxieties of color within this film.

The motion picture also reveals Irish American Dudley Murphy's increased investments in Blackness while also advancing his commitment to independent filmmaking and perceiving himself as an outsider to the film industry. Prior to his direction of *The Emperor Jones*, Murphy had directed two short films about Black life: *St. Louis Blues* (1929, with an all-Black cast) and *Black and Tan* (1929). "I like doing Negro things," Murphy once said.[24] Indeed, he was "best known for short films about Negroes," critic Creighton Peet put it in 1933.[25] Characterized by his biographer Susan B. Delson as "Hollywood['s] Wild Card" (the subtitle of her 2006 book), Murphy had a "conflicted relationship" with the film industry. The character of Brutus Jones "resonated with Murphy's perception of himself as an outsider in a rapidly changing, increasingly hostile industry."[26] Significantly, Murphy was working on his treatment for *The Emperor Jones* while filming *St. Louis Blues*, thus providing another through line between Murphy's previous work with Black actors and *The Emperor Jones*. In a letter to O'Neill, Murphy wrote: "I am so vitally interested in 'Emperor Jones' that it would nearly break my heart if I could not direct it myself. . . . I am so absolutely sure that I can make a great film out of 'Emperor Jones,' that I am willing to gamble or risk anything for the privilege of making it."[27] Murphy ultimately won over O'Neill, just as he would persuade Robeson to star in the film. O'Neill was convinced "not only by Murphy's passion for the material, but for his track record as an independent film maker not in the service of Hollywood clichés and formulas."[28] United in their rejection of Broadway and Hollywood and their interest in Black performance culture, these two Irish Americans created what would become the first white-produced, nationally distributed, studio picture in the U.S. with an African American lead.

Finally, actor Digges, who performed the role of colonialist Smithers in the film, was another important part of the artistic team with connections to Ireland. Born in Dublin, Digges was among the small group of actors who formed the Abbey Theatre (the theater company that made an indelible impression on O'Neill when he saw their legendary 1911 tour of the United States).[29] A souvenir program that accompanied *The Emperor Jones*'s 1933 premiere reminds readers that Digges "was first seen in this country with the Irish Players" in 1904.[30] Digges's assumption of the sneering Smithers, one of just three white roles in the film, provides a rich critical commentary on Britain's colonial history. His performance of the Cockney colonizer—as an *Irish* actor—literally embodied the contested history of Ireland and the British Empire.

Double exposure was not new when *The Emperor Jones* was filmed in 1933. David Bordwell observes that French filmmaker Georges Méliès pioneered methods such as double exposure during the early years of silent film.[31] Yet, even though the technique had been used for nearly two decades before filming *The Emperor Jones*, what Murphy and cinematographer Ernest Haller did with double exposure was new in assembling circum-Atlantic memories and embodied practices from the Black and green Atlantics. A 1934 study guide for students devoted two sections to describing dissolves and double exposures in the film.[32] While there are more than two dozen such instances throughout the film, I would like to return to the beginning sequence for a signature example of circum-Atlantic double exposure.

Directly following the title sequence, the camera swings above to an aerial crane shot, filming Haitian tribal dancers moving clockwise in a circle while singing and chanting. Next, a slow dissolve results in a double exposure of two sets of people (and, indeed, two continents): Afro-Caribbean performers are layered onto southern Black worshipers. The double exposure creates a palimpsest of Black diasporic performance practices. The dissolve continues until the double exposure resolves: the Caribbean fades away and the American South takes its place. Viewers

Fig. 25. The opening sequence of *The Emperor Jones* film featuring a double exposure of Haitian dancers and members from a Southern Baptist church. The African American celebrants move counterclockwise. Screenshot by Katie N. Johnson.

are now inside an African American church whose celebrants are moving counterclockwise.

Some film scholars have criticized this sequence for its primitivism. Cedric J. Robinson writes, for example, that the dissolve "from African or 'Haitian' tribal dancers to Black circle dancers in a backwoods church . . . made the point that Blacks were immune to history and civilization."[33] Even as the film suggests this, we could also see the dissolve as underscoring the notion that diasporic movements do not completely sever the link between homeland and new home. The dissolve, moreover, does not collapse the historicity of the people represented, for the performance practices and peoples in the opening sequence are not the same nor are they moving in sync. Whereas the Haitian dancers are moving clockwise, perhaps synchronized with circum-Atlantic flow, the Black southern worshipers move in the other direction, in what can be seen as oppositional movement. Double exposure allows both identities to be present at once. Rather than conflating cultural history, this doubly exposed frame invites critical commentary on the juxtaposition—and not merely how Haitian and African American performance practices are overlaid but also how the diasporic and genocidal histories of the circum-Atlantic world are invoked. *The Emperor Jones*'s use of circum-Atlantic double exposure reveals the connections between Irish and Caribbean figures in what Michael Malouf calls a "tactical politics of solidarity" in negotiating concerns regarding race, nationalism, and citizenship.[34] Insofar as film can function as a memory machine, *The Emperor Jones* serves as a case study not of surrogation— which Roach argues is a substitute of one thing for the other—but rather a doubling or "multiplication and simultaneity" of embodiedness.[35] This doubling—or, more accurately, *performative layering*—invites us to consider multiple iterations of imperial violence.

DOUBLE EXPOSURE AND RACE CUTS

André Bazin's 1946 essay "The Life and Death of Superimposition" is useful to highlight paradoxical tensions that can arise from double exposure (what he calls superimposition). Bazin writes: "Superimposition on the screen signals: 'Attention: unreal world, imaginary characters'; it does not portray in any way what hallucinations or dreams are really like, or, for that matter, how a ghost would look."[36] While Bazin dismisses superimposition as an ineffective technique for portraying ghosts in film, he does acknowledge that "supernatural phenomena are essential to verisimilitude."[37] Bazin never mentions *The Emperor Jones* in the essay, yet the paradoxical tension he maps between verisimilitude and "the escape from reality and into fantasy and the world of dreams" is crucial for understanding the film.[38] *The Emperor Jones* features several hallucination scenes shot with double exposures, which occur after Jones flees into the jungle and is hunted by the islanders. Tinted with an azure blue lens, the hallucinations are the film's most experimental—and expressionistic—moments.[39] These doubly exposed scenes are also powerful cinematic articulations of what Toni Morrison calls "rememory," a collision with collective history, "when you bump into a rememory that belongs to someone else," as Sethe from *Beloved* explains.[40] Jones experiences circum-Atlantic memories he could not possibly remember, including a slave auction, the Middle Passage, and a crocodile god invoked by a witch doctor. Bazin discredits superimposition, a viewpoint shared by a 1933 *New York Herald* review: "Double exposure is not the best way of making the phantoms terrifying."[41] Likewise, a *London Times* critic chastised director Dudley Murphy for using "some embarrassing and highly unconvincing ghosts."[42] This was echoed by the *New York Evening Post*, which found the "double-exposure wraiths" problematic and a mere "display of trick photography."[43] Yet these superimposed "tricks" delivered their significance far beyond the realm of realism. Indeed, the phony nature of such scenes allowed them to escape the censor's wrath and deliver footage of controversial themes, whereas more realistic scenes were cut.

Double exposure was not the only filmic technique that shaped the representation of, and engagement with, racialized hierarchies in *The Emperor Jones*. The film was also constituted by what I am calling "race cuts": disruptive gaps in the film that resulted from scenes that were spliced away, marking sites of contestation about representing race. "Race cuts" manifested from competing forces: due to censorship from organizations like the Motion Picture Producers and Distributors of America (MPPDA), or at the insistence of Black audiences who were protesting offensive racial epithets. As such, the multiple versions of *The Emperor Jones* constitute a celluloid archive of dichotomous racial hierarchies that shaped the film (or rather *versions* of the film). The ensuing gaps, and the lost footage, exposed breaks in continuity but also provided space for contemplating what was spliced away. My use of the term *race cut* builds upon the notion of a cine-matic jump cut. Bordwell defines a jump cut as "any bit of disjunctive or discontinuous editing" or "abrupt transitions between scenes."[44] Impor-tantly, "the jump cut is a fairly disruptive device. It assaults basic principles of continuity editing, confuses us about the placement of figures and vio-lates continuity of duration."[45] Indeed, the studio print of *The Emperor Jones* had many awkward gaps and seams. These cuts operated not only as era-sures or something lost but also as spaces in which the cut becomes visible when the film's action jumps awkwardly ahead and congruency is dis-rupted. Such gaps expose the double process of exposing and hiding the racialized epistemologies at work in the film. The jump cut need not be merely disruptive or assaultive; it can also unsettle film viewing in a criti-cally productive way, drawing spectators' attention to the apparatus of filmmaking, especially the often-invisible process of editing, as well as to the discursive forces of racialization. These awkward moments of spliced film are spaces where time jumps, where meaning is paused—or, con-versely, is moved too quickly forward—prompting the viewer to ask what has been omitted. Crucially, race cuts work *together* with double exposure in *The Emperor Jones* as entwined, oppositional forces that both excise and double meaning.

Consider, for example, the scene in which Brutus Jones is working on the chain gang, part of the pre-story that screenwriter Heyward created. Before he ends up on the Caribbean island, Jones has been sentenced to a U.S. prison that forces convicts to work in a quarry. The jail sentence is another miscarriage of justice, as Jones has accidentally killed his friend, Jeff, during a fight in which Jeff pulls a knife on him. As Robinson has pointed out, this scene demonstrates "the film's intertextuality with post-bellum Black labor" where the chain gang "meld[s] into the natural land-scape, a fitting deposit for Black men who lacked the talent or disposition for right behavior."[46] The scene begins with a medium shot of prisoners' feet chained together. During this shot, we hear Paul Robeson (as Jones) singing "John Henry"—a work ballad meant to coordinate the rhythm of the prisoners swinging their hammers. "This old hammer killed John Henry / but it won't kill me," Robeson sings. The lyrics attest to Jones's resilience in the face of the hammer's violence; they also foreshadow the deadly force of the hammer in his hands (Robeson added "John Henry" not only to the film but also to the stage revival in 1925). The shot next dissolves

Fig. 26. Shot with a low-angle camera, Robeson appears larger than life in the quarry scene of *The Emperor Jones*. Screenshot by Katie N. Johnson.

to a double exposure: the anonymous convicts' feet are superimposed onto a powerful image of Robeson holding a sledgehammer. Even though he is chained and in prison, Robeson embodies folk legend John Henry, a symbol of strength, pride, and endurance; this image was so commanding, that it was used on lobby cards and promotional materials.[47] Next, "John Henry" transitions into "Water Boy," another African American folk song (and one that Robeson incorporated into his concert tour). The quarry scene showcases Robeson's physical and vocal powers, for he appears shirtless, his muscled torso powerfully occupying the center of the frame. Some critics have interpreted this and other scenes as fetishizing Robeson. "Those shirtless, well-oiled, muscular glimpses of him singing while shoveling coal or busting rocks in *The Emperor Jones*" were careful constructions, Ed Guerro writes, "packaged for the gaze of an admiring public."[48] Yet, rather than reading the scene as strictly fetishistic, it can be seen differently. Holding a sledgehammer and singing with a booming baritone voice, Robeson is the epitome of strength and talent. Moreover, a low-angle shot amplifies Robeson's authority, making him appear larger than life, dwarfing other prisoners, who appear miniscule in the background.

The camerawork does not treat the white prison guard in the same way. When he commands Jones to beat another prisoner, the camera is at eye level, not granting him the same power it had bestowed on Jones.

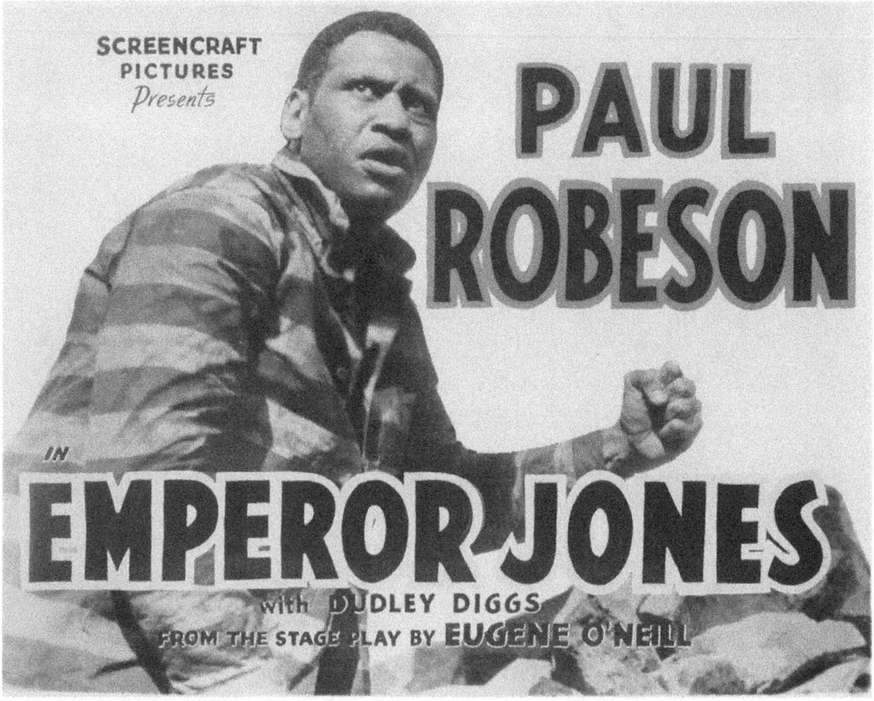

Fig. 27. Lobby card for *The Emperor Jones* film, featuring Paul Robeson in prison attire and fighting back. Distributed by Screencraft Pictures, 1933. Collection of the Smithsonian National Museum of African American History and Culture, Washington, DC.

Jones refuses, and, in retaliation, the guard hits Jones twice with a large stick before beating the prisoner himself. A jump cut is used to transition to the next frame, beginning with a close-up shot of Jones as he contemplates what to do. It is a subjective shot, freezing the action for a second time in the sequence—a stillness amid the violence. Then, in the next shot, Jones grabs a nearby shovel, lifts it up to strike the guard and JUMP!—there is an awkward gap, a race cut. The cut reads like an editing mistake. But the excision was not in the original print of the film; the expurgation was mandated by the censors postproduction: "The idea of a black man attacking a white man was unthinkable," reflected producer Krimsky.[49] We never see Jones hit the prison guard, but we can guess he has done so, for the film skips ahead to Jones fleeing while the guard lies lifeless on the ground. The gap points to the violence that cannot be shown, to the censoring mechanisms that excluded images of Black peo-

Fig. 28. Screenshot from the film version of *The Emperor Jones*, 1933. Robeson raises his shovel to strike the prison guard. The actual striking was censored out, creating an awkward jump cut. Screenshot by Katie N. Johnson.

ple fighting against oppression. As jarring as the race cut is, however, it also points to a space in which possibilities beyond the frame can occur. When Jones picks up the shovel, the significance of the "John Henry" lyrics becomes clear in an uncanny return: the hammer will not kill him, nor will it kill other prisoners. However, it will kill white oppressors. Try as they might, the censors could not excise Robeson triumphing over white abuse. Within the gap of the race cut, he gets away.

If the shot of Jones killing the prison guard was censored out, it lives on in a later hallucination scene—through another double exposure. In scene 175 of Heyward's shooting script, a little more than an hour into the film, Jones has fled to the jungle while being pursued by the Indigenous people of the island.[50] Remembering his past, Jones has numerous hallucinations, including a return to the chain gang scene. Jones not only sees these visions but also interacts with them, hammering in the stone quarry with the doubly exposed figures. Shot with an azure lens, this hallucination is a reenactment of the scene from the beginning of the film, except with a difference. As the white guard beats Jones viciously with a baton, Jones retaliates. According to the screenplay, "With arms upraised as if his hammer were a club in his hands, he springs murderously at the unsuspecting Guard. In the act of crashing down his hammer on the white man's skull, Jones suddenly becomes aware that his hands are empty."[51] This scene stages a dialectical moment that the double exposure lays bare: Jones both "crashes"/ crushes the white guard's skull and does not crush it. The pantomime shows Jones bringing the hammer down—yet the figure whom he is striking, or *pantomiming* that he is striking, is a superimposed figure, slightly out of reach of Jones's mimed hammer. Importantly, we see what was censored out in the earlier quarry scene: the hammer rises, the hammer falls. While he does not bash the guard's skull, given that his hands are empty, this does not stop Jones. He tries another tactic, expressing his intention to kill the guard for a *second* time, and with a second weapon. Jones now brandishes a gun, no longer pantomimed, and shoots the prison guard; the hallucination disappears. Double exposure thus facilitates a double death, and it allows Black retaliation against white oppressors.

At first glance, it is surprising that this violence—a double murder, conveyed with double exposure—was not hacked away. Given that it was a hallucination and filmed with superimpositions, however, the censors likely thought of it as only a figment of Jones's imagination. Circum-Atlantic double exposure therefore provided a technique that flew below the regulatory radar in the guise of hallucinations, lap dissolves, and circum-Atlantic apparitions. Contrary to Bazin's dismissal of celluloid ghosts, double exposures performed important anti-imperial work.

The race cut disrupting the quarry scene was not the only excision of resistance to white oppression from *The Emperor Jones*. The "most egregious of the cuts," as Library of Congress film historian Jennie Saxena notes, are, regrettably, those which are also forever lost to us: the slave auction and Middle Passage scenes.[52] Records show that the Library of Congress restoration team made great efforts to locate these excised slavery scenes, which were spliced from reels 8 and 9.[53] These scenes were also cut from the 1933 Metropolitan Opera production, which featured the lead baritone Lawrence Tibbett as Jones in blackface. (See chapter 4; Tibbett was initially proposed to star in the film version, an idea which Murphy, O'Neill, Krimsky, and Cochran all emphatically rejected).[54] Both the Middle Passage and slave auction scenes were in the script submitted to the New York Review Board for approval in 1933, implying that the cuts were made postproduction. Not only are these censored scenes crucial to Brutus Jones's psychological arc, they also are two of the central moments in the film featuring the historical significance of slavery and the oppression of Black people. Censoring these scenes had grave consequences because, as Richard Koszarski notes, "the lack of these scenes has the effect of eliminating any white responsibility for the bad behavior of Jones and those around him."[55] Indeed, without the slave auction or Middle Passage scenes, "the entire balance of the film is upset. White shame is spared while Jones, and the play, have a large dimension removed."[56] Crucially, the slave auction scene provides another astonishing moment in which Jones fights back against white oppressors, who appear via a double exposure. During this scene, Jones resists being sold into slavery, "convuls[ing] with raging hatred and fear."

Fig. 29. Paul Robeson in *The Emperor Jones* (film version, 1933). This scene, which portrayed the Middle Passage and enslaved people with double exposure, was censored. However, a film still of the scene appeared in *The Crisis* in October 1933. Photo by George Rhinehart via Getty Images.

According to the screenplay, Jones rejoins: "What yo' all doin', white folks? What's all dis? What yo' all lookin' at me fo'? What yo' doin' to me, anyhow? Is dis a auction? Is yo' sellin' me like dey uster befo' de war? An' yo' sells me? [A]n yo' buys me? I shows you I'se a free 'n— —r'!"[57] This dialogue lays bare the bitter contradictions of the film: Jones resists the auctioneer but does so while also using the n-word (one of thirty-three instances that are problematically splattered throughout the film). Yet, what happens subsequently is a remarkable scene of resistance and retribution. Next, Jones "fires [a gun] at the Auctioneer and at the Planter with such rapidity that the two shots are almost simultaneous."[58] Jones fights back, shooting not one but *two* white oppressors: double oppressors, doubly murdered.

While this moment of fighting back was censored, and the footage lost, the residue of the cut scene had an afterlife in popular culture. A film still of the Middle Passage scene was included in a lobby card montage used for publicity, demonstrating that the scene was cut postproduction.[59] This image was also published in the October 1933 issue of *The Crisis*, the African American periodical founded by W. E. B. Du Bois and devoted to bearing witness to racial injustice, one month after the film opened.[60] By printing a photo of the censored scene, the *Crisis* not only reminded its readers of the spliced-away footage but also reinserted the image back into the visual record, constituting an alternative archive. Given that the restored image of the Middle Passage appeared in the *Crisis*, the photo moreover exemplified a kind of "second sight."[61] Indeed, the *Crisis* addressed this dialectal dynamic by showing two images of Robeson in its October 1933 issue: on the cover, in full Emperor regalia, and another in the middle of the issue, in tattered clothing with the doubly exposed enslaved people.[62] Within the broader context of film Blackness, the censored scene lived on as a vital representation of the legacy of slavery and rising up against white supremacy.

Just as *The Emperor Jones* was doubly exposed and cut, so it was doubly screened: for Black and white audiences. At first, this was a matter of venue—and segregation.[63] On September 19, 1933, *The Emperor Jones* premiered at two cinemas in Manhattan: uptown at the Roosevelt Theater in Harlem and midtown at the Rivoli, known as Dudley Murphy's "Broadway standby."[64] Murphy rolled out a gala premiere and padded his box with distinguished guests, including former president Theodore Roosevelt's family.[65] Harlem's screening was auspicious as well, attended by Black luminaries such as dancer Bill Robinson, actress Ada Brown, and boxer Jack Johnson. There was a sense of pride that African Americans had "a special presentation of its own," featuring the first Black screen star, Paul Robeson, an actor "beloved by his people."[66] The *Chicago Defender* reported that "Paul Robeson emerged as one of the giants . . . and made him the hero of critics and the public."[67] As the *New York Amsterdam News* put it on their front page, "He's the Emperor."[68] Edward Steichen's iconic photograph, which appeared in *Vanity Fair* in August 1933, made clear Robeson's regal, defiant image. At first, the Harlem screening was meant to be a one-night event. However, as the *Amsterdam News* reported, "the crowds became so insistent the management was forced to open the doors of the theatre early and the picture went into two presentations with the crowd just as large at one as at the other."[69] Because Harlem had been "drawing unprecedented crowds," the run had been extended "for two or three weeks longer."[70] The extended run was a money-maker, reports Saxena: "The film appears to have made back most of its budget, earning $10,000 in its first week at the Harlem Roosevelt Theatre."[71]

Fig. 30. Photographer: Edward Steichen. Paul Robeson as 'The Emperor Jones,' 1933. Toned gelatin silver print. 34.9 × 27.3 cm (13 3/4 × 10 3/4 in.). The J. Paul Getty Museum, Los Angeles. © Condé Nast. © 2022 The Estate of Edward Steichen/Artists Rights Society (ARS), New York.

Fig. 31. Censored scene from *The Emperor Jones* 1933 film version when Smithers lights Jones's cigarette. The Library of Congress restored this scene in 2002. Screenshot by Katie N. Johnson.

Yet, in what will become clear in what follows, other audiences called the film "a damnable insult to the Negro race."[72] As objections to the film by the Black community intensified, the producers realized they needed to respond. What survives is a *film-in-motion*, with unexpected twists and turns.

FILM-IN-MOTION

The story of *The Emperor Jones*'s censorship is as complex as its restoration—and it, too, is plagued by cuts and omissions. *The Emperor Jones* might be one of the best examples of a *film-in-motion*—a picture that had multiple versions and receptions—for even after the cuts mentioned above, there were more to come. It was a film that was cut, censored, cut again, and screened for multiple audiences, only to be restored—from several different versions—by the Library of Congress Motion Picture Division in 2002.[73] There was no definitive master copy of the film, for, as Koszarski observes, "the film continued to circulate in cut and uncut versions throughout its release."[74] As detailed by the Library of Congress restoration team, "After the filming was complete, the censorship began in earnest, and it continued even after the premiere of the film."[75] It was an ever-changing set of celluloid reels.

One example of a scene that was censored and restored—or, we might say, "reraced"—was in the first half of the film, when Smithers deferentially lights a cigarette for Jones. The framing of the scene underscores Robeson's authority: he stands center frame, with the diminutive Smithers off to one side. Having commanded Smithers to fetch him a cigarette and then light it, Robeson (as Jones) stares beyond the camera while pondering his ascension to the throne, exhaling smoke in a close-up shot. Robeson's next line cements the moment: "Smithers, you has just had an audience with the Emperor Jones." The cigarette scene is "another symbol of the reversal of white supremacy in many of the images of the film," observes film scholar Jeffrey C. Stewart.[76] Given the scene's disruption of racial hierarchies, administrators of the Motion Picture Producers and Distributors of America (MPPDA), in adhering to the early roll out of the Production Code's prohibitions (or the Hays Code as it would become known), initially objected to this scene even before the film was released and debated censoring it. Ultimately, however, the scene was permitted.[77] But after release was another matter. Some markets insisted that this scene be cut, and it was especially advocated by distributors "so they could sell *The Emperor Jones* to white theatre owners in the South."[78] In other markets (likely in the North), the cigarette scene was kept. Fortunately, the Library of Congress team was able to restore it—reracing the cut.

The repeated use of racial epithets could have been handled—which is to say, removed—before the film was released by MPPDA. This had been done with offensive language in *Hallelujah* in 1929. By refusing to take a stand against the racist language in *The Emperor Jones*, the MPPDA missed an opportunity, and aligned its interests with white supremacy. "While it would have been logical for the MPPDA to simply ban the word 'n——r'— ostensibly the most direct insult to Black people," writes Ellen Scott, its inclusion demonstrates "the normalizing force of its national distribution to whites."[79] Indeed, the film was pitched "for consumption by whites," as *Variety* reported, although that was another misjudgment.[80]

The MPPDA and Universal Studio miscalculated the opposition the film would encounter from Black audiences and cinema workers: "It is understood already that colored operators below the Mason-Dixon Line are objecting to the use of the term 'n——r,' noted one review a week after its release."[81] Objections came from throughout the U.S., clarified the *Pittsburgh Courier*: "Negroes from every section of the country have been in a furore [*sic*]" about the offensive language and some plot elements.[82] This *New York Amsterdam News* headline says it all: "Harlem Dislikes 'N— —r' in Emperor Jones."[83] In response to objections after the initial release, producers Krimsky and Cochran proposed editing the film once again—this time for Black audiences. As the *Chicago Defender* reported, the producers proclaimed: "We are eliminating the word 'n— —r' from all new prints that [we] will make on *Emperor Jones*."[84] The *Afro-American* reprinted a portion of Krimsky's telegram to the Black community:

> Pursuant to your request we are eliminating the word 'n— — —' from all new prints that will make on Emperor Jones. We have no intention of offending the Negroes who were largely instrumental in making the screen version of 'Emperor Jones' one of the greatest pictures of the season.[85]

Controversy over the offensive language was not new to the 1933 film adaptation. The 1920 stage play was likewise met by criticism from the Black community, and both Gilpin and Robeson famously rewrote the script, removing objectional language (see chapter 1).[86] At least two different prints of *The Emperor Jones* circulated after the initial censorship: one that played in white cinemas, with racial epithets intact, and a Black-house version, which came later, with offensive language cut. When the Library of Congress restored the film, they remained true to the shooting script, and kept the racial epithets.

RACING THE CUT: A BLACK-HOUSE VERSION

There is another untold story—a ghostly return from the archive. The Black-house version of *The Emperor Jones* has been given little attention, even though it was hidden in plain sight.[87] This print, cut specifically for African American audiences, reshaped the contours of the "official" film's ontology by deleting the offensive language, excising scenes with abusive white power, and eliminating the expressionistic blue tint from the forest scenes. This version of the film "raced" the official cut, constituting a competing celluloid archive—and should be thought of as a performative diptych with the restored version.

In viewing the two versions side-by-side, I began to observe small cuts:

excisions of a second or two of film at a whack.[88] It then dawned on me that the shorter film was the Black-house version, running 4 minutes shorter, though it was not attributed as such. At first, the cuts were barely noticeable and appeared to respond to early Production Code prohibitions: the elimination of extended kissing with Undine (Fredi Washington) and a suitor, Undine tucking money into her garter belt, and two women dancing together in the Harlem club scene. Then, around the 21:00 minute mark of the film, the fight scene between Brutus Jones and Jeff in "Baby Jim's Juk" joint was markedly shorter: a close-up of Jeff's knife was cut, as were subsequent medium shots of the weapon while they fought (scenes 67–69 in the shooting script). With these excisions, Black-on-Black violence was tamed, as well as images of African American men wielding weapons, thus disallowing stereotypes about Black male criminality. More importantly for my argument, the white police officer who rushes into the all-Black space to respond to the murder was cut (time stamp 22:24). In the Library of Congress restored version, it's a seemingly insignificant scene, lasting a few seconds. Here's how MacQueen describes what he calls the "bizarre coda" of the scene: "When a white Irish cop bursts in he is met by Jeff's body lying on the floor, but the crap table has become a pool table, and the occupants of the room singing, playing piano, generally minding their own business and ignoring the dead man in their midst."[89] In the official version, the cop's shrill whistle summons reinforcements, signaling a larger racialized (and anti-Black racist) system of policing, capture, and internment of people of color. In the Black-house version, however, there's no white police presence at all; the scene ends with Brutus Jones fleeing the crime scene. The excision of the officer, and an Irish one at that (at least as MacQueen sees it), rewrites the narrative so that there is no police intrusion into this African American space. With a twenty-first century perspective in light of the #BlackLivesMatter movement, it also suggests that entanglements between the police and the Black community were problematic long ago. This version rewrites—or *races*—the film to exclude white policing of the Black community.

The next noteworthy cut occurs in the quarry scene, where Jones is working on a prison chain gang hammering stone. About eight seconds of film are gone in the Black-house version. Missing is the footage where Jones fights back and hits the guard with a shovel. (This is also missing from the Library of Congress restored version and believed to be lost; I call this a race cut in the section above).[90] In addition, the Black-house print also cuts the white guard beating Brutus Jones prior to his retaliation (24:51). Significantly, it is another excision of white physical abuse, jumping to Brutus Jones escaping.

There is a third expurgation of intruding white power in the Black-house version: the search posse that hunts Jones has been removed. In the original version, Jones flees from the prison chain gang with bloodhounds and an armed mob on his track, recalling the emotional flights of enslaved people portrayed in nineteenth-century slave narratives. Jones finds momentary refuge with Dolly, his girlfriend, before the sheriff appears. Then, "the door is kicked open and Brutus flattens himself behind it, a poker raised in his hand. The sheriff grabs Dolly brutally by the wrist and screams at her to tell him where Jones is. The posse calls, having picked up the false scent and the sheriff departs."[91] Gone is the white sheriff brutalizing Dolly; gone are the bloodhounds; and gone is the posse. With the specter of lynching underwriting the danger here—a threat so pronounced that Robeson stipulated in his contract that he would not film below the Mason Dixon line—this newly cut version removes police brutality and vigilante violence (the lost footage was not recovered for the Library of Congress restoration). Once again, Brutus Jones escapes without the direct interference of white oppressors.

Most significantly, the remaining cuts involved the removal of "n——r" from this version of the film. All thirty-three instances are gone. At times, these cuts are one or two second blips that stand out as awkward jumps; at other times, the cuts are barely recognizable. In addition to these cuts, Robeson also omitted some of the racial epithets prior to filming.[92] It is appropriate to consider the importance of these changes, which, on one level, appear to be merely linguistic. From a speech act perspective, the repetitive use of "n——r" in *The Emperor Jones* is not only insulting, as the Black community repeatedly claimed, but also injurious. Language not only assists violence, as Judith Butler has observed, but also "wields its own violence."[93] By jettisoning the offensive language—by racing the cut, in other words—the Black-house version provides a celluloid example of "talking back" to injurious speech.[94] As such, it may be one of the best early examples of a film responding to objections concerning the injurious nature of language. The resulting film moreover might be the closest artifact of the versions that Gilpin and Robeson performed when they excised offensive language from O'Neill's stage script.

Finally, the blue tint once Jones enters the forest is gone from the Black-house print (at 57:33 and at 1:00:05 in the restored version). As Saxena observes, the hallucination double exposure scenes were originally shot with Kodak tint No. 10, azure, described in the Eastman Kodak catalogue as being "suggestive of the sedate and reserved, even approaching the austere or forbidding; under certain conditions slightly gloomy."[95] The Library of Congress restored the tinting, "to add to the terror," as film restorer James Cozart noted, although they were concerned about the darkness of the color saturation.[96] The azure-tinted scenes constitute about ten minutes of darkly tinted film to accent the expressionistic encounters with Jones's hallucinations in the forest—with low visibility. However, the Black-house version kept the film in black and white, choosing visibility over mood, thus eschewing the "forbidding" and "gloomy" atmosphere in order to let Robeson shine. Film editors for this version may also have chosen to reduce the expressionistic elements after the failure of *The Emperor Jones* in 1927, when Bledsoe was booed off the stage. Absent the azure tinting, the black-and-white film is not only less experimental; it is also easier on the eye.

The version for Black audiences was test marketed in Harlem on October 19, 1933, about a month after the premiere of the official film. Two different versions were screened to fifty selected guests to get their reactions: the original version that "insulted the intelligence of Negroes" and another "with the word 'n——r' deleted," according to the *Pittsburgh Courier*. The revised version was, as the title of the article put it, "Well Received." The *Courier* noted that by viewing this print Black spectators could "maintain your race pride and self-respect, without being insulted or offended."[97] The news of the reedited version spread in the Black press. According to a headline in the *Afro-American*, "33 Insults [Were] Cut Out of Robeson's Film."[98]

After test marketing the recut film, the Black-house version was screened nationally for limited engagements, although it is uncertain how long it ran or in which cities. When *The Emperor Jones* was screened in Washington, D.C., in October 1933, the film had been altered and "all those insulting remarks about which critics cussed have been removed." The cinema's manager promised his patrons that they "need fear nothing offensive in 'Emperor Jones' when it appears here."[99] The film grossed $11,000 in the nation's capital.[100] A special October viewing with the recut film in Baltimore for members of the Black community was likewise met with approval.[101] The white manager of this Baltimore theater (and owner of a Black theater chain), A. R. Lichtman, moreover challenged the producers to make the Black house version the definitive print to circulate nationally, although this was never executed.[102] Tellingly, to make his case, he referenced a film called *The Callahans and the Murphys*, which "the reaction as far the Irish was concerned was so tremendous that it was taken out of release and the prints junked."[103] Thus, like previous Irish audiences, Black theatergoers protested offensive images in film, demanding that changes be made. And changes were made, racing the cut. Film historian Thomas Cripps has documented *The Emperor Jones*'s success throughout the U.S.: "In Baltimore, its first experimental Southern date, it made money and opened the way for mass booking in the South. In a western run it was the top grosser for its week."[104] In addition, *The Emperor Jones* played in Hollywood, California for four weeks for "colored patrons . . . were generous in their praise of it." It's unclear whether this was the Black-house version or not.[105]

With its many versions, *The Emperor Jones* was a film-in-motion: a movie that broke color lines, was censored, cut, recut, and restored. Its fluidity demonstrates the important interchanges between the repertoire and archive, while attending to racial performativity and film Blackness.

CIRCUM-CARIBBEAN SIMULATION

Just as O'Neill and director Dudley Murphy utilized Blackness to reconcile their own contested Irish American identities, so the plotline of *The Emperor Jones* drew upon the Caribbean world, specifically Haiti, creating what John Lowe has called the circum-Caribbean imaginary.[106] While *The Emperor Jones* was often critiqued by Black commentators of O'Neill's day (just as it is currently debated), it is important to examine the circum-Caribbean setting: an island in the West Indies preceding white colonial rule. Indeed, the West Indies can be characterized as a veritable playground of colonial misrule. Yet *The Emperor Jones*'s invocation of the Haitian Revolution resonates powerfully for Black power within circum-Atlantic spheres. As has often been recounted, O'Neill was inspired by revolutionary figures such as "Henri Christophe and Haiti's President Sam, who, like Jones, had a silver bullet." This citationality was not lost on the press: "There is a suggestion of Toussaint L'Ouverture and Jean [*sic*] Christophe in the air," a 1933 review observed, "as Mr. Robeson . . . plunges into the jungle."[107] The *New York Times* observed that Brutus Jones "is destined to emulate another Jean [*sic*] Christophe."[108] Murphy and O'Neill's citation of Caribbean revolutionaries was especially timely, given that the United States' unsuccessful occupation of Haiti was waning (the occupation lasted from 1915 to 1934): "'We played Christophe,' Heyward told O'Neill after writing the 1933 film script, 'as close as we dared.'"[109] This reference to past uprisings against imperial tyranny indexed a powerful archive of revolt and resistance. As Ruby Cohn has observed, such invocations of Haitian revolutionaries cited the legacy of power throughout the Black diaspora.[110] Just as the 1920 stage play referenced the 1915 assassination of Haiti's president, so the 1933 film version hinted at the impending failure of the American occupation.

While Haiti was the island the filmmakers had in mind, and initially nearly a third of the filming was scheduled to be shot on location there, *The Emperor Jones* was filmed entirely in the United States but on a different isle—Long Island—in an abandoned studio in Astoria.[111] One cartoon described the location bluntly as "In the Jungles of Astoria, L. I.," exposing a circum-Atlantic simulation.[112] The production lot was (mis)characterized as "a jungle, with palms and cacti imported from Haiti and Florida."[113] Remapping Long Island as a West Indian island was not perceived as a problem but rather as a cinematic virtue. The "jungle episodes are admirable," the *New York Sun* observed, effacing the long history of colonial violence throughout the circum-Atlantic world.[114]

Much like Jean Baudrillard's simulacrum, the simulated jungle stood in for "the real" while also being characterized as *better* than filming in the Caribbean—a place believed to be tainted with swamps and disease. John Mosher's 1933 piece in *The New Yorker* epitomizes this fallacious logic: "They have built a wonderful jungle. Swamp with heaters to warm water so Paul Robeson won't get rheumatism during rehearsals. Decided could built [*sic*] better jungle on lot than go to Haiti. 250 flies ordered to add reality. Etherized so wouldn't fly off set. Negroes secured from Harlem."[115] The glib tone of the piece not only catalogues what constitutes a simulated jungle (swamp, flies, "Negroes"), but also implies that the Caribbean is amok with decay and infection. Robert Garland described the setting as "a cactus-strewn, agave-infested jungle, a jungle that is at once a morass and a pitfall."[116] The contagion motif was extended even when journalists discussed a clearly simulated jungle. The jungle episodes are so "forbidding," wrote the *New York Sun*, that "when Mr. Heyward first walked through its mossy network last spring, he remarked he was going to get out of it quickly for fear that he might get malaria."[117] Another critic called the set a "savage island" where Jones's "frenzied screams in the black swamps of the jungle" could be heard.[118] Robert Garland's article in the *New York World-Telegram* described "diablerie and exorcism and voodoo rites are being practiced these steaming afternoons" on the Astoria set.[119] Such reviews revealed racialized panic, as well as a collapse between reality and performance ("exorcism and voodoo rites are being *practiced*," it says, not performed for the camera). Yet, the *New York Amsterdam News* challenged the "jungle fever" rhetoric by calling attention to "what they claim to be voodoo-infested Haiti."[120] Another article in the *New York Times* bizarrely characterized the setting as a nineteenth-century insurgent Native American uprising: "For the past six weeks the ominous throb of the tomtom has been heard on the plains of Astoria and the Queens trappers, fearing an uprising of the Arapahoes [*sic*] or a pillaging expedition of the crafty Sioux along the banks of the Interborough, have been feverishly engaged in reinforcing their stockades and burnishing their flintlocks."[121] Characterizations of the supporting cast as "contagious," "savage," or "pillaging" reveals racialized rhetoric that would extend to perceptions of the actors' work ethic.

The actors were hardly the "pillaging expedition" described by the *New York Times*, although they were a resistant workforce for their Irish American director. The Harlem extras were "trouble!" as one article put it, refusing to do menial tasks in the sweltering heat.[122] Examining the film's labor practices reveals another doubled significance: on the one hand, the supporting actors and extras were supposedly a "headache" for Murphy, who moaned in an interview, "Oh, if only I'd known!" Murphy called the project "the worst flock of grief ever handed to a director!," revealing that in spite of the film's antiracist aims, the director still espoused white supremacist views of the labor.[123] On the other hand, the actors challenged exploitative labor practices. Just as the actors resisted unfair work conditions, so Robeson commanded top billing and the second-highest salary of anyone on the artistic team, except for O'Neill, earning $18,000 (by contrast, Digges made just $5,000 and Murphy earned $7,500).[124] The work on the film afforded both opportunity and insult for actors of color, as the *Chicago Defender* reported:

> The Race audiences find the O'Neill play a little rough in spots upon the sensibilities. . . . However, as Frank Wilson, the actor, said on opening night [of the film], there should be a spirit of tolerance because herein was opened up a new field of activity for Race actors and actresses which will afford new opportunities to portray different types of Race members.[125]

Given that the film provided jobs for "race members," as the *Defender* put it, *The Emperor Jones* might best be understood as a race film, as Anna Siomopoulos claims,[126] not only because there are only three white actors in it (with second billing) but also because the camerawork fortifies Robeson's authority. And it was also created, filmed, and shaped by an Irish American team negotiating their own liminal, racialized identity within white U.S. culture.

At the end of *The Emperor Jones*, Brutus Jones's body lies lifeless on a stone slab. However, the film would live on, in various iterations. In 1999, *The Emperor Jones* was selected for the Library of Congress's National Film

Registry, and the Library of Congress restored it in 2002. Repeatedly edited, censored, and recut, *The Emperor Jones* was a film whose alterations revealed the entanglements with, and resistance to, regimes of power. An imperfect, if not flawed, film, *The Emperor Jones* nonetheless constitutes a celluloid archive of moments that raced, and doubly exposed, the legacy of colonial violence and racism. Its use of circum-Atlantic double exposures and race cuts disclose how Irish American film artists used Black performance culture to negotiate their own racialized positionality. Created by a team of Irish Americans at the crossroads of film Blackness and diasporic circum-Atlantic reverberations, *The Emperor Jones* reveals the complex terrain of performing (anti)imperialist representations.

Conclusion: What Remains?

What remains of O'Neill's legacy for twenty-first-century theater?

My search for those remains took me to Tao House in Danville, California: Eugene O'Neill's last home, which is nestled above the San Ramon Valley and in the Las Trampas hills with a breathtaking view of Mount Diablo. As a Travis Bogard writer-in-residence supported by the Eugene O'Neill Foundation, I was set up in the trunk room, a cottage-like space (formerly housing Carlotta Monterey O'Neill's Louis Vuitton trunks) that had been converted into a study for visiting scholars. Tao House is where O'Neill wrote his final masterpieces, where he crafted heart-wrenching dramas about his broken family: plays written in "tears and blood," as he put it in the dedication to *Long Day's Journey Into Night*. I went there to finish my book: to dig in the archives and be inspired by Tao House's beauty and O'Neill's creative imagination. There, the book began writing itself. It took a turn I did not anticipate. The archive kept pointing me to O'Neill's breakthroughs. Various archives had pointed me there for over a decade, but the salience of those findings didn't strike me until my residency at Tao House. Now, having finished this book, I step back to reflect upon what questions still remain for future projects.

Theater artists are driving the conversations about O'Neill's place and importance for contemporary theater. For two decades, Robert Falls, artistic director of the Goodman Theatre, has turned his artistic energies to O'Neill, remarking: "I think Eugene O'Neill is the American Shakespeare." Dubbing O'Neill "the father of American drama," Falls observed, "I think he almost single-handedly created it as a serious art form in the early part of the 20th century."[1] Falls should know: he not only produced a revival of *A Moon for the Misbegotten* (directed by Daniel Sullivan on Broadway in 2000 and starring Gabriel Byrne and Cherry Jones), but also directed a 2003 production of *Long Day's Journey Into Night* starring Brian Dennehy, Philip Seymour Hoffman, Vanessa Redgrave, and Robert Sean Leonard; it garnered three Tony Awards, including Best Revival of a Play. Attuned to O'Neill's international contributions, Falls curated a season at the Goodman Theatre called "A Global Exploration: Eugene O'Neill in the 21st Century" in 2009. The season showcased productions from New York's Wooster Group (*The Emperor Jones*), Brazil's Comanhia Triptal (*Three Sea Plays*), Chicago's The Hypocrites (*The Hairy Ape*), Amsterdam's Toneelgroep (*Rouw Siert Electra*), Chicago's Neo-Futurists (*Strange Interlude*), and the Goodman's own *Desire Under the Elms* (with Brian Dennehy, Carla Cugino, and Pablo Schreiber—with a Broadway transfer).[2] Falls's twin Tony Award-winning productions of *The Iceman Cometh* (with Brian Dennehy in the role of Hickey in 2009, and Nathan Lane in 2012) demonstrate the appeal of O'Neill in contemporary commercial theater.

In recent years, O'Neill's plays have not only returned to Broadway with critical success but also appeared on stages across the Atlantic, often with star-studded casts and impresario directors. O'Neill's dramas have attracted stage celebrities such as Ruby Dee, Colleen Dewhurst, Anne-Marie Duff, Katherine Hepburn, William Hurt, Jack Lemon, Al Pacino, Christopher Plummer, Jason Robards, and Kevin Spacey. His works have also captivated luminary directors such as Ivo Van Hove, Robert O'Hara, José Quintero, Lloyd Richards, and George C. Wolfe. Among the many revivals on Broadway, one of the most notable triumphs was *Long Day's Journey Into Night* with Jessica Lange and Gabriel Byrne, which garnered several Tony and Outer Critics Circle awards in 2016. Other recent high-profile London stagings of *Long Day's Journey Into Night* include productions with David Suchet and Laurie Metcalf in 2012, and Lesley Manville and Jeremy Irons in 2018. *Long Day's Journey* has been raced as well—adapted into a 1982 made-for-TV film featuring an all-Black cast that included Earle Hyman and Ruby Dee. And the 2022 production of *Long Day's Journey* (directed by Robert O'Hara) included a colorblind cast featuring Bill Camp, Elizabeth Marvel, Jason Bowen, and Ato Blankson-Wood. The Theater of War company has used *Long Day's Journey* in their Addiction Performance Project to raise awareness about opioid and alcohol addiction. In fact, it could be said that O'Neill is not only the father of American drama (to return to Falls's formation) but also an important figure for global theater, with productions of his works having recently appeared in Australia, Brazil, Canada, China, Europe, Japan, South Africa, and beyond. This renewed interest in staging contemporary interpretations of O'Neill throughout the world reveals not only that O'Neill works are still being received with great acclaim but also that these dramas ignite global conversations about racial tensions, gender inequities, immigrant precarity, and the challenges of addiction seen through a twenty-first-century lens.

O'Neill's drama about an iconoclastic hooker-with-a-heart-of gold,

"Anna Christie," has similarly seen a resurgence on both sides of the Atlantic, demonstrating that this play still sheds light on the plight of abused women who have turned to sex work out of desperation. Fresh, award-winning productions of "Anna Christie" have illuminated related contemporary issues, such as sexual assault, unequal wages for women, and sex trafficking. Liam Neeson and his wife, Natasha Richardson, breathed new life into a 1993 revival on Broadway, winning the Tony, Outer Critics Circle, and Drama Desk Awards for Best Revival of a Play. Jude Law and Ruth Wilson delivered remarkable performances in "Anna Christie" at London's Donmar Warehouse, which garnered the Olivier Award for Best Revival in 2011. "Anna Christie" returned to Paris in 2015 with an original, modern adaptation by Jean-Claude Carrière and featuring Mélanie Thierry. Contemporary revivals of "Anna Christie" demonstrate important insights not only about gender and sexuality but also intersectional concerns like race and class. An all-Black production directed by Scott Edmiston at the Lyric Stage Company in Boston addressed issues of racial inequities and the #MeToo movement in 2018.

O'Neill's The Hairy Ape has prompted timely conversations about labor and class exploitation, captured by the neon-jolting Richard Jones's production starring Bobby Cannavale that was staged first in London and then transferred to the cavernous New York Park Avenue Armory in 2017. The Wooster Group's controversial Hairy Ape production with Willem Dafoe and Kate Valk in 2006 sparked controversies still unresolved, while the 2012 Southwark Theatre Playhouse production (staged under a wet tunnel) brought a much-needed focus to the precarity of the lower depths. I have been fortunate to review several of these productions, which led me on a path to writing this book on O'Neill.

Color lines are still being broken with O'Neill's work, often "raced" by actors of color depicting "white" characters, such as Forest Whittaker playing the title role in Hughie (2016) and Denzel Washington portraying Hickey in The Iceman Cometh (2018). Although it may appear that the urgency of casting breakthroughs has diminished since Gilpin broke the color line a hundred years ago, Broadway is still shockingly white, as captured by the #Broadwaysowhite hashtag. There is still much work to do.

O'Neill's legacy of racing the Great White Way can also be found in recent revivals of shows that were resurrected from the archive of Black Broadway: Shuffle Along: or, the Making of the Musical Sensation of 1921 and All That Followed (directed by George C. Wolfe in 2016) and The Gershwins' Porgy and Bess (adapted by Suzan-Lori Parks and directed by Diane Paulus in 2011). While the original versions of both shows—Shuffle Along (1921) and *Porgy and Bess* (1935)—were seen as breakthrough productions in the history of Black performance culture, through a modern lens, they seem dated, if not problematic (much like O'Neill's *The Emperor Jones*). *Shuffle Along* was notable for featuring an all-Black cast and creators (Noble Sissle, Eubie Blake, Fleurnoy Miller, and Aubrey Lyle); it also portrayed a love story between two African American leads that wasn't ridiculed or burlesqued.[3] *Shuffle Along* delivered hits like "I'm Just Wild about Harry," and a cast that included Josephine Baker, Paul Robeson, Florence Mills, and Fredi Washington. Yet, as an artifact of its time, *Shuffle Along* negotiated the tension between satirizing stereotypes while also performing them (for example, some of the Black performers utilized blackface). In the hands of George C. Wolfe ninety years later, *Shuffle Along: or, the Making of the Musical Sensation of 1921 and All That Followed*—as the lengthy title implies—brought the dramaturgical backstory center stage. Wolfe's *Shuffle Along* performatively engaged with the archive by not only focusing on the show-stopping numbers (and there were plenty of them, with a star-studded cast and choreography by Savion Glover), but also on the challenges of making such musical entertainments—and all that followed—on the Great White Way.

Similarly, *The Gershwins' Porgy and Bess* is another show resurrected from the archive of Black entertainments that incorporated modern commentary. The title encapsulates its Jewish-authored genealogy as well as the power of the Gershwin estate to shape artistic production ninety years later. The original jazz-opera *Porgy and Bess*, set in Catfish Row in Charleston, South Carolina, featured a large cast of African American characters and substantial leading roles; it also gave birth to hits like "Summertime," recorded memorably by Billie Holliday in 1936. On the other hand, this controversial opera was authored by a white and Jewish creative team with mixed receptions. The story was originally penned by DuBose Heyward, a white, Southern novelist and playwright (who also wrote the screenplay to *The Emperor Jones* in 1933). Together with his wife, Dorothy, Heyward had written a novel about Black life, *Porgy* (1925), and adapted it to the stage in 1928; *Porgy and Bess* as an opera appeared in 1935. The 2011 adaptation by Suzan-Lori Parks and directed by Diana Paulus engaged critically with this history, while also paring down the length of the production, clarifying Porgy's disability, and changing the tragic ending. The Parks-Paulus adaptation sparked controversy, epitomized by Stephen Sondheim's letter to the editor of the *New York Times*, in which he charged the creative team with "willful ignorance," distorting the source material, and "condescension to the audience."[4] Yet the strength of both the new *Porgy and Bess* and

Wolfe's *Shuffle Along* is precisely due to how these Black theater artists interrogated the neglected archives of Black performance culture *through* performance. In both of these revived productions, theater artists of color wrestled with, and raced, the archive through performative dramaturgy and artistic interventions.

And what of the Emperor's remains? As the case studies in this book have shown, *The Emperor Jones* broke color lines and critiqued empire, even while deploying tropes of imperialism. The tensions and dichotomies presented in *The Emperor Jones* are still with us one hundred years later: we live in a postcolonial moment, but as the Black Lives Matter movements have shown, the persistent problem of racism and imperial destruction remains throughout the world. Perhaps this is why *The Emperor Jones* has seen several recent revivals and sparked scholarly and artistic debates that still linger. Under the artistic leadership of Ciarán O'Reilly, the Irish Repertory Theater has produced *The Emperor Jones* twice of late: in 2009 with John Douglas Thompson, and in 2017 with Obi Abili. Both productions were *New York Times* Critic's Picks. "Boundary-pushing in its day," wrote the *New York Times*, "the play still has plenty to say—about tyranny and greed and corruption, sure, but more potently about our culture's long history of race-based violence and degradation."[5] *Theater Mania* summed it up: "The racial and political anxieties that *The Emperor Jones* explores are ripe for renewed discussion in our time."[6]

What is it about O'Neill's body of work that continues to draw creative engagement? Why has O'Neill not gone the way of Paul Green or Edward Sheldon, two white playwrights who wrote on similar themes, but have passed into obscurity? Is it because of the contradictions and the dichotomies of O'Neill's plays—the ways that his texts do not provide satisfactory clear readings? Or is it due to his theatrical innovations? Or is it because O'Neill's works continue to speak to our current cultural moment? It may be any number of these reasons—or others—but one thing is clear: O'Neill's theater continues to inspire creative adaptations. The Neo-Futurists have crafted playful deconstructive versions of O'Neill: *Strange Interlude* (a production that provoked an elderly audience member to boo before storming out) and *The Complete and Condensed Stage Directions of Eugene O'Neill, vol. 2.* Some of O'Neill's dramaturgical innovations—like the interior monologues portrayed on stage for the first time in *Strange Interlude* and memorably mocked by Groucho Marx—could be said to have found contemporary application in the television series *Fleabag.* Adrienne Earle Pender's new play *"N"* charts Charles Gilpin's interventions in *The Emperor Jones* and provides the source material for a film adaptation, *The Black Emperor of Broadway* (directed by Arthur Egeli, 2020). Tony Kushner and Jeannine Tesori's opera, *A Blizzard on Marblehead Neck* (2011), charts a near-fatal night with a bitter fight between Gene and Carlotta during a New England snowstorm. Indeed, Kushner's investment in O'Neill is far from over: he is working on a documentary film about O'Neill (and appears in Ken Burns's O'Neill documentary). In an essay called "The Genius of O'Neill," Kushner lauds O'Neill's legacy for the American theater: "Much that an American playwright needs to know can be learned by studying Eugene Gladstone O'Neill."[7]

And what do we make of O'Neill's cameo appearance in Paula Vogel's Tony Award–winning *Indecent* (2017)? It's a surprising choice to pen O'Neill as a character in a play that performatively engages with *God of Vengeance*, a Yiddish play featuring Broadway's first lesbian kiss in 1923.[8] In a scene from *Indecent* that is appropriately set in the Hell Hole, one of O'Neill's favorite dive New York bars during his early drinking days, O'Neill delivers an abridged version of the testimony he would have given at the 1923 obscenity trial if they had let him speak: "The court dismissed all the defense witnesses," he tells Lemml, the stage manager for *God of Vengeance*. "We are all barred from testifying. You all are up the shite's creek without a paddle."[9] O'Neill's perspective, including his Irish American phrasing of "shite," functions as unofficial testimony to counter the official court transcript. Having recently won the Pulitzer Prize for *"Anna Christie"* at this moment of action in the play (a detail that Vogel lists in the stage directions), his perspective on what I have elsewhere called brothel dramas is finally put into the record, even as the court has barred it. Regardless of the fact that O'Neill belts back three shots during this short scene, he has remarkable clarity: "They're gonna claim they're closing [the show] because of *Homo sexualis*. That's bunk," says O'Neill. It's a smokescreen for the real reason—the hypocrisy of religions. O'Neill continues: "He's [Asch, the playwright of *God of Vengeance*] crafted a play that shrouds us in a deep, deep fog of human depravity: then like a lighthouse, those two girls. That's a beacon I will remember."[10] Even from the grave, O'Neill has weighed in on matters of obscenity, sexuality, and hypocrisy in modern theater.

Finally, we must examine the virtual performances of O'Neill works during the Covid pandemic.[11] Innovative programming and artistic vision can be found with multiple theaters and directors. Eric Fraisher Hayes of the Eugene O'Neill Foundation directed riveting productions of O'Neill's "Lost Plays" (*Abortion*, *The Web*), and also *Beyond the Horizon* and *Welded*. The Metropolitan Playhouse has offered excellent virtual series, which includes O'Neill's early play *Shell Shock*, directed by Hayes, and also *Where the Cross Is Made* and *The Rope*, directed by Alexander Roe. The Irish Repertory Theater is making its 2021 digital production of *A Touch of the Poet* available to stream with Irish Rep @Home.

The future of O'Neill's legacy still remains to be seen. One thing is for certain: his dramatic works provide platforms for experimentation; for responding to racial, gender, and class hierarchies; and for exploring the depths of human suffering and tragedy. It seems likely that world theater will continue racing toward Eugene O'Neill in future artistic explorations, and I for one will relish opportunities to see this work.

Notes

1. Cheryl Black and Jonathan Shandell, *Experiments in Democracy: Interracial and Cross-Cultural Exchange in American Theatre, 1912–1945* (Carbondale: Southern Illinois University Press, 2016).

2. W. E. B. Du Bois, *The Souls of Black Folk* (New York: New American Library, 1903), 10.

3. Du Bois, "The Negro and Our Stage," *Sunday World*, May 4, 1924. Du Bois's essay also appeared in the 1923–24 playbill for the Provincetown revival of *The Emperor Jones* featuring Paul Robeson. *Emperor Jones* Clipping File, Hatch-Billops Collection, New York City (now the Camille Billops and James V. Hatch Archive housed at Emory University). "The Negro and Our Stage" was also printed in the playbill for the 1924 production of *All God's Chillun Got Wings*. Program for *All God's Chillun Got Wings*, Provincetown Players Season 1923–24, no. 5, page 2. Program File: *All God's Chillun Got Wings*, Manuscripts and Archives, Schomburg Center for Research in Black Culture, New York Public Library.

4. Brandi Wilkins Catanese, *The Problem of the Color[blind]: Racial Transgression and the Politics of Black Performance* (Ann Arbor: University of Michigan Press, 2011), 6.

5. Brutus Jones was not the first Broadway role for Charles Gilpin, but it was his first Broadway leading role in a serious drama. Gilpin had appeared in John Drinkwater's Broadway production of *Abraham Lincoln* in 1919 in the role of William Curtis, a Black preacher. While this was an important role and Gilpin received good reviews, it was a not a leading character (he appears in one scene), and, as James Weldon Johnson observed, the dialect was demeaning. See James Weldon Johnson, *Black Manhattan* (New York: Alfred A. Knopf, 1930), 182–83.

6. Bernth Lindfors, "'Mislike Me Not for My Complexion . . . .': Ira Aldridge in Whiteface," *African American Review* 33, no. 2 (Summer 1999): 347–54. As Anita Gonzales notes, Aldridge was not only a respected Shakespearean actor but also wrote his own play, *The Black Doctor*, about "an educated mulatto hero with a tragic love for a white French heroine." Anita Gonzalez, "Aldridge in

Action: Building a Visual Digital Interface," *Theatre Journal* 68, no. 4 (2016): E-1–E-17; at E-4, doi:10.1353/tj.2016.0136

7. Gonzalez, "Aldridge in Action," E-4.

8. The 1822 rival productions of *Richard III* were portrayed by Carlyle Brown in his play *The African Company Presents Richard III* (New York: Dramatists Play Service, 1994).

9. The three one-acts constituting *Three Plays for a Negro Theater* were *Granny Maumee*, *The Rider of Dreams*, and *Simon the Cyrenian*, all written by white playwright Ridley Torrence; they were performed April 5–24, 1917. Drama critic Alexander Woollcott scorned "the preposterous production of the Torrence plays" with Black actors as "utterly inadequate for the dramatic needs of the roles" other than possessing a "naturing makeup box." Woollcott's critique of Torrence's three one-act plays was included in his review of *The Dreamy Kid*. Alexander Woollcott, "Second Thoughts on First Night," review of *The Dreamy Kid*, by Eugene O'Neill, directed by Ida Rauh, Provincetown Playhouse, *New York Times*, November 9, 1919, XX2.

10. Early African American–authored plays were *The Chip Woman's Fortune* by Willis Richardson (1923), *The Fool's Errand* by Eulalie Spence (1927), *Meek Mose* by Frank Wilson (1928), *Appearances* by Garland Anderson (1925), and *Harlem* by William Jourdan Rapp and Wallace Thurman (1926). All of these plays appeared after *The Emperor Jones*. See Errol Hill and James V. Hatch, *A History of African American Theatre* (Cambridge: Cambridge University Press, 2003), 234–42; David Krasner, *A Beautiful Pageant: African American Theatre, Drama, and Performance in the Harlem Renaissance, 1910–1927* (New York: Palgrave, 2002); John G. Monroe, "The Harlem Little Theatre Movement, 1920–1929," *Journal of American Culture* 6, no. 4 (1983): 63–70; Freda Scott, "Five African-American Playwrights on Broadway, 1923–1929" (PhD diss., City University of New York, 1990); and Jeanne-Marie A. Miller, "The First Serious Dramas on Broadway by African American Playwrights," in *Experimenters, Rebels, and Disparate Voices: The Theatre of the 1920s Celebrates Diversity*, ed. Arthur Gewirtz and James J. Kolb (Westport, CT: Praeger, 2003), 71–81.

11. Susan Curtis, *The First Black Actors on the Great White Way* (Columbia: University of Missouri Press, 1998), 41.

12. Eugene O'Neill, *Thirst, The Moon of the Caribbees*, and *The Dreamy Kid*, in *Eugene O'Neill: Complete Plays, 1913–1920*, ed. Travis Bogard (New York: Library of America, 1988); and *The Emperor Jones* and *All God's Chillun Got Wings* in *Eugene O'Neill: Complete Plays, 1920 -31*, ed. Travis Bogard (New York: Library of America, 1988). See also Gary Jay Williams, "*The Dreamy Kid*: O'Neill's Darker Brother," *Theatre Annual* 43 (1988): 3–14; and Shahed Ahmed, "Evolution of Black Characterization in American Theater: Eugene O'Neill's *The Dreamy Kid* and Entrée into 'Authentic Negro' Experience," *SUST Studies* 15, no. 1 (2012): 21–33.

13. Deborah Wood Holton, "Revealing Blindness, Revealing Vision: Interpreting O'Neill's Black Female Characters in *Moon of the Caribbees, The Dreamy*

Kid, and *All God's Chillun Got Wings,"* *Eugene O'Neill Review* 19, nos. 1–2 (1995): 29–44, at 29.

14. John Gilbert Monroe, "A Record of the Black Theatre in New York City, 1920–29" (PhD diss., University of Texas at Austin, 1980), 62 and 95.

15. Critics such as Kurt Eisen, Glenda Frank, Cedric J. Robinson, Jeffrey C. Stewart, Michelle Ann Stephens, and Shannon Steen have examined O'Neill's works for their primitivism and stereotypes.

16. Alain Locke, "The Negro and the American Theatre," *Theatre Arts Monthly* 10 (October 1926): 701–6, reprinted in *Theatre Essays on the Arts of the Theatre,* ed. Edith Isaacs (New York: Little, Brown, 1927), 290–303, at 292.

17. Montgomery Gregory, "The Drama of Negro Life," in *The New Negro,* ed. Alaine Locke (1925; reprint, New York: Atheneum, 1992), 153. The essay was excerpted and printed in the playbill for the 1925 revival of *The Emperor Jones.* Playbill, *The Emperor Jones,* directed by James Light with Paul Robeson, Provincetown Playhouse, Season 1924-25, no. 3.

18. James Weldon Johnson, *Black Manhattan* (1930; New York: Da Capo Press, 1991), 184.

19. W. E. B. Du Bois, "Negro Art," *The Crisis* 22, no. 2 (June 1921), 56; see also Booker T. Washington, "Why Not a Negro Drama for Negroes by Negroes," *Current Opinion* 72, no. 5 (May 1922): 639–40; William Stanley Brainwaithe, "The Negro in American Literature," and Gregory, "The Drama of Negro Life," 157; both in *The New Negro,* ed. Alain Locke (New York: Albert and Charles Boni, 1925).

20. Locke, *New Negro,* 35.

21. Rena Fraden, *Blueprints for a Black Federal Theatre* (Cambridge: Cambridge University Press, 1996), 11.

22. O'Neill: "Eugene O'Neill on the Negro Actor," *Messenger* 7.1 (January 1925): 17. Qtd. in Fraden, *Blueprints,* 11.

23. Du Bois, "Krigwa, 1926," *The Crisis* 31 (August 1926), 134.

24. Letter from W. E. B. Du Bois to Eugene O'Neill, September 16, 1924. O'Neill said it would be "an honor" to judge the Spingarn Medal and called his participation on the advisory board "a damn fine thing." Letter from Eugene O'Neill to W. E. B. Du Bois, September 24, 1924; see also Letter from W. E. B. Du Bois to Eugene O'Neill, August 17, 1925, Letter from [likely John La Farge] to Eugene O'Neill, May 25, 1931. The citation of this letter on the website incorrectly attributes the recipient as Du Bois. All letters can be found at the W. E. B. Du Bois Papers (MS 312). Special Collections and University Archives, University of Massachusetts Amherst Libraries.

25. Alain Locke, "Broadway and the Negro Drama," *Theatre Arts* 25, no. 10 (October 1941): 745–50, at 745.

26. Kevin Whelan, "The Green Atlantic: Radical Reciprocities between Ireland and America in the Long Eighteenth Century," in *A New Imperial History: Culture, Identity, and Modernity in Britain and the Empire, 1660–1840,* ed. Kathleen Wilson (Cambridge: Cambridge University Press, 2004), 216–38.

27. See David A. Roediger, *Working Toward Whiteness: How America's Immi-*

grants Became White: The Strange Journey from Ellis Island to the Suburbs (New York: Basic Books, 2005).

28. Robyn Wiegman, *American Anatomies: Theorizing Race and Gender* (Durham, NC: Duke University Press, 1995), 9.

29. Noel Ignatiev, *How the Irish Became White* (London: Routledge, 2012), 3.

30. Cedric J. Robinson, *Forgeries of Memory and Meaning: Blacks and the Regimes of Race in American Theater and Film before World War II* (Chapel Hill: University of North Carolina Press, 2007).

31. Diana Taylor, *The Archive and the Repertoire: Performing Cultural Memory in the Americas* (Durham, NC: Duke University Press, 2003), 31.

32. Catanese, *The Problem of the Color[blind]*, 21.

33. Daphne A. Brooks, *Bodies in Dissent: Spectacular Performances of Race and Freedom, 1850–1910* (Durham, NC: Duke University Press, 2006), 40.

34. Susan Manning, *Modern Dance, Negro Dance: Race in Motion* (Minneapolis: University of Minnesota Press), 2004.

35. Rebecca Schneider, *Performing Remains: Art and War in Times of Theatrical Reenactment* (London: Routledge, 2011), 15 and 22; italics in the original.

36. Dwight Conquergood, *Cultural Struggles: Performance, Ethnography, Praxis* (Ann Arbor: University of Michigan Press, 2013), 57.

37. For more about Black polytemporality within the framework of afro-fabulation, see the introduction to Tavia Nyong'o, *Afro-Fabulations: The Queer Drama of Black Life* (New York: New York University Press, 2019). Such performative interventions build upon what Michelle Wright calls "epiphenomenal time," where the "now" is constituted through "the past, present, and future" taken together. Michelle M. Wright, *Physics of Blackness: Beyond the Middle Passage Epistemology* (Minneapolis: University of Minnesota Press, 2015), 2.

38. My use of "racing spectatorship" extends Manthia Diawara's notion of resisting spectatorship and bell hooks's formulation of the oppositional gaze in film. See Diawara, "Black British Cinema: Spectatorship and Identity Formation in *Territories*," *Public Culture* 3, no. 1 (1990): 33–48. See also hooks, *Black Looks: Race and Representation* (Boston: South End Press, 1992): 115–31.

39. Dora Cole Norman, "From Hattie's Point of View," *Messenger* 7, no. 1 (January 1925): 32–33, at 32. From the Hatch-Billops Collection, New York City (now the Camille Billops and James V. Hatch Archive housed at Emory University).

40. E. Patrick Johnson, "Black Performance Studies: Genealogies, Politics, Futures," in *The Sage Handbook of Performance Studies* (Thousand Oaks, CA: SAGE, 2006), 446–63, at 449.

41. Curtis, *First Black Actors on the Great White Way*, 9.

42. See Stephanie Leigh Batiste, *Darkening Mirrors: Imperial Representation in Depression-Era African American Performance* (Durham, NC: Duke University Press, 2011); Warren Hoffman, *The Great White Way: Race and the Broadway Musical* (New Brunswick, NJ: Rutgers University Press, 2014); David Savran, *High-*

brow/Lowdown: Theater, Jazz, and the Making of the New Middle Class (Ann Arbor: University of Michigan Press, 2009); Shane Vogel, *The Scene of Harlem Cabaret: Race, Sexuality, Performance* (Chicago: University of Chicago Press, 2009); James F. Wilson, *Bulldaggers, Pansies, and Chocolate Babies: Performance, Race, and Sexuality in the Harlem Renaissance* (Ann Arbor: University of Michigan Press, 2010); and Harvey Young, *Embodying Blackness: Stillness, Critical Memory, and the Black Body* (Ann Arbor: University of Michigan Press, 2010).

43. Mary C. Henderson, *The City and the Theatre: New York Playhouses from Bowling Green to Times Square* (Clifton, NJ: James T. White, 1973), 88.

44. Brooks Atkinson, *Broadway* (New York: Macmillan, 1970), 177–78.

45. Henderson, *The City and the Theatre*, 174–75.

46. Siobhan B. Somerville, *Queering the Color Line: Race and the Invention of Homosexuality in American Culture* (Durham, NC: Duke University Press, 2000), 3.

47. See chapter 4 in David Román, *Performance in America: Contemporary U.S. Culture and the Performing Arts* (Durham, NC: Duke University Press, 2005), 174.

48. "From Broadway to the Bowery," *Theatre Magazine* 7 (April 1907): 121.

40. "From Broadway to the Bowery," 121.

50. Loften Mitchell noted "that more than a dozen major theater groups were formed [in Harlem] between 1910 and 1930." See Mitchell, "Harlem Has Broadway on Its Mind," *Theater Arts* 37 (June 1953): 68–69. See also Nellie McKay, "Black Theater and Drama in the 1920s: Years of Growing Pains," *Massachusetts Review* 28, no. 4 (Winter 1987): 615–26, at 617. An excellent history of the Lafayette Players can be found in Sister Mary Francesca Thompson's dissertation (she was the daughter of actress Evelyn Preer). See Thompson, "The Lafayette Players, 1915–1932" (PhD diss., University of Michigan, 1972). I am grateful to her insights over email in 2010. See also Monroe, "The Harlem Little Theatre Movement," 63–70; and Adrienne Macki Braconi, *Harlem's Theaters: A Staging Ground for Community, Class, and Contradiction, 1923–1939* (Evanston, IL: Northwestern University Press, 2015).

51. Lester Walton, title unknown, *New York Age*, January 17, 1920.

52. Eric Lott, *Love and Theft: Blackface Minstrelsy and the American Working Class* (Oxford: Oxford University Press, 2013), 4.

53. Chappy Gardner, "White Actors Steal Your Art, Take Your Place and Your Job," *Pittsburgh Courier*, July 18, 1931, A8.

54. Gardner, "White Actors Steal Your Art, Take Your Place and Your Job," A8.

55. Monroe, "Harlem Little Theatre Movement," 64.

56. Marvin McAllister, *Whiting Up: Whiteface Minstrels and State Europeans in African American Performance* (Chapel Hill: University of North Carolina Press, 2011), 1.

57. Faedra C. Carpenter, *Coloring Whiteness: Acts of Critique in Black Performance* (Ann Arbor: University of Michigan Press, 2014), 3.

58. Anita Bush, qtd. in Thompson, "The Lafayette Players, 1915–1932," 30.

59. *New York Age*, January 13, 1916, 6. Cited in Thompson, "The Lafayette Players, 1915–1932," 32.

60. New York theaters catering to white audiences presented some Afrocentric entertainments written by, and starring, race stars, such as *Black Boy* (1926, with Paul Robeson); *Africana* (1927, with Ethel Waters); *Harlem* (1929, an all-Black drama written by William Jourdan Rapp and Wallace Thurman featuring Hemsley Winfield); *Deep Harlem* (1929, written by the Tutt brothers), and the musical *Broadway to Harlem* (1932, also featuring Ethel Waters).

61. Louis A. Hirsch, Gene Buck, and Dave Stamper, "It's Getting Dark on Broadway," 1922, Sheet Music Collection. 38. http://digitalcommons.ithaca.edu /sheetmusic/38

62. Harvey Anderson, "Race Stage Stars Are Numerous on Broadway," *Pittsburgh Courier*, October 29, 1927.

63. Anderson, "Race Stage Stars Are Numerous on Broadway."

64. Shannon Steen, *Racial Geometries of The Black Atlantic, Asian Pacific and American Theatre* (New York: Palgrave Macmillan, 2010), 5; and Joseph Roach, *Cities of the Dead: Circum-Atlantic Performance* (New York: Columbia University Press, 1996).

65. Playbill, *The Emperor Jones* with Paul Robeson at the Provincetown Playhouse, NY. Season 1923–24. *Emperor Jones* Clipping File, Hatch-Billops Collection, New York City (now the Camille Billops and James V. Hatch Archive housed at Emory University).

66. Homi K. Bhabha, "Of Mimicry and Man: The Ambivalence of Colonial Discourse," in "Discipleship: A Special Issue on Psychoanalysis," *October* 28 (Spring 1984): 125–33.

67. Brent Hayes Edwards, *The Practice of Diaspora: Literature, Translation, and the Rise of Black Internationalism* (Cambridge, MA: Harvard University Press, 2003), 7.

CHAPTER 1

Portions of this chapter appeared in my essay "Racing O'Neill," in *The Theatre of Eugene O'Neill: American Modernism on Stage*, ed. Kurt Eisen (London: Bloomsbury, 2017) and appears with permission. It has been significantly revised and expanded here.

1. Eugene O'Neill, *Selected Letters of Eugene O'Neill*, ed. Travis Bogard and Jackson Bryer (New Haven: Yale University Press, 1988), 475.

2. Charles Gilpin, qtd. in Arthur Gelb and Barbara Gelb, *O'Neill*, rev. ed. (New York: Harper and Row, 1973), 450.

3. "He's the Emperor," *New York Amsterdam News*, July 19, 1933, 1.

4. Paul Robeson was the first Black actor in a studio-produced feature film

(*The Emperor Jones*), but this does not overlook the race film industry during this time, about which I say more later in the chapter.

5. Originally intended to be a Broadway play, *The Black King* by Trinidadian-American writer (and composer) Donald Heywood was released as a race film in 1932 by Southland Pictures Corporation. The film was based on Marcus Garvey's conviction for mail fraud (1925), deportation (1927), and fall from Black leadership. Also known as *Harlem Hotshot*, the film is intertextual with *The Emperor Jones* in a number of ways: the king iconography, the chanting, and the protagonist's fall from power. See Kate Dossett, "Staging the Garveyite Home: Black Masculinity, Failure, and Redemption in Theodore Ward's 'Big White Fog'," *African American Review* 43, no. 4 (2009): 557–76; and Judith Weisenfeld, *Hollywood Be Thy Name: African American Religion in American Film, 1929–1949* (Berkeley: University of California Press, 2007).

6. The initial title for *The Emperor Jones* was "The Silver Bullet."

7. W. E. B. Du Bois, qtd. in Christopher William Edgar Bigsby, *Confrontation and Commitment: A Study of Contemporary American Drama 1959–66* (Columbia: University of Missouri Press, 1968), 116.

8. Gregory, "Drama of Negro Life," 153–60. Gregory's essay was excerpted in the 1925–26 playbill for *The Emperor Jones*. Playbill, *The Emperor Jones*, directed by James Light with Charles Gilpin, Provincetown Playhouse, Season 1925–26, no. 4. Gregory played Brutus Jones in 1921 with the Howard Players from Howard University before a nonsegregated audience at the Shubert-Belasco Theatre in Washington, DC.

9. Robinson, *Forgeries of Memory and Meaning*.

10. Aaron Douglas's *Emperor Jones Series* was commissioned and published in several periodicals from 1925 to 1927 in a number of variations. Two of the four illustrations from the *Series* accompanied Alain Locke's 1926 article, "The Negro and The American Stage." See Jeffrey Garrison, "Aaron Douglas's *Emperor Jones Series*: The Illustrations," *Journal of Komazawa Junior College* 28 (March 2000): 253–94. See also Alain Locke, "The Negro and the American Stage," *Theatre Arts Monthly* 10, no. 2 (February 1926): 112–20.

11. As Felicia Hardison Londré observes, "Besides Gilpin, some of the outstanding black actors who have portrayed Jones in revivals of the play are Paul Robeson (1924, 1930, 1939, and in the 1933 film version), Habib Benglia (1923, 1950), Wayland Rudd (1930), Rex Ingram (1936), Arthur Rich (1945), Ossie Davis (1955), James Earl Jones (1964), Rodney Hudson (1977), John Amos (1982), and Cleavon Little (1984)." See Londré's *Words at Play: Creative Writing and Dramaturgy* (Carbondale: Southern Illinois University Press, 2005).

12. Charles Musser, "Troubled Relations: Paul Robeson, Eugene O'Neill, and Oscar Micheaux," in *Paul Robeson: Artist and Citizen*, ed. Jeffrey C. Stewart (New Brunswick, NJ: Rutgers University Press, 1998), 85.

13. Soyica Diggs Colbert, Douglas A. Jones Jr., and Shane Vogel, eds., *Race and Performance after Repetition* (Durham, NC: Duke University Press, 2020), 15.

14. I thank Alexander Pettit for this insight about the use of blackface for the original role of Lem. See James H. Cox and Alexander Pettit, "Black Indigeneity and Anti-Colonial Rebellion in Eugene O'Neill's *The Emperor Jones*," *Modern Drama* 64, no. 3 (Fall 2021): 259–82.

15. J. J. Hayes, "An Irish 'Emperor Jones,'" *New York Times*, February 13, 1927, X4. The Irish premiere of *Emperor Jones* opened at the Abbey Theatre in Dublin, Ireland, on January 24, 1927 and ran for seven performances. The cast included Irish actor Rutherford Mayne as Brutus Jones in blackface. It was revived again with the same cast in July 25, 1927 for seven performances. The *New York Times* reported that Mayne was not convincing in blackface, for the audience could see "the white man beneath the dark make-up" Hayes X4.

16. Al Jolson wanted to perform serious roles and had his sights on *The Emperor Jones*, but was repeatedly turned down—except for the radio. See Charles Musser, "Why Did Negroes Love Al Jolson and *The Jazz Singer*? Melodrama, Blackface and Cosmopolitan Theatrical Culture," *Film History: An International Journal* 23, no. 2 (June 2011): 196–222. O'Neill granted Jolson permission to perform *The Emperor Jones* on the air in 1934. O'Neill was both amused and worried about Jolson's radio performance, captured in this letter he wrote to his agent: "The Jolson broadcast is a bit of velvet all right. It will be amusing to hear what he does with it. I hope Brutus Jones won't burst into 'Mammy!'" See O'Neill, Letter to Richard Madden, March 8, 1934. Folder: Letters, Madden, Richard, 1933–37. Accession Number: MAR340308. Eugene O'Neill Foundation Library, Tao House, Danville, California.

17. Carpenter, *Coloring Whiteness*.

18. Playbill, *The Emperor Jones*. Salem, MA, February 7, 1938. Library of Congress, accessed May 20, 2020, https://www.loc.gov/item/musftpplaybills.20022 0584/. See also the poster at https://www.loc.gov/item/musftpplaybills.200220 585/. Another "all-Negro" Federal Theatre production of *The Emperor Jones* occurred October 21–23, 1938, in Hartford, CT.

19. Oscar Fernández, "Black Theatre in Brazil," *Educational Theatre Journal* 29, no. 1 (1977): 5–17.

20. Habib Benglia staged a one-month revival of *L'Empereur Jones* in Paris on July 2, 1950. "Paris Does 'Emperor Jones' with African Voodoo Troupe" (1950), an otherwise unidentified clipping, *The Emperor Jones* Clipping File, Billy Rose Theatre Division, New York Public Library for the Performing Arts.

21. Johan Callens, "'Black Is White, I Yells It out Louder 'n Dier Loudest': Unraveling the Wooster Group's *The Emperor Jones*," *Eugene O'Neill Review* 26 (2004): 43–69, at 52.

22. Lott, *Love and Theft*. See also Hill and Hatch, *History of African American Theatre*.

23. Cedric J. Robinson, "Ventriloquizing Blackness: Eugene O'Neill and Irish-American Racial Performance," in *The Black and Green Atlantic: Cross-Currents of the African and Irish Diaspora*, ed. Peter D. O'Neill and David Lloyd (New York: Palgrave, 2009), 49–63, at 54.

24. Charles S. Gilpin, qtd. in Arthur and Barbara Gelb, *O'Neill* (New York: Harper & Row, 1962), 450.

25. Aoife Monks, "'Genuine Negroes and Real Bloodhounds': Cross-Dressing, Eugene O'Neill, the Wooster Group, and *The Emperor Jones*," *Modern Drama* 48, no. 3 (Fall 2005): 540–64, at 545.

26. Robinson, "Ventriloquizing Blackness," 57. O'Neill appeared in the 1916 production of *Thirst* as the mulatto Sailor.

27. Louis Sheaffer, *O'Neill: Son and Artist* (Boston: Little, Brown, 1973), 118.

28. Ignatiev, *How the Irish Became White*.

29. Edward L. Shaughnessy, "O'Neill's African and Irish-Americans: Stereotypes or 'Faithful Realism'?," in *The Cambridge Companion to Eugene O'Neill*, ed. Michael Manheim (New York: Cambridge University Press, 1998), 148–63, at 149.

30. Sheaffer, *O'Neill: Son and Artist*, 49. In an interview with Oona O'Neill, Gene's daughter, about whether she identified as "shanty Irish" or "lace curtain Irish," she replied, "shanty Irish." Gene was not amused.

31. Gelb and Gelb, *O'Neill*, 136.

32. Sean O'Casey, qtd. in Croswell Bowen, *The Curse of the Misbegotten: A Tale of the House of O'Neill* (New York: McGraw-Hill, 1959), 314.

33. Arthur Gelb and Barbara Gelb, *By Women Possessed: A Life of Eugene O'Neill* (New York: Marian Wood Books, 2016), 669.

34. Shannon Steen, "Melancholy Bodies: Racial Subjectivity and Whiteness in O'Neill's *The Emperor Jones*," *Theatre Journal* 52, no. 3 (2000): 339–59, at 340. In this essay, Steen argues that *The Emperor Jones* "actively constitutes qualities of white subjectivity in the spectator" (340), but as this chapter seeks to demonstrate, the play also ignited Black spectatorship.

35. O'Neill, qtd. in Sheaffer, *O'Neill: Son and Artist*, 302.

36. Croswell Bowen, "The Black Irishman," *PM*, November 3, 1946, 13–17. Parts of that essay are revised and reprinted in Bowen's *The Curse of the Misbegotten* (New York: McGraw Hill, 1959) and in *O'Neill and His Plays: Four Decades of Criticism*, ed. Oscar Cargill et al. (New York: New York University Press, 1961), 64–84.

37. See Gelb and Gelb, *O'Neill*, 49, 51, 65, and 179.

38. George Bernard Shaw, qtd. in St. J[ohn] E[rvine], Review of *The Emperor Jones*, *Observer* (London), September 15, 1925. V&A Theatre Collection.

39. "Tantee" and "Fanti." *Merriam-Webster.com Dictionary*, Merriam-Webster, accessed May 26, 2020, https://www.merriam-webster.com/dictionary/fantee

40. Anne McClintock, *Imperial Leather: Race, Gender and Sexuality in the Colonial Context* (New York: Routledge, 1995), 53.

41. Roach, *Cities of the Dead*, 2–7, 38, and 68.

42. Taylor, *The Archive and the Repertoire*, 46.

43. Gwendolyn Bennett, "The Emperors Jones," *Opportunity* 8 (September 1930): 270.

44. My use of the term *Emperor's remains* is indebted to Rebecca Schneider's work on performative traces in embodied practice; see her *Performing Remains*.

45. Gilpin was not the first actor approached to play Brutus Jones. Opal Cooper was originally considered, but was overseas and unable to take the part. Paul Robeson was next asked, but he turned down the role, only to perform it four years later. For more, see Michael A. Morrison, "Emperors Before Gilpin: Opal Cooper and Paul Robeson," *Eugene O'Neill Review* 33, no. 2 (2012): 159–73. See also John G. Monroe, "Charles Gilpin and the Drama League Controversy," *Black American Literature Forum* 16, no. 4 (School of Education, Indiana State University, 1982): 139–141, at 141.

46. Charles S. Gilpin, qtd. in Gelb and Gelb, *O'Neill*, 450.

47. David Krasner, "Whose Role Is It Anyway? Charles Gilpin and the Harlem Renaissance," *African American Review* 29, no. 3 (1995): 483–96, at 484.

48. Sheaffer, *O'Neill: Son and Artist*, 35.

49. Ronald H. Wainscott, *Staging O'Neill: The Experimental Years, 1920–1934* (New Haven: Yale University Press, 1988), 57. See also Krasner, "Whose Role Is It Anyway?," 493.

50. The *Pittsburgh Courier* reported: "A letter with a Ku Klux Klan signature was received by Gilpin while in Virginia. It threatened: 'not to attempt to continue in the South with his company, which contains white players.' It was then that the route was changed and the troupe is now in Ohio." *Pittsburgh Courier*, January 29, 1922, section 6, page 4.

51. "Entertains Prisoners," *Pittsburgh Courier*, June 30, 1923, 4.

52. Paul Packard, "'Emperor Jones' Gilpin's Last Stand," *New York Amsterdam News*, July 25, 1928, 7.

53. "Black and White," March 30, 1922. Otherwise unidentified clipping from the Charles Gilpin Clipping File, Hatch-Billops Collection, New York City (now the Camille Billops and James V. Hatch Archive housed at Emory University).

54. Gilpin directed *The Emperor Jones* at the Mayfair Theatre, which ran November 10, 1926 through January 15, 1927, for a total of about 150 performances, by my calculations. See Moss Hart, *Act One* (New York: St. Martin's Press, 1959), 98–99. See also Monroe, "Charles Gilpin and the Drama League Controversy," 107, and Krasner, "Whose Role Is It Anyway?," 484.

55. "Color Line in Art," *Chicago Defender*, April 24, 1926, A8.

56. "Gilpin's Return in Old Role Hailed by Metropolitan Critics," *New York Amsterdam News*, February 24, 1926, 5.

57. Packard, "'Emperor Jones' Gilpin's Last Stand," 7.

58. "Negro as Dramatic Artist Finds Opportunity at Last," *New York World*, May 13, 1923. Alexander Gumby Collection of Negroiana, 1800–1981; Box 82, Little Theatres, Part 2. Rare Book and Manuscript Library, Columbia University Library.

59. Mary B. Mulett, "Where Do I Go From Here?," *American Magazine*, June 1921, 54–56. Alexander Gumby Collection of Negroiana, 1800–1981; Box 120,

Negro In Drama 1, Rare Book and Manuscript Library, Columbia University Library.

60. *The Crisis* reported in 1921: "Charles S. Gilpin, the Negro star in Eugene O'Neill's *The Emperor Jones,* has been received in private audience by President Harding," *Crisis,* November 1921. Otherwise unidentified clipping from the Alexander Gumby Collection of Negroiana, 1800–1981; Box 120, Negro In Drama 1, Rare Book and Manuscript Library, Columbia University Library.

61. "Gilpin Dines," *Chicago Defender,* March 12, 1921, 5.

62. O'Neill, qtd. in Schaeffer, *O'Neill: Son and Artist,* 157.

63. "Seeking Play for Gilpin," *New York Amsterdam News,* November 24, 1926, 13.

64. "Seeking Play for Gilpin," 13.

65. Four years after directing *The Emperor Jones* on Broadway, Gilpin died at an early age, having retired from the stage.

66. Glenda E. Gill, "Eugene O'Neill and Paul Robeson: An Uneasy Collaboration in Three of O'Neill's Early Plays," *Laconics* 1 (2006).

67. Tony Perucci, *Paul Robeson and the Cold War Performance Complex: Race, Madness, Activism* (Ann Arbor: University of Michigan Press 2012), 8.

68. The comparison of Robeson to Gilpin happened mostly after the fact. Given that Robeson's 1924 performance of *The Emperor Jones* was staged by the Provincetown Players, it wasn't covered that extensively in the press. By comparison, the clippings for Gilpin are extensive.

69. John Corbin, "'Emperor Jones' Revived," *New York Times,* May 7, 1924, 18.

70. Marvin A. Carlson, *The Haunted Stage: The Theatre as Memory Machine* (Ann Arbor: University of Michigan Press, 2003). In addition to attending Robeson's *Emperor Jones* performances, Gilpin also was in the audience for Robeson's *All God's Chillun Got Wings,* and his presence suggested his legacy, as seen in this headline, "Gilpin Play Read," *Chicago Defender,* March 8, 1924, 7.

71. *"The Emperor Jones* Reappears at Provincetown with a New Emperor," *New York Post,* May 7, 1924.

72. Eslanda Robeson's diary, qtd. in Paul Robeson Jr., *The Undiscovered Paul Robeson: An Artist's Journey, 1898–1939* (New York: John Wiley & Sons, 2001), 116.

73. *"The Emperor Jones* Reappears at Provincetown with a New Emperor."

74. P. V., "At the Provincetown," *New York Morning World,* May 7, 1924. *The Emperor Jones* Clipping File, Billy Rose Theatre Division, New York Public Library for the Performing Arts.

75. Young, *Embodying Blackness,* 7.

76. P. V., "At the Provincetown."

77. P. V., "At the Provincetown." Harry Willis, known as the "Black Panther," was a talented boxer who, like Jack Johnson, was at the top of his sport, but he was never allowed to box with white athletes or to challenge Jack Dempsey with a title match.

78. "A New Emperor," *New York World,* May 8, 1924.

79. P. P., "Eugene O'Neill's Plays," *Evening Standard* (London), September 11, 1925. Clippings file of the James Weldon Johnson Memorial Papers, Series II: Personal/Corporate Names, Box 149, Paul Robeson File, 1922–25, in the Yale Collection of American Literature, Beinecke Rare Book and Manuscript Library. The *Pittsburgh Courier* reprinted the London review as "Robeson Wins Praise of Critics in London," *Pittsburgh Courier*, October 10, 1925.

80. Review of *The Emperor Jones* by Eugene O'Neill, Ambassadors Theatre, London, 1925. V&A Collections, Department of Theatre and Performance.

81. This review appeared in the London *Daily Graphic* on September 11, 1925. The *Chicago Defender* reprinted it as "Reviews: Paul Robeson," *Chicago Defender*, October 31, 1925, 7.

82. "Giant Negro Actor," *Daily Mail* (London), September 11, 1925. See also "Giant Negro-Actor on His Ambition to Sing," *Evening News* (London), September 11, 1925. British feminist playwright Cicely Hamilton also referred to Robeson as a "giant" in her article. Cicely Hamilton, "The Theatre: Foreign Importations," *Time and Tide*, September 25, 1925. Clippings File of the James Weldon Johnson Memorial Papers, Series II: Personal/Corporate Names, Box 149, Paul Robeson File, 1922–25 in the Yale Collection of American Literature, Beinecke Rare Book and Manuscript Library.

83. "6 ft. 4 in. Negro Actor's Triumph," *Star* (London), September, 1925. Clippings File of the James Weldon Johnson Memorial Papers, Series II: Personal/Corporate Names, Box 149, Paul Robeson File, 1922–25, in the Yale Collection of American Literature, Beinecke Rare Book and Manuscript Library.

84. Brown qtd. in Deborah Willis, "The Image and Paul Robeson," in *Paul Robeson: Artist and Citizen*, ed. Jeffrey C. Stewart (New Brunswick, NJ: Rutgers University Press, 1998), 61. See also Lloyd L. Brown, *The Young Paul Robeson: "On My Journey Now"* (New York: Westview Press, 1997), 3.

85. Jeffrey C. Stewart, "The Black Body: Paul Robeson as a Work of Art and Politics," in *Paul Robeson: Artist and Citizen* (New Brunswick, NJ: Rutgers University Press, 1988), 134–63, at 139.

86. Stewart, "Black Body," 140.

87. Callens, "'Black Is White, I Yells It out Louder 'n Dier Loudest'," 52.

88. Stewart, "Black Body," 142.

89. Hazel Carby, *Race Men* (Cambridge, MA: Harvard University Press, 2009), 48–49.

90. Michelle Ann Stephens, *Black Empire: The Masculine Global Imaginary of Caribbean Intellectuals in the United States, 1914–1962* (Durham, NC: Duke University Press, 2005), 79.

91. See chapter 2, "Still Standing: Daguerreotypes, Photography, and the Black Body," in Young, *Embodying Blackness*, 26–75.

92. Paul Robeson, "Reflections on O'Neill's Plays," *Opportunity* 2, no. 25 (December 1924): 368.

93. Eugene O'Neill, Letter to Harry Weinberger, June 4, 1933. Folder: Letters, Weinberger, Harry, 1932–37. Accession Number: WEH330604. Eugene O'Neill Foundation Archive, Tao House, Danville, California.

94. In April 1925, Robeson performed a "Program of Negro Music" with Lawrence Brown on the piano at the Greenwich Theatre. Part of the program included "Water Boy," which would appear in the 1933 version of *The Emperor Jones*. The playbill is in the Clippings File of the James Weldon Johnson Memorial Papers, Series II: Personal/Corporate Names, Box 149, Paul Robeson File, 1922–25, in the Yale Collection of American Literature, Beinecke Rare Book and Manuscript Library.

95. "Rialto Gossip," *New York Times*, January 4, 1925, X1.

96. "London Likes O'Neill Play: 'The Emperor Jones' and Paul Robeson Win Applause," *New York Times*, September 11, 1925, 20. *The Emperor Jones* at the Ambassadors Theatre was paired with O'Neill's *The Long Voyage Home* as a curtain raiser. In Britain during the 1920s, "the growing interest in avant-garde American drama, especially the plays of Eugene O'Neill which featured black characters, began to stimulate the employment of black actors." See Claire Cochrane, *Twentieth-Century British Theatre: Industry, Art and Empire* (Cambridge: Cambridge University Press, 2011), 107.

97. Caption from an unidentified clipping. Clippings of *The Emperor Jones*, by Eugene O'Neill, The Ambassadors Theatre, London; 1925. V&A Theatre Collections.

98. Caption from an unidentified clipping. Clippings of *The Emperor Jones*, by Eugene O'Neill, The Ambassadors Theatre, London; 1925. V&A Theatre Collections.

99. Caption from an unidentified clipping. Clippings of *The Emperor Jones*, by Eugene O'Neill, The Ambassadors Theatre, London; 1925. V&A Theatre Collections.

100. St. J[ohn] E[rvine], Review of *The Emperor Jones*, by Eugene O'Neill, The Ambassadors Theatre, London, *Observer* (London), September 15, 1925. V&A Theatre Collection.

101. Caption from a photo in an unidentified clipping by The White Studio and Stage Photo Company. Clippings of *The Emperor Jones*, by Eugene O'Neill, The Ambassadors Theatre, London; 1925. V&A Theatre Collections.

102. Stephens, *Black Empire*, 77.

103. Unidentified clipping of *The Emperor Jones*, by Eugene O'Neill, The Ambassadors Theatre, London; 1925. V&A Theatre Collections.

104. Calling this 1930 adaptation an "experiment" orchestrated by Robeson, the *New York Times* wrote: "It begins and ends with two groups of Negro songs and its centre is the first act of 'The Emperor Jones,' which we are invited to consider, apart from what follows it in the text, as a self-contained play." Charles Morgan, "Mr. Robeson Tries an Experiment," *New York Times*, September 14, 1930, 108.

105. C. Hooper Trask, "Berlin's Year at the Spring," *New York Times*, May 25, 1930, 1 and 2. See also Trask, "Berlin Calls It a Season," *New York Times*, June 15, 1930, X6. According to an online archive, the 1930 production at the Deutsches Künstlertheater was played in English with Robeson in the title role and director James Light as Smithers. The website referred to O'Neill as an "irischen Dramatiker" (Irish playwright; translation mine) and reported inaccurately that it took place on March 31, instead of May 31. See "An einem 31. März," accessed October 23, 2020, https://www.dhm.de/archiv/gaeste/luise/tagesfakten/tf03/0331.htm

106. Paul Robeson Jr., *Undiscovered Paul Robeson*, 326. The 1939 *Emperor Jones* revival was at the Ridgeway Theatre in White Plains, New York.

107. Eugene O'Neill, Telegram to Richard Madden, July 21, 1940. Folder: Letters, Madden, Richard, 1937–42. Accession Number: MAR400731. Eugene O'Neill Foundation, Tao House, Danville, California.

108. "Stay Is Extended of 'Tobacco Road,'" *New York Times*, August 8, 1940, 23. See also Eugene O'Neill, typed letter to Richard Madden, March 23, 1940. Folder: Letters, Madden, Richard, 1937–42. Accession Number: MAR400323. Eugene O'Neill Foundation, Tao House, Danville, California.

109. Review of *The Emperor Jones* by Eugene O'Neill, *New York Herald Tribune*, August 4, 1940.

110. Olin Downes, "Robeson Soloist with Orchestra: 'Emperor Jones' Excerpts Are Feature of the Philadelphia Organization's Program," *New York Times*, December 18, 1940, 32. See also Paul Robeson, *Paul Robeson Speaks: Writings, Speeches, and Interviews, a Centennial Celebration* (New York: Citadel Press, 1978), 32. There was talk of reviving the operatic version of *The Emperor Jones* in 1960 with Robeson in the title role, but it never came to fruition. "Emperor," *New York Times*, August 28, 1960, X9.

111. "News of the Stage," *New York Times*, May 29, 1941, 14. See also "To Open in Old Role," *New York Times*, July 26, 1941, 18; "Ted Hammerstein Gets Saratoga Post: Will Operate the Spa Theatre, Which Plans 8-Week Season," *New York Times*, June 17, 1941, 24; and "This Week's Summer Bills," *New York Times*, July 13, 1941, X2.

112. Laurent Dubois, foreword to *Toussaint Louverture: The Story of the Only Successful Slave Revolt in History*, by C. L. R. James (Durham, NC: Duke University Press, 2013), viii.

113. Christian Høgsbjerg, introduction to *Toussaint Louverture: The Story of the Only Successful Slave Revolt in History*, by C. L. R. James (Durham, NC: Duke University Press, 2013), 2. Høgsbjerg is citing Colin Chambers, *Black and Asian Theatre in Britain: A History* (London: Routledge, 2011), 98.

114. Carlson, The *Haunted Stage*, 142.

115. Roach, *Cities of the Dead*, 25.

116. Shana L. Redmond, *Everything Man: The Form and Function of Paul Robeson* (Ann Arbor: University of Michigan Press, 2019), 3.

117. A[lan] D[ent], "Mr. Paul Robeson as Toussaint: A Documentary Play,"

Manchester Guardian, March 17, 1936. The publicity photo was printed in *The Sketch*, March 25, 1936, 63.

118. O'Neill's drama commences "on an island in the West Indies as yet not self-determined by White Marines," whereas James's *Toussaint Louverture* takes place in Cap François, "the largest town in the West Indian island of San Domingo." Eugene O'Neill, *The Emperor Jones*, in *Eugene O'Neill: Complete Plays, 1913–1920*, edited by Travis Bogard (New York: Library of America, 1988), 1030. See also act 1, scene 1 of C. L. R. James, *Toussaint Louverture: The Story of the Only Successful Slave Revolt in History* (Durham, NC: Duke University Press, 2013).

119. In *The Emperor Jones*, action from all but one scene takes place in the "Great Forest," where Jones is being pursued by the Indigenous people over whom he once ruled. Similarly, the second scene of *Toussaint Louverture* takes place in "the depths of the forest," where the "Negro slaves" gather to plot their revolution. James, *Toussaint Louverture*, 54.

120. O'Neill's stage directions read: "From the distant hills comes the faint, steady thump of a tom-tom, low and vibrating. It starts at a rate exactly corresponding to normal pulse beat—72 to the minute—and continues at a gradually accelerating rate from this point uninterruptedly to the very end of the play. Jones starts at the sound. A strange look of apprehension creeps into his face for a moment as he listens." O'Neill, *The Emperor Jones*, 1041.

121. *Toussaint Louverture* opens with "a faint but insistent beating of drums. In moments of tenseness the drums beat louder and with accelerated rhythm," providing a sonic backdrop for the enslaved people who have gathered to plot their revolution. James, *Toussaint Louverture*, 49.

122. Høgsbjerg, *Toussaint Louverture*, 25.

123. "Paul Robeson in Negro Play—a Dignified Study: Toussaint Louverture, by C. L. R. James," *Morning Post* (London), March 17, 1936. Qtd. in Høgsbjerg, *Toussaint Louverture*, 169–70. Høgsbjerg also observed that "Toussaint [was] singing a spiritual hymn in captivity," 10.

124. "Stage Society: 'Toussaint Louverture' by C. L. R. James," *Times* (London), March 17, 1936.

125. Steven Williams, "Robeson as Negro Leader," *Evening Standard* (London), March 17, 1936.

126. E. A. Baughan, "Robeson in Play by Negro—Author Takes Part," *News Chronicle* (London), March 17, 1936.

127. P. L. M. [Annock], "Paul Robeson as Slave Leader," *Daily Herald* (London), March 17, 1936.

128. Paul Robeson, "The Black Emperor," conducted by Eric Ansell, recorded May 21, 1936. EMI Classics, track number 5–8 on *Paul Robeson: The Complete EMI Sessions, (1928–1939)*, 2008, CD box set. Robeson had been in discussion with the great Russian director Sergei Eisenstein to film *The Black Majesty* (later renamed *The Black Consul*), which never came to fruition.

129. "Robeson to Form London Repertory: Plans to Organize Permanent

Company as Soon as His Engagements Permit," *New York Times*, October 28, 1932, 22.

130. "London Applauds Robeson in 'Toussaint Louverture,'" *Negro Star* (Wichita, Kansas), March 27, 1936, 3. Robeson "managed to sandwich this play in toward the end of a long, successful concert tour of the British Isles begun immediately following his return from Hollywood after making the film 'Show Boat.' . . . Thereafter may come his own Negro theatre here." See "Robeson a Success in Drama by Negro," *New York Times*, March 16, 1936, 21.

131. Paul Robeson, "I Want Negro Culture," *News Chronicle* (London), May 30, 1935. Cited in Høgsbjerg, *Toussaint Louverture*, 213–14.

132. Robeson, "I Want Negro Culture."

133. Whitman Alden, "Paul Robeson Dead at 77," *New York Times*, January 24, 1976, 1.

134. "Robeson 'Recaptures' Chicago," *Chicago Defender*, July 1940. Qtd. in Robeson Jr., *Undiscovered Paul Robeson*, 18.

135. Eugene O'Neill, Typewritten letter to Martin Birnbaum on March 26, 1942. Folder: Letters, Martin Birnbaum. Accession Number: BIM420326. Eugene O'Neill Foundation Archive, Tao House, Danville, California.

136. Eugene O'Neill, Typewritten letter to Martin Birnbaum on March 26, 1942. Folder: Letters, Martin Birnbaum. Accession Number: BIM420326. Eugene O'Neill Foundation Archive, Tao House, Danville, California.

CHAPTER 2

An earlier version of this chapter appeared in *Theatre Journal* 69, no. 1 (2017): 21–41, which won the Association for Theatre in Higher Education's 2018 Outstanding Article Award. It appears by permission, and has been revised and expanded here.

1. The 1923 Paris production of *The Emperor Jones* was translated by Maurice Bourgeois as *L'Empereur Jones* and was staged by Firmin Gemiér at Théâtre de l'Odéon; it premiered on October 31, 1923 and ran through January 1924.

2. Homi K. Bhabha, *The Location of Culture* (London: Routledge, 1994).

3. My use of the term "racial amnesia" builds upon Susan Curtis's notion of *cultural amnesia*, the pattern of forgetting Black actors on Broadway, and extends it to transnational performance. See Curtis, *First Black Actors on the Great White Way*, 18.

4. Stephanie Leigh Batiste, *Darkening Mirrors: Imperial Representation in Depression-Era African American Performance* (Durham, NC: Duke University Press, 2011).

5. Paul Gilroy, *The Black Atlantic: Modernity and Double Consciousness* (Cambridge, MA: Harvard University Press, 1993), 15.

6. "Will Play 'Emperor Jones' in Paris," *New York Amsterdam News*, May 16, 1923, 4; see also "Horizon," *The Crisis* 26, no. 3 (1923): 130.

7. According to a listing in *L'Œuvre* on October 28, 1923 (which was a Sunday), the *L'Empereur Jones* was slated to premiere at the Théâtre de l'Odéon on Wednesday, so that would have been October 31, 1923. See "L'Avante Scène," *L'Œuvre* (Paris), October 28, 1923, 7. The weekly arts magazine *La Rampe* lists performances of *L'Empereur Jones* on November 16, 20, 24, and 27, and December 1, 1923 (it is possible other performances occurred as well). See Jean Mangéat, "Les Spectacles de la Semaine dans les Théâtres subventionnés," *La Rampe* (Paris), November 15, 1923, 10; December 2, 1923, 14; December 9, 1923, 12. Clippings can be found at the Bibliothèque nationale de France (abbreviated as BnF [National Library of France]), Paris in the Arts du spectacle division. This production was also revived in January 1925 for an evening of international artistic exchange under the auspices of the Association Française d'Expansion et d'Échanges Artistiques sponsored by the Ministries of Foreign Affairs, Education and Fine Arts. See *La Renaissance*, January 1, 1925.

8. M[arshall] A. B[est], "O'Neill in Paris," *New York Times*, November 18, 1923, X2.

9. B[est], "O'Neill in Paris," X2.

10. Brent Hayes Edwards, *The Practice of Diaspora: Literature, Translation, and the Rise of Black Internationalism* (Cambridge, MA: Harvard University Press, 2003), 14. Taking up questions of Black internationalism alongside transnationalism, mobility, and translation in *The Practice of Diaspora*, Edwards observes the importance of "the ways that discourses of internationalism *travel*, the ways they are translated, disseminated, reformulated, and debated in transnational contexts marked by difference," (7; emphasis in original).

11. Benglia's publicity photograph as Brutus Jones can be found in the Randolph Linsly Simpson African-American Collection, Visual Material (Early 20th-Century Photographs), Box 17, Folder 1022. Photo by Underwood & Underwood. Beinecke Rare Book and Manuscript Library, Yale University, New Haven, Connecticut.

12. The word *unheimlich* contains two opposing meanings within it: *heim/heimlich* (home or homey) and *unheimlich* (strange), or what Hélène Cixous calls the "disquieting strangeness," a dichotomy that was crucial for Sigmund Freud. Freud uses the noun construction, *das Unheimliche*, to connote the uncanny, a term he borrows from Ernst Jentsch to craft his own theory. Freud writes, "Das deutsche Wort 'unheimlich' ist offenbar der Gegensatz zu heimisch, vertraut, und der Schluß liegt nahe, es sei etwas eben darum schreckhaft, weil es nicht bekannt und vertraut ist" (The German word "unheimlich" is seemingly the opposite to "heimisch," familiar, and the key lies in the fact that there is something frightening about it, because it is not known or familiar. Translation mine). See Sigmund Freud, *Das Unheimliche* (Freiburg im Breisgau: Outlook Verlag, 2020). First published in 1919 by Imago Verlag (Vienna). See also Hélène Cixous, "Fiction and Its Phantoms: A Reading of Freud's *Das Unheimliche* (The 'Uncanny')," *New Literary History* 7, no. 3 (1976): 525–645.

13. Qtd. in "Belated Recognition," *Chicago Defender*, November 24, 1923, A12.

14. Roland Barthes, *Camera Lucida* (New York: Hill and Wang, 1982), 26.

15. Paige A. McGinley, *Staging the Blues: From Tent Shows to Tourism* (Durham, NC: Duke University Press, 2014), 77.

16. Richard Schechner, *Between Theatre and Anthropology* (Chicago: University of Chicago Press, 1985), 36.

17. Bhabha, *Location of Culture*, 126.

18. Bhabha, *Location of Culture*, 126.

19. Young, *Embodying Blackness: Stillness, Critical Memory, and the Black Body* (Ann Arbor: University of Michigan Press, 2010), 46–49.

20. Schneider, *Performing Remains: Art and War in Times of Theatrical Reenactment* (London: Routledge, 2011), 94.

21. "New Emperor Jones: A Bengali 'Discovery' Expected to Be a Sensation in Paris," *New York Times*, May 11, 1923, 20. Bengal is now Bangladesh; it is nowhere near Algeria, as the author claims.

22. "Will Play 'Emperor Jones' in Paris."

23. "'Emperor Jones' in France," 1; and "The Theatre in France," *Forum* 72 (1924): 798.

24. Salini writes, "Beng (c'est ainsi que l'appellent ses amis)/ Beng ('as he's called by his friends')." Formose Salini, "Le grand acteur noir: Habib Benglia," *La Rampe* (Paris), December 1, 1931, 43–44, at 44. Most of the translations throughout this chapter are mine with help from Michel Pactat, unless otherwise noted.

25. "New Emperor Jones."

26. "Will Play 'Emperor Jones' in Paris." The director who "discovered" Benglia is incorrectly listed as "Clara" Laparcerie in this article. Her correct first name is Cora. The Théâtre de la Renaissance, where Benglia got his start in French theater, was home to many famous artists, including Sarah Bernhardt and Eleanora Duse.

27. Taylor, *The Archive and the Repertoire*, 54.

28. Christophe Konkobo, "Dark Continent, Dark Stage: Body Performance in Colonial Theatre and Cinema," *Journal of Black Studies* 40, no. 6 (2010): 1094–1106, at 1097.

29. Kurt Eisen, "Theatrical Ethnography and Modernist Primitivism in Eugene O'Neill and Zora Neale Hurston," *South Central Review* 25, no. 1 (2008): 56–73.

30. Bennetta Jules-Rosette, *Black Paris: The African Writers' Landscape* (Urbana: University of Illinois Press, 1998), 26.

31. "Negro Theatrical Invasion of Europe," *New York Age*, May 19, 1923, 4.

32. "Algerian Star Thrills Paris in Gilpin Role," *Chicago Defender*, November 17, 1923, 3. For more on Gilpin's claims about authoring the role of Brutus Jones, see David Krasner, "Whose Role Is It Anyway? Charles Gilpin and the Harlem Renaissance," *African American Review* 29, no. 3 (1995): 483–96.

33. "He's No Charles Gilpin," *Afro-American* (Baltimore), November 16, 1923, A1.

34. "'The Emperor Jones' Flops without C. Gilpin," *New York Amsterdam News*, November 7, 1923, 5.

35. "'The Emperor Jones' Flops without C. Gilpin," 5.

36. "'The Emperor Jones' Flops without C. Gilpin," 5.

37. B[est], "O'Neill in Paris," X2.

38. J. L. Austin, *How to Do Things with Words*, ed. J. O. Urmson and Marina Sbisà (Cambridge, MA: Harvard University Press, 1975), 14.

39. Edwards, *Practice of Diaspora*, 14.

40. René Wisner, "La Semaine Théâtrale," *La Rampe* (Paris), November 11, 1923, 7–11, at 8. Bibliothèque nationale de France (BnF [National Library of France]), Paris, Arts du spectacle division.

41. O'Neill, *The Emperor Jones*, 1033.

42. Bourgeois, trans., *L'Empereur Jones*.

43. Bourgeois, *L'Empereur Jones*, 6.

44. B[est], "O'Neill in Paris," X2. See also "'Emperor Jones' in France," *Cleveland Gazette*, November 17, 1923, 1.

45. Achille Mbembe, *Critique of Black Reason* (Durham, NC: Duke University Press, 2017).

46. O'Neill, *The Emperor Jones*, 1036. Bourgeois, *L'Empereur Jones*, 9.

47. B[est], "O'Neill in Paris," X2.

48. Rudolf Kommer, "O'Neill in Europe," *New York Times*, November 9, 1924, X2.

49. "The Theatre in France," 798.

50. Playbill, *The Emperor Jones*, 1924, with Paul Robeson, Hatch-Billops Collection, New York City (now the Camille Billops and James V. Hatch Archive housed at Emory University).

51. Wisner, "La Semaine Théâtrale," 10.

52. Wisner, "La Semaine Théâtrale," 10.

53. B[est], "O'Neill in Paris," X2.

54. Review of *The Emperor Jones*, Paris, March 5, 1923, by a critic with last name of Mosk, an otherwise unidentified clipping in *The Emperor Jones* Clipping File, Billy Rose Theatre Collection, New York Public Library for the Performing Arts.

55. "He's No Charles Gilpin."

56. B[est], "O'Neill in Paris," X2.

57. "Eugene O'Neill in Paris," *New York Transcript*, January 14, 1923. *The Emperor Jones* Clipping File, Billy Rose Theatre Collection, New York Public Library for the Performing Arts.

58. "Eugene O'Neill in Paris."

59. "Eugene O'Neill in Paris."

60. The *Evening Mail*'s review was quoted in "Belated Recognition."

61. "Paris and 'The Emperor Jones,'" *The Crisis* 27, no. 5 (1924): 223.

62. B[est], "O'Neill in Paris," X2.

63. Rudolf Kommer, "Broadway in Central Europe," *New York Times*, September 28, 1924, X2, in *The Emperor Jones* Clipping File, Billy Rose Theatre Collection, New York Public Library for the Performing Arts.

64. The original French review reads: "M. Benglia, lui, joue avec ses muscles. On peut dire de M. Benglia que sa poitrine parle, et que ses omoplates crient. La sueur l'inonde, fait reluire son torse bronzé. . . . C'est de la sculpture sur soi." Thanks to Jeanne De Groote-Strauss for help with this translation. See René Wisner, "Théâtre de l'Odéon," *La Rampe* (Paris), November 11, 1923. Clippings can be found at the Bibliothèque nationale de France (BnF [National Library of France]) in Paris in the Arts du spectacle division. Cited in Nathalie Coutelet, "Habib Benglia, le 'nègrérotique' du spectacle français," *Genre, sexualité & société* [En ligne], footnote 9. Posted online June 29, 2009, https://gss.rev ues.org/688#quotation

65. The first quote is from Antoine André, Review of *L'Empereur Jones*, *L'Information*, November 12, 1923; the second from Jean Botrot, "À l'Odéon *L'Empereur Jones*," periodical unknown, November 3, 1923. Both are qtd. in Coutelet, "Habib Benglia," footnote 9.

66. Armory, "La Matinée" (1923), qtd. in Coutelet, "Habib Benglia," footnote 9.

67. Coutelet, "Habib Benglia."

68. Wisner, "La Semaine Théâtrale," 8.

69. "Horizon."

70. This same *New York Times* review noted that while no dialect was used, Brutus Jones's speech was "different enough to give the right suggestion, even to a Frenchman." See "Eugene O'Neill in Paris."

71. "Eugene O'Neill in Paris."

72. This review from *L'Eclair* was reprinted in "Paris and 'The Emperor Jones.'"

73. This review from *L'Avenir* was reprinted in "Paris and 'The Emperor Jones.'"

74. "Will Play 'Emperor Jones' in Paris."

75. "Paris and 'The Emperor Jones.'"

76. "Eugene O'Neill in Paris."

77. As historian W. Scott Haine has noted, the term *apache* "emerged when a journalist in 1902 grafted the term from the North American Indian tribe onto the 'savage' gangs of adolescent youth—ranging in age from the middle teens to the middle twenties—who seemed to roam the 'frontiers' of the outlying districts of eastern Paris and who periodically descended on central Paris to terrorize the bourgeois"; see Haine, "The Development of Leisure and the Transformation of Working-Class Adolescences, Paris 1830–1940," *Journal of Family History* 17, no. 4 (1992): 451–76, at 452.

78. Jules-Rosette, *Black Paris*, x.

79. Batiste, *Darkening Mirrors*, 8–15.

80. Richard Brender, "Reinventing Africa in Their Own Image: The Ballets Suédois' 'Ballet nègre,' *La Création du monde*," *Dance Chronicle* 9, no. 1 (1986): 119–47, at 120.

81. Brender, "Reinventing Africa," 121.

82. Brender, "Reinventing Africa," 125.

83. Coutelet, "Habib Benglia."

84. "Electrifies French Capital," *Afro-American* (Baltimore), June 23, 1923, 8.

85. Jules-Rosette, *Black Paris*, 10.

86. The author describes Benglia's dancing at his club as follows: "danse chaque soir à Montparnasse, dans une boîte qu'il a créée." Salini, "Le grand acteur noir," 44.

87. "Spotlight Highlights," *Philadelphia Tribune*, September 3, 1931, 7.

88. I wish to thank Bob Lipartito, Music Reference Specialist at the Library of Congress, who hypothesizes that Benglia is holding a musical instrument called a quwaytara from Algeria. *The Grove Dictionary of Musical Instruments* describes the quwaytara as a "small unfretted, short-necked lute of the Maghreb. Its body is smaller and narrower, and the neck longer than those of the ūd. It has four pairs of strings; a typical Moroccan tuning is G-e-A-d." Email, Bob Lipartito, October 8, 2021.

89. Susan Foster, "The Ballerina's Phallic Pointe," in *Corporalities: Dancing Knowledge, Culture and Power* (New York: Taylor & Francis, 2004), 1–26.

90. Jennifer Anne Boittin, *Colonial Metropolis: The Urban Grounds of Anti-Imperialism and Feminism in Interwar Paris* (Lincoln: University of Nebraska Press, 2010), 44.

91. Patricia A. Morton, "National and Colonial: The Musée des Colonies at the Colonial Exposition, Paris, 1931," *Art Bulletin* 80, no. 2 (1998): 357–77.

92. Boittin, *Colonial Metropolis*, 37.

93. "In Europe with J. A. Rogers," *New York Amsterdam News*, September 2, 1931, 10.

94. "In Europe with J. A. Rogers," 10. The *Philadelphia Tribune* noted the voyeuristic pleasures of racial mixing at Benglia's club: "White American tourists have discovered the place and some visit it to get the thrill of seeing black and white folk dancing together." "Spotlight Highlights."

95. "Spotlight Highlights."

96. For more on the Négritude movement in dance and Benglia's contributions, see Hélène Neveu Kringelbach, "Moving Shadows of Casamance: Performance and Regionalism in Senegal," in *Dancing Cultures: Globalization, Tourism, and Identity in the Anthropology of Dance*, ed. Hélène Neveu Kringelbach and Jonathan Skinner (New York: Berghahn Books, 2012), 143–60, at 146.

97. The ballet *Le train bleu* premiered at Paris's Théâtre des Champs-Élysées on June 20, 1924. Created by Serge Diaghilev and Jean Cocteau (libretto), with choreography by Bronislava Nijinska (Nijinsky's sister), the ballet's production

team reads like a veritable who's who of modernism, with costumes by Coco Chanel, sets by sculptor Henri Laurens, and stage curtain and program by Pablo Picasso. For more on how alternative masculinities were performed in French ballet, see Charles R. Batson, *Dance, Desire, and Anxiety in Early Twentieth-Century French Theater: Playing Identities* (Aldershot, UK: Ashgate, 2005); see also Frank William David Ries, *The Dance Theatre of Jean Cocteau* (Ann Arbor, MI: UMI Research Press, 1986).

98. I take the term *symbolic inversion* from Peter Stallybrass and Allon White's *The Poetics and Politics of Transgression* (London: Methuen, 1986).

99. George Hutchinson, *In Search of Nella Larsen: A Biography of the Color Line* (Cambridge, MA: Harvard University Press, 2009), 382. It is also noteworthy that Benglia avoided locating his club in touristy Montmartre, where Josephine Baker originally established her legendary club, choosing instead Montparnasse, the heart of Black Paris. See William A. Shack, *Harlem in Montmartre: A Paris Jazz Story between the Great Wars* (Berkeley: University of California Press, 2001).

100. Edward W. Said, *Orientalism* (New York: Pantheon Books, 1978).

101. "Napoléon Noir," *L'Avenir normand* (Paris), January 15, 1947.

102. Cécile Dupouy, "Ce soir, pour l'inauguration de 'Point 50' les 'Argonautes' présentent 'Empereur Jones' et 'Bagatelles,'" *L'Aube* (Paris), January 7, 1950.

103. Sylvie Chalay, "Habib Benglia: Premier grand acteur noir en France," *Africultures*, last modified March 31, 2000. http://africultures.com/habib-bengl ia-premier-grand-acteur-noir-en-france-1312/; "Benglia a souvent déclaré dans la presse son désir de voir naître en France un théâtre noir qui révèle l'évidence de l'Art nègre."

104. The 1950 revival of *L'Empereur Jones* was directed by Sylvain Dhomme featuring set design by Jacques Noël at the Maison de la Pensée Française with Habib Benglia as Brutus Jones, Paul Chevalier as Smithers, and the company Segg. This production used Maurice Bourgeois's translation once again, but it was composed of just seven scenes (implying the Middle Passage scene was cut). It played for about eight weeks, with three performances per week. Records can be found at the Bibliothèque national de France at http://data.bnf .fr/39465695/empereur_jones_spectacle_1950/

105. André Ransan, "Empereur Jones," *Le Matinée Pays* (Paris), February 11–12, 1950.

106. Ransan, "Empereur Jones."

107. Jean Ganrey-Rety, "Empereur Jones et Bagatelles," *Le Soir* (Paris), February 11, 1950.

108. Georges Lerminier, "A 'Point 50' Les Argonautes présentent 'Bagatelles' et 'Empereur Jones'," *L'Aube* (Paris), February 13, 1950.

109. Elsa Triolet, "'Empereur Jones' la célèbre pièce," *Lettres Française*, February 16, 1950, 7. O'Neill's stage directions stipulate that Brutus Jones wears "a

light blue uniform coat, sprayed with brass buttons, heavy gold chevrons and his shoulders," and "bright red" pants "with a blue strip down the side." O'Neill, *The Emperor Jones*, 1033.

110. Unidentified review of *L'Empereur Jones* Clipping File, Bibliothèque national de France, Paris, page 10.

111. C. L. R. James, *The Black Jacobins: Toussaint Louverture and the San Domingo Revolution*, 2d ed., rev. (New York: Vintage Books, 1989).

112. Review of *L'Empereur Jones*, *L'Aurore* (Paris), February 12, 1950.

113. Triolet, "'Empereur Jones' la célèbre pièce," 7.

114. Triolet, "'Empereur Jones' la célèbre pièce," 7.

115. Francis Ambrière, "Le 'Point 50'," *Opéra*, February 15, 1950.

116. "Paris Does 'Emperor Jones' with African Voodoo Troupe" (1950), an otherwise unidentified clipping from *The Emperor Jones* Clipping File, Billy Rose Theatre Division, New York Public Library for the Performing Arts. While not covered extensively in the United States, this production was briefly reported in the *Afro-American*. See E. B. Rea, "Encores and Echoes," *Afro-American* (Baltimore), March 4, 1950, 8. See also Rosey E. Pool, "The Negro Actor in Europe," *Phylon* 14, no. 3 (1953): 258–67, at 264.

117. Claudine Chonez, "Bonne Chance à Point 50," *Les Nouvelles Littéraires*, February 23, 1950.

118. "A la Maison de la Pensée: Habib Benglia dans 'Empereur Jones,'" *Le Liberation* (Paris), February 20, 1950.

119. Chonez, "Bonne Chance à Point 50."

120. Triolet, "'Empereur Jones' la célèbre pièce," 7.

121. Shelby T. McCloy, *The Negro in France* (Lexington: University Press of Kentucky, 1961).

CHAPTER 3

1. L. S. McClelland, "All God's Chillun Got Wings," *Pittsburgh Courier*, August 1, 1936, 15. See also Dave Harrington, "All God's Chillun," *New York Amsterdam News*, July 18, 1936, 16.

2. "U.S. Coaches Declare That Tolan Conditioned Himself," *Afro-American* (Baltimore), August 13, 1932, 15.

3. According to a search in the African American Newspapers & Periodicals databases (which covers 1827–1998), the use of "All God's Chillun" in articles referencing events other than theatrical productions occurred mostly after the 1924 stage production of O'Neill's *All God's Chillun Got Wings* with Paul Robeson. When Paul Robeson premiered in the staged adaptation of *Black Boy*, drama critic Theophilus Lewis's headline read "All God's Chillun Still Got Wings." See Lewis, "All God's Chillun Still Got Wings," *Messenger* (New York) 8, no. 11 (November 1924): 333–34. Mainstream papers also featured the title in

articles about racial equality such as "All God's Chillun Got Feelings," *Arkansas State Press*, city ed., June 6, 1952, 5. The Federal Council of Churches used the title to explicitly denounce the South's "pattern of segregation," and to make the case for "a more complete democracy." See "'All God's Chillun,'" *New York Times*, December 5, 1948, E8. A 1954 editorial in the *New York Times* also referenced the play, claiming that "morally and constitutionally, in these United States, 'All God's Chillun Got Wings.'" See "'All God's Chillun,'" *New York Times*, February 1, 1954, 22.

4. Glenda E. Gill, "Love in Black and White: Miscegenation on the Stage," *Journal of American Drama and Theatre* 10, no. 3 (Fall 1998): 32–51, at 22.

5. Italics in original. Kevin J. Mumford, *Interzones: Black/White Sex Districts in Chicago and New York in the Early Twentieth Century* (New York: Columbia University Press, 1997), 122.

6. Glenda Frank, "Tempest in Black and White: The 1924 Premiere of Eugene O'Neill's *All God's Chillun Got Wings*," *Resources for American Literary Study* 26, no. 1 (2000): 75–89, at 84.

7. Unlike in *The Emperor Jones*, the use of "n——r" in *All God's Chillun Got Wings* is mostly said by other characters *to* Jim as a sign of their racism, which the play critiques. Given that *All God's Chillun*'s characters demonstrate the injurious nature of racial epithets, there is evidence of O'Neill changing his views about the performative force of language as a mechanism of racism. While "n——r" is problematically peppered throughout the script, it is significant that Jim stands up to those who call him so, responding "(*fiercely*) Don't you call me that—not before them!" (O'Neill, *All God's Chillun Got Wings*, 285). This is something Brutus Jones never does. At times, O'Neill used more socially accepted terms to describe Black people. In the original typescript, he crossed out "colored" on the first page scene description and wrote "black" three times; another time he used the word "sugar." O'Neill, "*All God's Chillun Got Wings*," draft, typescript and typescript carbon, corrected, n.d. Series III, Writings, 1914–1970, Plays, *All God's Chillun Got Wings*. Box 41, Folder 876. Eugene O'Neill Papers, Yale Collection of American Literature, Beinecke Rare Book and Manuscript Library.

8. *All God's Chillun Got Wings* was performed at the Provincetown Playhouse from May 15 to July 5, 1924 with Paul Robeson and Mary Blair in the title roles. It was directed by James (Jimmy) Light with set design by Cleon ("Throck") Throckmorton; it was produced by the "triumvirate": Kenneth Macgowen, Robert Edmund Jones, and Eugene O'Neill. *All God's Chillun* next transferred to the Greenwich Village Theatre and ran from August 18 to October 4, 1924, again with Robeson in the title role of Jim Harris. Dorothy Petersen replaced Mary Blair in the Greenwich Village Theatre production. Because the May 1924 production of *All God's Chillun Got Wings* was shown exclusively to Provincetown Players subscribers, the August production was the first time that tickets were sold to the general public. See Margaret Loftus Ranald, *The Eugene O'Neill Companion* (Westport, CT: Greenwood Press, 1984), 20.

9. Charles Musser, "To Redream the Dream of White Playwrights: Reappropriation and Resistance in Oscar Micheaux's *Body and Soul*," in *Oscar Micheaux and His Circle: African American Filmmaking and Race Cinema of the Silent Era*, ed. Pearl Bowser, Jane Gaines, and Charles Musser (Bloomington: Indiana University Press, 2001), 97–131, at 100.

10. Tony Perucci has argued that "Paul Robeson's performances emerged as a central domestic site for the waging of the Cold War," but I understand Robeson's performances of O'Neill's *early* plays as "part of a broad-based African American struggle against American imperialism and capitalism." See Perucci, *Paul Robeson and the Cold War Performance Complex*, 2. See also Cedric R. Tolliver, *Of Vagabonds and Fellow Travelers: African Diaspora Literary Culture and the Cultural Cold War* (Ann Arbor: University of Michigan Press, 2019).

11. "Augustus Thomas Scores Casting in O'Neil [*sic*] Play," *Brooklyn Daily Eagle*, February 25, 1924, 9.

12. John Corbin, "Among the New Plays," *New York Times*, May 18, 1924, XI.

13. "Augustus Thomas Scores Casting in O'Neil [*sic*] Play," 9.

14. "An Ill-Advised Performance," *New York World*, March 4, 1924. Alexander Gumby Collection of Negroiana, 1800–1981; Box 141; Scrapbook 112, Paul Robeson Folder; Rare Book and Manuscript Library, Columbia University Library.

15. "An Ill-Advised Performance."

16. William McAdoo, "Public Protests Ignored: O'Neill Play to Be Seen," *New York World*, March 3, 1924, 1 and 4.

17. "Race Strife Seen if 'God's Chillun' Is Staged," *New York American*, March 15, 1924, 1.

18. Frank, "Tempest in Black and White," 79. Travis Bogard, as well as Arthur Gelb and Barbara Gelb, have written that there were bomb threats as well. See Bogard, *Contour in Time: The Plays of Eugene O'Neill*, rev. ed. (New York: Oxford University Press, 1988), 192; and Arthur Gelb and Barbara Gelb, *O'Neill* (New York: Harper and Row, 1962), 552. Mary Blair's husband observed that during the run of *All God's Chillun Got Wings* she received several "insulting letters." See David Castronovo and Janet Groth, *Critic in Love: A Romantic Biography of Edmund Wilson* (Berkeley, CA: Counterpoint Press, 2005), 24.

19. C. H. Bell, "Objects to Play," letter to the editor, *Chicago Defender*, March 15, 1924, 12.

20. McAdoo, "Public Protests Ignored," 1 and 4. See also Frank, "Tempest in Black and White," 80.

21. "Legislative League Acts," *Chicago Defender*, March 15, 1924, 6.

22. Cheryl Black, "After the Emperor: Interracial Collaborations Between Provincetown Alumni and Black Theatre Artists c. 1924–1946," *Journal of American Drama and Theatre* 20, no. 1 (Winter 2008): 5–26, at 8. See also Frank, "Tempest in Black and White," 77.

23. Eugene O'Neill, *All God's Chillun Got Wings*, in *American Mercury* 1, no. 2 (February 1924): 129–48.

24. An article in the *New York Post* pointed out that "the controversy has been based on the published text. It's quite a different matter on the stage, as any one might have known it would be." See "New O'Neill Play and the Mayor," *New York Post*, May 16, 1924. Qtd. in John Houchin, ed., *The Critical Response to Eugene O'Neill* (Westport, CT: Greenwood Press, 1997), 59.

25. Arthur Pollock, Review of *All God's Chillun Got Wings*, *Brooklyn Daily News*, May 16, 1924, 5.

26. Kenneth McGowan, "O'Neill's Play Again," *New York Times*, August 31, 1924, X2.

27. On February 21, 1924, O'Neill wrote in his work diary: "sensational stuff in papers all over country for past week about 'All God's Chillun.'" And on March 11: "More stink in papers about 'All G[od's]. C[hillun].'" Eugene O'Neill, *Work Diary 1924–1943*, transcribed by Donald Gallup, preliminary edition, vol. 1 (New Haven: Yale University Library, 1981), 5.

28. "O'Neill to Rescue of 'All God's Chillun,'" *New York World*, March 19, 1924. *All God's Chillun Got Wings* Clipping File, Billy Rose Theatre Division, New York Public Library for the Performing Arts.

29. Corbin, "Among the New Plays," XI.

30. Frank, "Tempest in Black and White," 79.

31. O'Neill, *Work Diary 1924–1943*, 4.

32. Black, "After the Emperor," 8.

33. Frank, "Tempest in Black and White," 80. See also Cary D. Winz, *Black Culture and the Harlem Renaissance* (Houston: Rice University Press, 1988), 192.

34. Helen Deutsch and Stella Hanau, *The Provincetown: A Story of the Theatre* (New York: Farrar & Rinehart, 1931), 108.

35. Johnson, *Black Manhattan*, 196.

36. Loften Mitchell, *Black Drama: The Story of the American Negro in the Theatre* (New York: Hawthorn Press, 1967), 83. See also Joe Weixlmann, "Staged Segregation: Baldwin's *Blues for Mister Charlie* and O'Neill's *All God's Chillun Got Wings*," *Black American Literature Forum* 11, no. 1 (Spring 1977): 35–36.

37. Frank, "Tempest in Black and White," 75.

38. Will Anthony Madden, "Why Did Eugene O'Neill Write 'All God's Chillun Got Wings'?," *Pittsburgh Courier*, April 12, 1924, 13.

39. Mumford, *Interzones*, 122.

40. "O'Neill to Rescue of 'God's Chillun.'" *All God's Chillun Got Wings* Clipping File, Billy Rose Theatre Division, New York Public Library for the Performing Arts. Noting the hypocrisy of those who objected to Robeson in this role, O'Neill pointed out, "Right in this city two years ago, in a public theatre, he played opposite a distinguished white actress, Margaret Wycherly, in a play called 'Voodoo.'" The correct title of the play was *Taboo*, which had a short run in April 1922 at the Sam H. Harris Theatre on Broadway. Written by white author Mary Hoyt Viborg, the play was set in Africa and starred Robeson and Wycherly. It was in Harlem's highly respected Lafayette Players' production of *Taboo* that Robeson was spotted by

Provincetowners Robert (Bobby) Edmond Jones and Kenneth Macgowan who then considered him for *All God's Chillun Got Wings* in 1924.

41. Gill, "Eugene O'Neill and Paul Robeson."

42. Robeson, "Reflections on O'Neill's Plays," 368–70; reprinted in *The Portable Harlem Renaissance Reader*, ed. David Levering Lewis (New York: Viking, 1994), 59–60, at 59.

43. Robeson, "Reflections on O'Neill's Plays," 60.

44. "6 ft 4 in Negro Actor's Triumph," *Star* (London), September 11, 1925. Clippings File of the James Weldon Johnson Memorial Collection, Series II: Personal/Corporate Names, Box 149, Robeson, Paul 1922–1925 in the Yale Collection of American Literature, Beinecke Rare Book and Manuscript Library.

45. Frank, "Tempest in Black and White," 86. See also Martin Duberman, *Paul Robeson: A Biography* (New York: Alfred Knopf, 1988), 59; and Wainscott, *Staging O'Neill*, 148.

46. Burns Mantle, "*All God's Chillun* Plays without a Single Protest," *Chicago Daily Tribune*, May 25, 1924, F1. Arthur Pollock concurred: "instead of causing a riot, it was greeted with cheers and loud whistlings." Pollock, Review of *All God's Chillun Got Wings*, 5.

47. O'Neill, qtd. in Gelb and Gelb, *O'Neill*, 555. In his working diary O'Neill recorded the night succinctly: "went over well—none of the expected trouble." Eugene O'Neill, *Diary 1924–1943*, 489.

48. Madden, "Why Did Eugene O'Neill Write 'All God's Chillun' Got Wings'?," 13.

49. Sheaffer, *O'Neill: Son and Artist*, 119.

50. O'Neill, qtd. in Virginia Floyd, *Eugene O'Neill at Work: Newly Released Ideas for Plays* (New York: Ungar Publishing, 1981), 53.

51. Weeks before she shot herself, Etta Johnson said the following: "I am a white woman . . . and am tired of being a social outcast. I deserve all of my misery for marrying a black man. Even the Negroes don't respect me; they hate me. I intend to end it all." Qtd. in Sheaffer, *O'Neill: Son and Artist*, 119. See also Werner Sollors, *Neither Black Nor White Yet Both: Thematic Explorations of Interracial Literature* (Cambridge, MA: Harvard University Press, 1991), 36.

52. O'Neill's daughter, Oona, referred to herself in a public interview as "shanty Irish." See Sheaffer, *O'Neill: Son and Artist*, 49. For more about the interracial marriage of Jack Johnson and Etta Duryea, see Ken Burns, dir., *Unforgiveable Blackness: The Rise and Fall of Jack Johnson*. 2004; Arlington County, VA: PBS, 2005. DVD.

53. Black, "After the Emperor," 8.

54. Monks, "'Genuine Negroes and Real Bloodhounds,'" 540–64, at 549.

55. O'Neill, *All God's Chillun Got Wings*, 280.

56. O'Neill, "All God's Chillun Got Wings" (typescript), page 3.

57. Ignatiev, *How the Irish Became White*.

58. O'Neill, *All God's Chillun Got Wings*, 282.

59. Johnson, *Appropriating Blackness*, 5.

60. Johnson, *Appropriating Blackness*, 3.

61. O'Neill, *All God's Chillun Got Wings*, 280.

62. Somerville, *Queering the Color Line*, 3.

63. Hatch, qtd. in Gill, "Eugene O'Neill and Paul Robeson: An Uneasy Collaboration." See also James V. Hatch, Camille Billops, and Ted Shine, *Black Theatre, USA. Revised and Expanded Edition, The Early Period, 1847–1938* (New York: Free Press, 1996), 96.

64. Gill, "Eugene O'Neill and Paul Robeson: An Uneasy Collaboration." The second part of the quote is found in this clipping: "New Racial Play Stirs Stage World: Mary Blair, White Actress, Revealed as Co-Star With Colored Actor," *Broad Ax* (Chicago), March 1, 1924, 2.

65. See "Actress Quits Play with Negroes in Cast," *New York Times*, September 12, 1925, 9.

66. As Glenda Frank reminds us, "the text [of *All God's Chillun*] was not the primary problem, the casting was." Frank, "Tempest in Black and White," 82.

67. "Deems It an Honor to Play in Show with Negro, Says Mary Blair; Shows No Bias," *Brooklyn Daily Eagle*, February 22, 1924, 1.

68. "Hylan Bars Scene in O'Neill's Play," *New York Times*, May 16, 1924, 1. Integrating child actors in the prologue also sparked objections from some African American commentators. Writing for the *Chicago Defender*, critic William Pickens called *All God's Chillun Got Wings* a "vicious" play, fearing that the portrayal of Black and white children playing together would backfire and justify school segregation. Referencing the efforts to establish "separate but equal" schools for black children, he wrote: "It is the play's insidious attack upon the common public school and its direct or indirect support of the devilish sentiment to put Negro children out of the public schools." He hoped that "Negroes who have brains will not 'root' for it," and oppose it lawfully." W. [William] M. Pickens, "O'Neill's Drama Supports Race Discrimination," *Chicago Defender*, March 22, 1924, 8.

69. Robin Bernstein, *Racial Innocence: Performing American Childhood and Race from Slavery to Civil Rights* (New York: New York University Press, 2011), 4.

70. "Mayor Still Bars Children in Play," *New York Times*, May 17, 1924, 18. Given that *All God's Chillun* was performed for a subscription-only crowd at the Provincetown Playhouse, the authorities had no other way to stop the show than by withholding the license for the child actors.

71. "Hylan Bars Scene in O'Neill's Play," 1.

72. In Frederick Bond's 1940 study of Black drama, he notes: "The Mayor's office . . . may have felt that it was a bit too unusual to permit a colored boy to carry a white girl's book to school, which kindness on the boy's part precipitated admiration for the lad." Frederick Weldon Bond, *The Negro and the Drama* (1940; College Park, MD: McGrath Publishing, 1969), 72.

73. As the council for the Provincetown Playhouse argued, "a number of

children of this age (10–13) and several who are younger, are appearing continually in New York productions." See "Mayor Still Bars Children in Play," 18.

74. E. W. Osborn, Review of *All God's Chillun Got Wings*, by Eugene O'Neill, directed by James Light, Provincetown Playhouse, *New York Evening World*, May 16, 1924. *All God's Chillun Got Wings* Clipping File, Billy Rose Theatre Division, New York Public Library for the Performing Arts. See also Alexander Woollcott, "*All God's Chillun Got Wings*: O'Neill's Play Tranquilly Produced in Macdougal Street," *New York Sun*, May 16, 1924, 24.

75. "Hylan Bars Scene in O'Neill's Play," 1. According to another account, "The prologue received considerable applause from the audience which was friendly to the play throughout." See "Prologue of 'All God's Chillun' Is Read, as Child Actors Are Barred," *New York World*, May 16, 1924. See also Percy Hammond, "The Mayor Interferes a Little Bit with *All God's Chillun Got Wings*," *New York Herald Tribune*, May 16, 1924, 10. Reviews can be found in the *All God's Chillun Got Wings* Clipping File, Billy Rose Theatre Division, New York Public Library for the Performing Arts.

76. Gilbert W. Gabriel, "*All God's Chillun*: First Scene of O'Neill's Play Reaches Public Performance at Last." Otherwise unidentified clipping, Series III, Writings, Plays, *All God's Chillun Got Wings*, Clippings of Reviews and Advertisements, 1925–68, n.d., Box 41, Folder 878. Eugene O'Neill Papers. Yale Collection of American Literature, Beinecke Rare Book and Manuscript Library.

77. "Passing the Grandstand," *Messenger* (New York) 6, no.7 (July 1924): 224.

78. Deutsch and Hanau, *The Provincetown*, 112. See also Stark Young, "*All God's Chillun* Again," *New York Times*, August 19, 1924, 9.

79. See chapter 2 in Nyong'o, *Afro-Fabulations*, 46–75.

80. Lester Walton, "Evelyn Preer Would Make Good 'Ella Downey' in 'All God's Chillun Got Wings,'" *Pittsburgh Courier*, March 15, 1924, 10.

81. Walton, "Evelyn Preer Would Make Good 'Ella Downey,'" 10.

82. Austin, *How to Do Things with Words*.

83. Austin conceded that "I do" is not the phrase used during marriage ceremonies, his editors note in a footnote. Austin, *How to Do Things with Words*, 5.

84. O'Neill, *All God's Chillun Got Wings*, 295.

85. Brenda Murphy, *The Provincetown Players and the Culture of Modernity* (Cambridge: Cambridge University Press, 2005), 219.

86. O'Neill, *All God's Chillun Got Wings*, 296.

87. O'Neill, *All God's Chillun Got Wings*, 315.

88. "Riots Feared from Drama," *New York American*, March 18, 1924, 1.

89. Madden, "Why Did O'Neill Write 'All God's Chillun' Got Wings'?," 13.

90. Deutsch and Hanau, *The Provincetown*, 108. See also "White Actress to Play Opposite Negro 'Lead,'" *Washington Post*, February 22, 1924, 3; "Public Protests Ignored," *New York World*, March 3, 1924; and "*All God's Chillun Got Wings* Calls for White Actress to Kiss Negro's Hand," *Washington Post*, February 22, 1924, 3.

91. Castronovo and Groth, *Critic in Love*, 24.

92. "Broadway Gasps as Mary Blair, White Actress, Stars in Play Featuring Infatuation of Caucasian for Race Man," *Pittsburgh Courier*, June 19, 1926, 1.

93. Gill observes: "Marcus Garvey, the famous Black nationalist of the 1920s, severely criticized Robeson for playing Jim Harris and Brutus *Jones*," but that doesn't discredit my point about the portrait in the production possibly referencing him. See Gill, "Eugene O'Neill and Paul Robeson: An Uneasy Collaboration."

94. O'Neill, *All God's Chillun Got Wings*, 304.

95. As Scott Allen Nollen observes, "The next day [after *Jones*'s opening], he [Robeson] began rehearsing *All God's Chillun Got Wings* during the day and continued to star in *The Emperor Jones* during the evening." See Nollen, *Paul Robeson: Film Pioneer* (Jefferson, NC: McFarland, 2010), 12.

96. O'Neill, *All God's Chillun Got Wings*, 292.

97. O'Neill, *All God's Chillun Got Wings*, 302.

98. Dora Cole Norman, "From Hattie's Point of View," *Messenger* (New York) 7, no. 1 (January 1925), 32. From the Hatch-Billops Collection in New York City (now the Camille Billops and James V. Hatch Archive housed at Emory University). In addition to acting and heading the Colored Players Guild of New York 1919–21, Norman was also a dancer, choreographer, and playwright. She was the dance director for Du Bois's *Star of Ethiopia*. See Bernard L. Peterson, *Profiles of African American Stage Performers and Theatre People, 1816–1960* (New York: Greenwood Press, 2001), 197.

99. Norman, "From Hattie's Point of View," 32.

100. O'Neill, *All God's Chillun Got Wings*, 313.

101. O'Neill, *All God's Chillun Got Wings*, 315.

102. Nollen, *Paul Robeson: Film Pioneer*, 11. Musser also makes this point. Musser, "Troubled Relations," 87.

103. An article in *Time Magazine* observed: "He [Robeson] is also a graduate of Columbia Law School, but theatrical interests have so far kept him from the practice of Law." See "The Theatre: *All God's Chillun* Monday," *Time Magazine*, March 17, 1924. Although Robeson worked for a short while at the Manhattan law firm Louis W. Stotesbury, he experienced discrimination while working there.

104. The *New York World* reported, "Rehearsals [of *All God's Chillun Got Wings*] have been halted temporarily and Paul Robeson, the Negro actor cast for the leading role opposite Mary Blair, is to appear for a while in the production of *Roseanne*, put on by a Negro cast at the Lafayette Theatre. Rehearsals will be resumed about May," no article title, *New York World*, May 19, 1924. *All God's Chillun Got Wings* Clipping File, Billy Rose Theatre Division, New York Public Library for the Performing Arts. In another bizarre twist to the Robeson/Gilpin collective performative, Robeson replaced Gilpin in *The Emperor Jones* after he quit *Roseanne*. See "Gilpin Quits 'Roseanne,' Paul Robeson Takes His Place," *New York Age*, March 22, 1924, 1.

105. Theophilus Lewis, "Roseanne," *Messenger* (New York) 6, no. 3 (March 1924), 73. *Roseanne* played at the Greenwich Village Theatre from December 29, 1923 to February 1924 for forty-one performances.

106. White actress Chrystal Herne played the lead role of Leola in *Roseanne* and John Harrington appeared as preacher Cicero Brown—both were in black-face. While Chrystal Herne was praised for rising to "admirable heights of emotion" in the role of Leola, the cast was also critiqued for their blackface performances. See Charles Belmont Davis, "'Roseanne' Somber Study of Primitive Customs of Negro," *New York Tribune*, December 31, 1923, 6. Theophilus Lewis praised Herne's "brilliant" performance, writing: "I never believed a Caucasian could portray Negro feeling with such fidelity to the subject. It was simply astounding." Lewis, "Roseanne," 73. For more, see Musser, "To Redream the Dream of White Playwrights," 106–7.

107. As the *New York Age* reported, "Charles S. Gilpin, the most distinguished and best known member of the cast, is a marked improvement of the white actor who played the part." Walton, "'Roseanne,' with All Negro Cast," 6. See also Musser, "To Redream the Dream of White Playwrights," 106n39.

108. "Gilpin Quits 'Roseanne'," 1.

109. "At the Lafayette Theatre," *New York Age*, March 29, 1924, 6.

110. Walton, "'Roseanne,' with All Negro Cast," 6.

111. Musser, "To Redream the Dream of White Playwrights," 119.

112. Musser, "To Redream the Dream of White Playwrights," 120.

113. Musser, "To Redream the Dream of White Playwrights," 121-22.

114. "'All God's Chillun' in Broadway Revival," *Broad Ax* (Chicago), July 2, 1927, 2. The *Broad Ax* mistakenly reported that this revival occurred at Broadway's Majestic Theatre. There is also a Majestic Theatre in Los Angeles, and this is the correct theater, which is corroborated by other reviews. "'All God's Chillun,'" *Afro-American* (Baltimore), February 12, 1927, 8. *All God's Chillun Got Wings* was performed earlier in the year at Hollywood's Vine Street Theatre in February 1927. This production had an all-white cast featuring Jessie Arnold as Sister Hattie and Irving Pichel as Jim; it was also paired with Negro spirituals featuring Aaron Jones. There was also a Los Angeles production of *All God's Chillun Got Wings* on March 6, 1927 with Irving Pichel and Violette Wilson at the El Capitan Theater. See "'All God's Chillun' Makes Its Third Los Angeles Appearance," *Pittsburgh Courier*, June 25, 1927, A2. See also "'All God's Chillun' in Broadw'y Revival," *Afro-American* (Baltimore), June 25, 1927, 7.

115. IMDb describes Pichel as an "ethnic character villain in early pre-Code talkies." IMDb, "Irving Pichel Biography," accessed September 5, 2021, https://www.imdb.com/name/nm0681635/bio?ref_=nm_ov_bio_sm. Pichel went on to perform ethnic roles such as Prince Yamadori in *Madame Butterfly* (1933), and Gen. Carbajal in *Juarez* (1939), although these are not his definitive roles. A tribute after his death mentions his role in *All God's Chillun Got Wings*. See Kenneth Macgowan et al., "Irving Pichel (1891–1954): Wonderful to Have Had You with Us," *Quarterly of Film Radio and Television* 9, no. 2 (1954): 109–23.

116. Michael Rogin, *Blackface, White Noise: Jewish Immigrants in the Hollywood Melting Pot* (Berkeley: University of California Press, 1998), 13. See also Henry Bial's *Acting Jewish: Negotiating Ethnicity on the American Stage and Screen* (Ann Arbor: University of Michigan Press, 2005); M. Alison Kibler, *Censoring Racial Ridicule: Irish, Jewish, and African American Struggles over Race and Representation, 1890–1930* (Chapel Hill: University of North Carolina Press, 2015); Roediger, *Wages of Whiteness*; Lott, *Love and Theft*; and Lester D. Friedman, *Hollywood's Image of the Jew* (New York: Ungar, 1982).

117. Esther Romeyn, *Street Scenes: Staging the Self in Immigrant New York, 1880–1924* (Minneapolis: University of Minnesota Press, 2008), 189.

118. "O'Neill Drama and 'Abie's Irish Rose' on Week's Calendar," *Los Angeles Times*, June 19, 1927, 17.

119. Musser, "Why Did Negroes Love Al Jolson and *The Jazz Singer?*," 198.

120. Chandler Owen, editorial, "New Opinion of the Negro," *Messenger* (New York) 9, no. 6 (June 1, 1927): 191 and 207, at 191.

121. Owen, editorial, 191 and 207.

122. "Hands across the Sea," letter to the editor, *New York Amsterdam News*, October 9, 1929, 8.

123. "Hands across the Sea, 8.

124. London's Royal Court Theatre production of *All God's Chillun Got Wings* opened on June 17, 1929 and ran for twenty-four performances. "Backstage with Stagestruck," *Inter-State Tattler* (New York), July 12, 1929, 9. See also Cochrane, *Twentieth-Century British Theatre*, 107.

125. "Hands across the Sea," 8.

126. *All God's Chillun Got Wings* Programmes File, Billy Rose Theatre Division, New York Public Library for the Performing Arts. According to Jozefina Komporaly, O'Neill was the most performed American dramatist at London's Gate Theatre during these years. See Komporaly, "The Gate Theatre: A Translation Powerhouse on the Inter-War British Stage," *Journal of Adaptation in Film & Performance* 4, no. 2 (2011): 129–43, at 134.

127. Production Photo, *All God's Chillun Got Wings*, by Eugene O'Neill, produced by Peter Godfrey, The Gate Theatre, London, 1929. From the Horst Frenz Collection. Box 27: Photographs of O'Neill's Plays European, Folder 7. Eugene O'Neill Foundation Archive, Tao House, Danville, California. For more details, see J. P. Wearing, *The London Stage 1920–1929: A Calendar of Productions, Performers, and Personnel* (New York: Rowman & Littlefield, 2014), 680.

128. Kamerny retitled *All God's Chillun Got Wings* as *"Negr"* for Russian audiences. See Katherine Weinstein, "Towards a Theatre of Creative Imagination: Alexander Tairov's O'Neill Productions," *Eugene O'Neill Review* 22, nos. 1–2 (1998): 157–70, at 165. According to Wiktionary, "The usage of the word негр (negr) or негритянка (negritjánka) in Russian is *generally* not considered pejorative. Until recently, it was considered a neutral word in Russian, and was not used derogatively." Wiktionary, "Негр," accessed May 20, 2020, https://en.wiktionary.org/wiki/%D0%BD%D0%B5%D0%B3%D1%80

129. John Martin, "The Dance: Russians in Paris," *New York Times*, June 15, 1930, X8.

130. Telegram from Eugene O'Neill to Richard Madden on May 15, 1930. Folder: Letters, Madden, Richard, 1919–32. Accession Number: MAR300515. Eugene O'Neill Foundation Archive, Tao House, Danville, California.

131. Telegram from Eugene O'Neill to Richard Madden on May 15, 1930. Folder: Letters, Madden, Richard, 1919–32. Accession Number: MAR300515. Eugene O'Neill Foundation Archive, Tao House, Danville, California.

132. Eugene O'Neill, *Work Diary*, vol. 1, 36. O'Neill described the Paris production of *All God's Chillun Got Wings* with excitement (and with an unusual exclamation point) in a letter to his agent, Dick Madden. Hand-written letter from Eugene O'Neill to Richard Madden, on February 17, 1934. Folder: Letters, Madden, Richard, 1933–37. Accession Number MAR340217. Eugene O'Neill Foundation Archive, Tao House, Danville, California.

133. Weinstein, "Towards a Theatre of Creative Imagination," 65.

134. Martin, "The Dance: Russians in Paris," X8.

135. Production photos from *All God's Chillun Got Wings*, produced by Alexander Tairov for the Kamery Theatre in Moscow. Horst Frenz Collection. Box 27: Photographs of O'Neill's Plays European, Folder 8, Photo 10, "All God's Chillun Got Wings," Eugene O'Neill Foundation Archive, Tao House, Danville, California.

136. The London revival of *All God's Chillun Got Wings* opened on March 13, 1933 at the Embassy Theatre where its run was extended to three weeks. It then transferred to the Piccadilly Theatre on April 3, 1933 and closed on April 29, 1933. This production starred Paul Robeson as Jim Harris and Flora Robson as Ella Harris; it was produced and directed by Andre Van Gyseghem. Gyseghem recounted that the 1933 London production of *Chillun* was an "unforgettable experience" with "blazing intensity." Andre Van Gyseghem, *Paul Robeson: The Great Forerunner* (New York: Dodd, Mead, 1978), 45–46. See also "Paul Robeson's Big Season in London," *Chicago Defender*, April 22, 1933, 5; Arnold H. Lubasch, *Robeson: An American Ballad* (Lanham, MD: Scarecrow Press, 2012), 72; "All God's Chillum Got Wings," *Times* (London), March 17, 1933, *All God's Chillun Got Wings* Clipping File, Billy Rose Theatre Division, New York Public Library for the Performing Arts; and "Robeson Wins Plaudits: Hailed in London in O'Neill's 'All God's Chillun,'" *New York Times*, March 14, 1933, 19.

137. "Rialto Gossip: The Theatre Guild Also Has Its Casting Problems," *New York Times*, April 2, 1933, X1.

138. *All God's Chillun Got Wings* T-Photo (B) file, Billy Role Theatre Division, New York Public Library for the Performing Arts.

139. Lubauch, *Robeson: An American Ballad*, 73.

140. W. E. B. Du Bois, Letter to Esther E. Wilson, November 12, 1930. W. E. B. Du Bois Papers (MS 312). Special Collections and University Archives, University of Massachusetts Amherst Libraries.

141. Review of *All God's Chillun Got Wings*, by Eugene O'Neill, directed by Ralph Coleman, *New York Herald*, November 1, 1931, otherwise unidentified clipping, *All God's Chillun Got Wings* Clipping File, Billy Rose Theatre Division, New York Public Library for the Performing Arts. See also Lisa Simmons, "The Negro Theater Project, 1935–1939," *Boston Black Theater: Its Golden Era*, accessed March 22, 2020. http://academics.wellesley.edu/AmerStudies/BostonBlackHistory/theatre/theatreproject.html

142. Programme for *All God's Chillun Got Wings* by Eugene O'Neill (1944), *Mercury Theatre Colchester*, accessed November 21, 2020, https://www.mercurytheatre.co.uk/mercury-voices/programme-for-all-gods-chillun-got-wings-by-eugene-oneill/

143. The cast of the Colchester Repertory Theatre's 1944 production of *All God's Chillun Got Wings* included Earl Cameron, Robert Adams (as Jim Harris), Elizabeth Jeppe, Joan MacArthur, George Brown, Orlando Martins, Leonard Maquire, Michael Logan, John Stock, C. B. Pulman, Lavinia Lewis, Ida Shepley (as Ella Harris), Patrick Barton, Renee Croome, Maurice Michel, and Robin Hood. See *Wikipedia*, "Ida Shepley," accessed November 20, 2020. https://en.wikipedia.org/wiki/Ida_Shepley#cite_note-3

144. "Black and Asian Performance in Britain, 1940–1969." Victoria & Albert Museum, accessed November 20, 2020, http://www.vam.ac.uk/content/articles/b/history-of-black-and-asian-performance-in-britain5/ (article is no longer posted).

145. Christine Douxami, "Brazilian Black Theatre: A Political Theatre against Racism," *TDR/The Drama Review* 63, no. 1 (2019): 32–51, at 36.

146. Fernández, "Black Theatre in Brazil," 9n16. O'Neill was not always generous in granting permission to produce *All God's Chillun Got Wings*. He withheld the rights from an all-Black production of *All God's Chillun Got Wings* in California during the Second World War. His wife, Carlotta, wrote in her diary on May 12, 1942: "A wire arrives from Los Angeles for Gene saying the Negro population wants to know why he cancelled the production of 'All God's Chillun?' He replied that never having given his okay for the production—how could he cancel it? He does not wish it to be produced during the war on account of the color line controversy." It's unclear what O'Neill meant by that, but his thinking changed once again after the war concluded. See Carlotta Monterey O'Neill, *Diary*, May 12, 1942. Copy at the Eugene O'Neill Foundation Archive, Tao House, Danville, California.

CHAPTER 4

1. Cover of *The Crisis* 40, no. 10 (October 1933).

2. Cover of *Time Magazine*, January 16, 1933.

3. Siobhan B. Somerville, *Queering the Color Line: Race and the Invention of*

Homosexuality in American Culture (Durham, NC: Duke University Press, 2000), 3.

4. See James Smalls, *The Homoerotic Photography of Carl Van Vechten* (Philadelphia: Temple University Press, 2006), 105; "An Interview with Bruce Nugent," in *Artists and Influences*, ed. James V. Hatch and Camille Billops (New York: Hatch-Billops Collection, 1982), 99; and Manning, *Modern Dance, Negro Dance*, 31.

5. Kristen M. Turner, "Class, Race, and Uplift in the Opera House; Theodore Drury and His Company Cross the Color Line," *Journal of Musicological Research* 34, no. 4 (2015): 320–51, at 321. See also Eileen Southern, *The Music of Black Americans: A History* (New York: W. W. Norton, 1997), 414–18 and 445–51; Twila L. Perry, "Race on the Opera Stage," in *The Routledge Companion to African American Theatre and Performance*, ed. Kathy A. Perkins, Sandra L. Richards, Renée Alexander Craft, and Thomas F. DeFrantz (London: Taylor & Francis, 2018), 77–82; and Lucy Kaplan, "The Improbable Rise of the First African American Opera Impresario," *Classic Voice*, February 6, 2017, accessed March 4, 2022, https://www.sfcv.org/articles/feature/improbable-rise-first-african-american -opera-impresario

6. Naomi André, *Black Opera: History, Power, Engagement* (Urbana: University of Illinois Press, 2018), 10.

7. "Well into the early twentieth century, minstrel stereotypes provided a coded norm for how blackness was performed in a musico-dramatic setting and thus became potent models for depicting blackness on the operatic stage, whether in terms of story lines, characterization, or the simple application of dark makeup." Naomi André, Karen M. Bryan, and Eric Saylor, eds., *Blackness in Opera* (Urbana: University of Illinois Press, 2012), 3.

8. The first performer portraying Otello *without* blacking up at the Metropolitan Opera House was José Cura (an Argentinian) in 2013. Michael Cooper, "An 'Otello' Without Blackface Highlights an Enduring Tradition in Opera," *New York Times*, September 17, 2015, accessed March 2, 2022, https://www.nyti mes.com/2015/09/20/arts/music/an-otello-without-the-blackface-nods-to-mode rn-tastes.html

9. Cooper, "An 'Otello' without Blackface Highlights an Enduring Tradition in Opera."

10. Olin Downes, "'Emperor Jones' Triumphs as Opera," *New York Times*, January 8, 1933, 1 and 26, at 26. Louis Gruenberg M Clippings File, Billy Rose Theatre Division, New York Public Library for the Performing Arts.

11. R. Vincent Ottley, "Are You Listenin'?," *New York Amsterdam News*, February 1, 1933, 16.

12. The Metropolitan Opera's world premiere of *The Emperor Jones* was broadcast on January 7, 1933; this production included debuts for Hemsley Winfield and set designer Jo Mielziner. See more at "World Premiere (The Emperor Jones)," Metropolitan Opera Online Archives, accessed March 2, 2022.

http://archives.metoperafamily.org/archives/scripts/cgiip.exe/WService=BibSp
eed/fullcit.w?xCID=112640&limit=500&xBranch=ALL&xsdate=&xedate=&thet
erm=&x=0&xhomepath=&xhome=

13. Downes, "'Emperor Jones' Triumphs as Opera," 26. See also Louis Gruenberg, *The Emperor Jones; Kaiser Jones Opera in Two Acts, a Prologue, an Interlude
and Six Scenes (after Eugene O'Neill's Play)*, Op. 36 (New York: Cos Cob Press,
1932).

14. See chapters one and seven in Savran, *Highbrow/Lowdown*.

15. David Metzer, "'A Wall of Darkness Dividing the World': Blackness and
Whiteness in Louis Gruenberg's *The Emperor Jones*," *Cambridge Opera Journal* 7,
no. 1 (1995): 55–72, at 57.

16. André et al., *Blackness in Opera*, 2.

17. Andrew Farkas, ed., *Lawrence Tibbett: Singing Actor* (Milwaukee: Hal
Leonard Corporation, 1989), 1.

18. "O'Neill into Opera," *Time Magazine*, January 16, 1933, 20. See also Leonard Liebling, "'Emperor Jones,' New American Opera Given Its Premier[e] Performance at Metropolitan," *Musical Courier*, January 14, 1933, 13.

19. Downes, "'Emperor Jones' Triumphs as Opera," 26.

20. "O'Neill into Opera," 20.

21. Tibbett qtd. in Farkas, *Lawrence Tibbett*, 78.

22. "The Negro in Opera," *New York Amsterdam News*, July 26, 1933, 6.

23. Manning, *Modern Dance, Negro Dance*, 64.

24. Harry Keelan, "The Emperor Jones," *Opportunity* 11, no. 2 (February
1933): 45, and 58; at 45.

25. Ottley, "Are You Listenin'?," 16.

26. Paul Jackson, *Sunday Afternoons at the Old Met: The Metropolitan Opera
Broadcasts, 1931–1950* (Portland: Amadeus Press, 1992), 49.

27. Gruenberg, *The Emperor Jones*, 172.

28. John O. Perpener III, *African-American Concert Dance: The Harlem Renaissance and Beyond* (Urbana: University of Illinois Press, 2001), 50. See also appen-
dix B in Ranald, *Eugene O'Neill Companion*. Ranald credits both Gruenberg and
de Jaffa for the libretto but adds that the "printed libretto [was] compiled, *but
not written*, by Kathleen de Jaffa" (italics original, 745). Ranald also notes that
the libretto was "prepared with the help of Dr. Irma Gruenberg" 746.

29. Olin Downes, "Gruenberg's 'Jones' in Premiere," *New York Times*, January 1, 1933, X6. Louis Gruenberg M Clippings File, Billy Rose Theatre Division,
New York Public Library for the Performing Arts.

30. Ottley, "Are You Listenin'?," 16.

31. Upset by his name being left off the playbill, O'Neill wrote to his lawyer
Harry Weinberger: "in keeping my name off the Metropolitan program Gruenberg was guilty of a breach of contract with me." O'Neill also warned, "and if
he doesn't lay off his stupid nonsense [I] will try to stop any further productions of the opera anywhere." Eugene O'Neill, Handwritten letter to Harry

Weinberger, June 4, 1933. Folder: Letters, Weinberger, 1932–37. Accession Number: WEH330604. Eugene O'Neill Foundation Library, Tao House, Danville, California.

32. Eugene O'Neill, Handwritten Letter to Harry Weinberger, July 9, 1933. Folder: Letters, Weinberger, 1932–37. Accession Number: WEH32330709. Eugene O'Neill Foundation Library, Tao House, Danville, California.

33. Carlotta Monterey O'Neill, Diary, Friday, Mary 21, 1937. Copy at the Eugene O'Neill Foundation Library, Tao House, Danville, California.

34. Nelson D. Neal, "Hemsley Winfield: First Black Modern Dancer," *Afro-Americans in New York Life and History* 36, no. 2 (2012): 66–85. See also Neal, *Hemsley Winfield: The Forgotten Pioneer of Modern Dance, an Annotated Bibliography* (Scotts Valley, CA: CreateSpace Independent Publishing Platform, 2016); Jessie Carney Smith, *Black Firsts: 4,000 Ground-Breaking and Pioneering Historical Events* (Canton, MI: Visible Ink Press, 2012); and Neal and Diane Harrison, "Hemsley Winfield: First African American Modern Dancer Contracted by the Metropolitan Opera," *Afro–Americans in New York Life and History* 40, no. 1 (2018): 137–51.

35. Horalde R. Stovall, "*The Emperor Jones* Hailed at the Metropolitan Opera," *New York Amsterdam News*, January 11, 1933, 8.

36. "Opera Will Get Emperor Jones Early in Year," *Chicago Defender*, January 7, 1933, 4.

37. Bruce Gulden, "Louis Gruenberg's Opera 'The Emperor Jones,'" *Dance Culture* (March 1933): 12. Louis Gruenberg M Clippings File, Billy Rose Theatre Division, New York Public Library for the Performing Arts.

38. Keelan, "The Emperor Jones," 58.

39. Perpener, *African-American Concert Dance*, 51.

40. Mary F. Watkins, "With the Dancers," *New York Herald Tribune*, January 15, 1933. Hemsley Winfield Clipping File, Billy Rose Theatre Division, New York Public Library for the Performing Arts.

41. Keelan, "The Emperor Jones," 45.

42. Keelan, "The Emperor Jones," 45.

43. Since the Metropolitan Opera House production of *The Emperor Jones* did not list the names of the Black chorus members and dancers, I relied on Stovall's review in the *New York Amsterdam News*. Stovall, "The 'Emperor Jones' Hailed," 8.

44. Keelan, "The Emperor Jones," 58.

45. Kathleen de Jaffa, *The Emperor Jones: Opera in Two Acts (after Eugene O'Neill's Play)* (New York: Fred Rullman, 1932), 7.

46. Rebecca Gauss observes that there was just one "virtually unseen chorus," a conclusion based likely on a textual, rather than a performance, analysis, since there were two choruses at the Metropolitan production. See Rebecca B. Gauss, "O'Neill, Gruenberg, and *The Emperor Jones*," *Eugene O'Neill Review* 18 (1994): 38–44, at 40.

47. Perpener, *African-American Concert Dance*, 51.

48. Gulden, "Louis Gruenberg's Opera 'The Emperor Jones,'" 12.

49. Downes, "Emperor Jones Triumphs," 26.

50. Downes, "Emperor Jones Triumphs," 26.

51. Winfield's dancers were called the "Hemsley Winfield Art and Dance Group" by Metropolitan Opera's assistant manager Edward Ziegler. Handwritten Letter on March 25, 1934 from Edie [Edward] Ziegler, Asst. Manager, to Edward Ellsworth Hipsher. Folder: Clippings File, *The Emperor Jones*. Metropolitan Opera Archives, New York City.

52. Gulden, "Louis Gruenberg's Opera 'The Emperor Jones,'" 12. In his production notes, set designer Jo Mielziner writes about "Voo Doo witch doctors" in the plural, but this may have been one idea that was ultimately cut. "The Emperor Jones: Notes on Production," August 30, 1932. Folder: Edward Ziegler Correspondence, 1932–1933. Metropolitan Opera Archives, New York City.

53. Watkins, "With the Dancers."

54. "Ledger Sheet for Hemsley Winfield & Troupe," 203. Metropolitan Opera Archives, New York City. Winfield received $200 for the first performance of *The Emperor Jones* on January 9, 1933 at the Metropolitan Opera House and $240 for out-of-town performances in Philadelphia and Baltimore. For performances on and after January 13, he received $200 per performance at the Metropolitan Opera House and $250 for out-of-town performances, according to ledger sheets (although a letter states that Winfield should have received $240 for the Met and $280 for out-of-town productions). Letter c/o Miss Barbara Williams, 115 W. 133rd Street, no date (likely January 1933). *The Emperor Jones* Clippings File, Metropolitan Opera Archives, New York City. I suspect the extra out-of-town stipend was because Winfield would have had to stay in separate housing, given segregation. Winfield was moreover paid $1 per day of rehearsal and $5 for being the director of the company. The dance company was paid $38 for each performance.

55. Metropolitan Opera star Lawrence Tibbett was paid nearly than twice as much as Hemsley Winfield, at $562.50 per performance. Email from John Pennino, Metropolitan Opera Archives, June 29, 2016. The matinee premiere on January 7, 1933 grossed $12,016.55. Total receipts for ten performances of *The Emperor Jones* in 1933 (January through March) were $1,165,996.05. An additional five performances in 1934, three of which were in Hartford or Boston and all without Winfield, yielded $42,959. The lower receipts are likely due to performing at venues other than the Met, where houses may have been smaller and profits split. "Ledger Sheet for *The Emperor Jones*," 177. Metropolitan Opera Archives, New York. Gruenberg was paid $500 for writing the opera, plus royalties. Edward Ziegler, Letter to Louis Gruenberg June 7, 1933. Edward Ziegler Correspondence File (F–G), 1932–1933. Metropolitan Opera Archives, New York City.

56. In the role of Smithers, Marek Windheim made only $150 per week in

1933 and $218.75 in 1934. Paid even less was Pearl Besuner in the role of Native Woman at $81 per week in 1933 (and then, puzzlingly, only $75.00 in 1934—it is unclear why her pay dropped). Email with John Pennino, Metropolitan Opera Archives on June 29, 2016.

57. Maude Roberts George, "'Emperor Jones' as Opera Wins Ovation in Chicago," *Chicago Defender*, May 6, 1933, 11.

58. Manning, *Modern Dance, Negro Dance*, 9.

59. "Winfield Dead at 27; 'Emperor Jones' Dancer," *New York Herald Tribune*, January 16, 1934, 15; Winfield's last performance as the Congo Witch-Doctor was during a matinee on March 18, 1933. He was replaced in 1934 with a member of his company, Leonardo Barres. See Letter from Edward Ziegler, assistant manager, to Edward Ellsworth Hispher on March 25, 1934. Metropolitan Opera Archives, New York City. Some newspapers incorrectly reported that Winfield died at the age of twenty-seven, but others, such as the *New York Times*, said Winfield was twenty-six, which is correct. Scholars Nelson D. Neal and John Perpener verify that Hemsley was twenty-six years (and nine months) old when he died. "Hemsley Winfield: Negro Actor Appeared in Opera 'The Emperor Jones'," *New York Times*, January 16, 1934, 21.

60. "Winfield Dead at 27," 15.

61. V. E. Johns, "Hemsley Winfield" [Obituary], *New York Age*, January 27, 1933, 6.

62. "The Negro in Opera," 6.

63. Unidentified clipping from the *Residentie-Bode* (The Hague), Jules Bledsoe's scrapbook, 118. Jules Bledsoe Papers, Accession #2086, Box 23: Oversized Scrapbook, 1934–43, The Texas Collection, Baylor University.

64. Jules Bledsoe, Scrapbook. Jules Bledsoe Papers, Accession #2086, Box 23: Oversized Scrapbook, 1934–43, The Texas Collection, Baylor University.

65. Somerville, *Queering the Color Line*, 11.

66. Bledsoe's and Huygens's relationship was often acknowledged as friendship. For example, Geary calls Freddy "his manager and closest friend." See Lynnette G. Geary, "Jules Bledsoe: The Original 'Ol' Man River,'" *The Black Perspective in Music* 17, nos. 1–2 (1989): 27–54, at 47. In his biography of Bledsoe, Charles P. Rhambo (Bledsoe's cousin) hints at Freddy's role as Jules's partner when he describes their shared home in West Hollywood. See Rhambo, *The Life of Jules Bledsoe* (Lima, OH: Fairway Press, 1989). Letters with family members give a more complex picture.

67. "Julius Bledsoe in First Straight Acting Part at the Provincetown," *New York Amsterdam News*, December 29, 1926, 11.

68. "'The Emperor Jones' Did Not Go at the Lincoln," *New York Amsterdam News*, August 31, 1927, 13.

69. See Ethel Pitts Walker, "Krigwa, a Theatre By, For, and About Black People," *Theatre Journal* 40, no. 3 (1988): 347–56.

70. "'The Emperor Jones' Did Not Go at the Lincoln," 13. See also "Ethio-

pian Art Advances to Nine Plays in Season," *New York Amsterdam News*, June 15, 1927, 14.

71. Mitchell, *Black Drama*, 83–84.

72. Langston Hughes, *The Big Sea: An Autobiography* (New York: Alfred Knopf, 1940), 258.

73. Hughes, *The Big Sea*, 258–59.

74. "Theatres and Performers—Big and Little," *New York Amsterdam News*, April 24, 1929, 13.

75. Hughes, *The Big Sea*, 258–59.

76. According to one review, Bledsoe appeared in a dramatic version of *The Emperor Jones* that lasted for eight weeks "before it was set to music by Louis Gruenberg for the Metropolitan Opera Company." I have not been able to locate where Bledsoe performed this role, but it is possible he toured the South with it. See "'The Emperor Jones' with Bledsoe Is Next N.Y. Opera," *Chicago Defender*, July 7, 1934, 7; and "Darktown Scandals to Play Columbia: Julius Bledsoe to Tour South in Emperor Jones," *Pittsburgh Courier*, July 16, 1927, A3. Another newspaper article suggests that Bledsoe toured the Pacific coast with *The Emperor Jones* before performing in Harlem. See "Jack Goldberg, with Six Shows in Rehearsal, Gets Ready for Busy Fall and Winter Season," *Pittsburgh Courier*, July 30, 1927, A2.

77. Jules Bledsoe, "Has the Negro a Place in the Theatre?," *Opportunity* 6 (July 1928): 215.

78. Bledsoe, "Has the Negro a Place in the Theatre?," 215.

79. Perpener mistakenly says O'Neill gave permission to Gruenberg to adapt the score in 1931, but according to O'Neill's own letter, he did so in March 1930. See Perpener, *African-American Concert Dance*, 49.

80. O'Neill, *Selected Letters of Eugene O'Neill*, 371.

81. O'Neill, *Selected Letters of Eugene O'Neill*, 371.

82. "N.Y. Raves over Bledsoe's Debut," *Chicago Defender*, July 21, 1934, 9.

83. Jules Bledsoe, Travel diary. Jules Bledsoe Papers, Accession #2086, Box 6, Folder 1 (Literary Journals), The Texas Collection, Baylor University. Bledsoe's French title for his adaptation of the opera may have been inspired by the 1923 Paris production.

84. One obituary noted that Bledsoe spoke seven languages. See "Negro Who Started Old Man River Buried on Brazos," *Dallas Morning News*, July 22, 1943, 5.

85. Bledsoe, Travel diary. Jules Bledsoe Papers, Accession #2086, Box 6, Folder 1 (Literary Journals), The Texas Collection, Baylor University.

86. Jules Bledsoe Papers, Box 4: "Sheet Music," SCM 86–16, Schomburg Center for Research in Black Culture, New York Public Library. Some items from the scenario, such as the inclusion of "Swing Low Sweet Chariot" and the invocation to the Hoodoo God, were not found in the fragments of the score at the Schomburg. Many thanks to Michael Dwinell for his assistance with reading and transcribing the score.

87. Jules Bledsoe, "The Emperor Jones," 8. Jules Bledsoe Papers, 1931–1939. Sc MG 255 BOX 4, Schomburg Center for Research in Black Culture, New York Public Library.

88. Bledsoe, "The Emperor Jones," 13.

89. O'Neill, *The Emperor Jones*, 1034.

90. Bledsoe, "The Emperor Jones," 13–14.

91. Bledsoe, "The Emperor Jones," unnumbered page.

92. Bledsoe, "The Emperor Jones," 22–23.

93. Bledsoe, "The Emperor Jones," unnumbered page.

94. Bledsoe, "The Emperor Jones," 22–23.

95. Jules Bledsoe, Letter to Nace [Naomi] Cobb, November 9, 1935. Jules Bledsoe Papers, Accession #2086, Box 1, Folder 5: Correspondence 1935–36, The Texas Collection, Baylor University.

96. Quote from Amsterdam's *Algemeen Handelsblad*. During 1933 and 1934, Bledsoe sang classical repertoire in Amsterdam, Rotterdam, Haarlem, and The Hague. Beyond Holland, he also performed in Vienna, Milan, Brussels, London, and Paris. Bledsoe's scrapbook. Jules Bledsoe Papers, Accession #2086, Box 23: Oversized Scrapbook, 1934–43, The Texas Collection, Baylor University.

97. Jules Bledsoe, Letter to Nace [Naomi] Cobb, February 4, 1934. Jules Bledsoe Papers, Accession #2086, Box 1, Folder 3, Correspondence 1934, The Texas Collection, Baylor University.

98. "Holland Goes Drama Dizzy as Bledsoe Plays 'Emperor," *Chicago Defender*, May 19, 1934, 9.

99. The Dutch review was reprinted in the *Chicago Defender*. See "Holland Goes Drama Dizzy," 9.

100. "Amsterdam Won by 'Emperor Jones,'" *New York Herald* (Paris edition), March 12, 1934. Jules Bledsoe Papers, Accession #2086, Box 23: Oversized Scrapbook, 1934–43, The Texas Collection, Baylor University.

101. Jules Bledsoe to Nace [Naomi] Cobb, March 22, 1934. Jules Bledsoe Papers, Accession #2086, Box 1, Folder 3: Correspondence 1934, The Texas Collection, Baylor University. See also Rhambo, *Life of Jules Bledsoe*, 24.

102. "Holland Goes Drama Dizzy," 9.

103. Publicity sheet with translated quotes from several Dutch reviews, Bledsoe scrapbook, 117. Jules Bledsoe Papers, Accession #2086, Box 23: Oversized Scrapbook, 1934–43, The Texas Collection, Baylor University.

104. Publicity sheet with translated quotes from several Dutch reviews, Bledsoe scrapbook, 117.

105. Bledsoe's copy of Gruenberg's *The Emperor Jones* score, 117. Jules Bledsoe Papers, Accession #2086, Box 16, Folder 5: Music--Opera Books "The Emperor Jones" (1932), The Texas Collection, Baylor University.

106. "Holland Goes Drama Dizzy," 9.

107. "Jules Bledsoe on Tour of Holland Singing 'The Emperor Jones,'" *New York Age*, April 14, 1934, 5.

108. "N.Y. Raves over Bledsoe's Debut in Opera," 9.

109. "N.Y. Raves over Bledsoe's Debut in Opera," 9.

110. On January 1, 1934, an operatic adaptation of *The Emperor Jones* was revived with Lawrence Tibbett in the lead role in blackface (with other cast changes), for five performances. Winfield no longer danced the role as the Congo Witch-Doctor.

111. "'The Emperor Jones' with Bledsoe Is Next N.Y. Opera," 7. As early as May 1934 the Black press reported on plans for a "colored grand opera in June" with "prominent Negro singers all lined up for the season with Jules Bledsoe in 'The Emperor Jones' heading the list." See "On the Air," *Washington Tribune*, May 24, 1934, 19.

112. The Aeolian Opera Association's first repertoire was organized by Peter Creatore, son of the famous bandleader. See "Bledsoe Gets an Important Role in Play," *Chicago Defender*, June 30, 1934, 8; and "Harlem's Finest Singers in Opera," *Chicago Defender*, July 7, 1934, 6.

113. "Bledsoe Gets an Important Role in Play," 8.

114. "Negro Opera Plans Debut," *New York Amsterdam News*, June 30, 1934, 17. By my count, there are twenty-eight instances of "n——r" in the libretto.

115. "'The Emperor Jones' with Bledsoe Is Next N.Y. Opera," 7; and "Bledsoe Will Sing Tuesday," *New York Amsterdam News*, July 7, 1934, 1.

116. "'The Emperor Jones' with Bledsoe Is Next N.Y. Opera," 7.

117. "Negro Opera Plans Debut," 17.

118. "N.Y. Raves over Bledsoe's Debut in Opera," 9.

119. "N.Y. Raves over Bledsoe's Debut in Opera," 9.

120. "Emperor Jones with Negro Cast," *New York Times*, July 11, 1934, 20.

121. The Aeolian Opera Association was not the first Black opera company in the U.S. The first was the Drury Grand Opera Company, which was founded in 1889 and ran sporadically for fifty years. See Robin Elliot, "Blacks and Blackface at the Opera," in *Opera in a Multicultural World: Coloniality, Culture, Performance*, ed. Mary Ingraham, Joseph So, and Roy Moodley (London: Taylor & Friends, 2015), 34–49, at 39–40.

122. "Bledsoe Sings in N.Y. Opera Before Throng," *Chicago Defender*, July 14, 1934, 9.

123. "Bledsoe Sings in N.Y. Opera Before Throng." See also "Cosmopolitan Opera Presents Gruenberg's 'Emperor Jones,'" December 8, 1934. Otherwise unidentified clipping, Louis Gruenberg M Clippings File, Billy Rose Theatre Division, New York Public Library for the Performing Arts. See also "'Emperor Jones' Bill at Hippodrome Tonight," *New York World-Telegram*, November 24, 1934, 22; and "Cosmopolitan Opera Announces New Bill," *New York Amsterdam News*, November 24, 1934, 4.

124. Display Ad for *The Emperor Jones*, *New York Amsterdam News*, November 24, 1934, 10.

125. Frances Moss Mann, "Music News," *New York Amsterdam News*, December 1, 1934, 4.

126. Robert Darden, interview, "Treasures of the Texas Collection: Jules Bledsoe," script for KWBU-FM and Texas NPR Stations, January 9, 2010, 1.

127. Bledsoe arranged his own spirituals and composed *African Suite,* a set of four songs for voice and orchestra. He also composed an opera based on *Uncle Tom's Cabin,* called *Bondage* (dated 1939; neither of these scores has been published). See Jules Bledsoe Papers, Accession #2086, Box 18 OVR, Folders 9 and 10, The Texas Collection, Baylor University.

128. "The Negro in Opera," *New York Amsterdam News,* July 26, 1933, 6.

129. "The Negro in Opera," 6. Caterina Jarboro was another pioneering Black performer in opera, appearing in the title role of New York Hippodrome's production of *Aida* in 1933.

130. "Colored Artists Play Big Part in Workers' Dance in New York," *Washington Tribune,* October 12, 1933.

131. "The Late Hemsley Winfield," *Harlem Heights Daily Citizen,* January 19, 1934, 4.

CHAPTER 5

An earlier version of this chapter appeared as "Black to Ireland: Circum-Atlantic Double Exposure and Racialized Jump Cuts in *The Emperor Jones,*" *MELUS* 44, no. 4 (Winter 2019): 147–76. It has been revised and expanded here.

1. As Kerstin Fest observes, "*Mädchen in Uniform* has repeatedly been hailed as a lesbian classic if not '*the* lesbian German movie'." See Fest, "Yesterday and/or Today: Time, History and Desire in Christa Winsloe's *Mädchen in Uniform,*" *German Life and Letters* 65, no. 4 (October 2012): 457–71. See also B. Ruby Rich, "From Repressive Tolerance to Erotic Liberation: *Maedchen in Uniform,*" *Gender and German Cinema: Feminist Interventions,* ed. Sandra Frieden et al., vol. 2 (Oxford: Berg, 1993), 61–96.

2. Norman Kagan, "The Return of *The Emperor Jones,*" *Negro History Bulletin* 34, no. 7 (1971): 160–66, at 161.

3. Scott MacQueen, "The Rise and Fall of *The Emperor Jones,* 1933," *American Cinematographer* 71, no. 2 (1990): 34–40, at 34.

4. Kevin Whelan, "The Green Atlantic: Radical Reciprocities between Ireland and America in the Long Eighteenth Century," in *A New Imperial History: Culture, Identity, and Modernity in Britain and the Empire, 1660–1840,* ed. Kathleen Wilson (Cambridge: Cambridge University Press, 2004), 216. See also Brian Dooley's *Black and Green: The Fight for Civil Rights in Northern Ireland and Black America* (London: Pluto Press, 1998); Nini Rodgers's *Ireland, Slavery, and Anti-Slavery: 1612–1865* (London: Palgrave Macmillan, 2007); Maria McGarrity's *Washed by the Gulf Stream: The Historic and Geographic Relation of Irish and Caribbean Literature* (Newark: University of Delaware Press, 2008); John Brannigan's *Race in Modern Irish Literature* (Edinburgh: Edinburgh University Press, 2009); George Bornstein's *The Colors of Zion: Blacks, Jews, and Irish from 1845 to 1945*

(Cambridge, MA: Harvard University Press, 2011); and Sinéad Moynihan's *Other People's Diasporas: Negotiating Race in Contemporary and Irish-American Culture* (Syracuse: Syracuse University Press, 2013).

5. Michael Boyce Gillespie, *Film Blackness: American Cinema and the Idea of Black Film* (Durham, NC: Duke University Press, 2016), 2.

6. Peter D. O'Neill and David Lloyd, introduction and eds., *The Black and Green Atlantic: Cross-Currents of the African and Irish Diaspora* (New York: Palgrave, 2009), xv–xx, at xvi.

7. Richard Rankin Russell, "The Black and Green Atlantic: Violence, History, and Memory in Natasha Trethewey's 'South' and Seamus Heaney's 'North,'" *Southern Literary Journal* 46, no. 2 (2014): 155–72, at 157.

8. Gilroy, *Black Atlantic*, 15.

9. Joseph Roach, *Cities of the Dead: Circum-Atlantic Performance* (New York: Columbia University Press, 1996), 4.

10. O'Neill was "working out a scheme for [the] filming" of *The Emperor Jones* as early as 1922. Eugene O'Neill, Letter to Harry Weinberger, January 26, 1922, Folder: Letters-Harry Weinberger, 1922–28. Accession Number WEH220126. Eugene O'Neill Foundation Archive, Tao House, Danville, California.

11. Another important member of *The Emperor Jones* production team who had investments in Black performance culture was screenwriter DuBose Heyward. A white, Southern novelist and playwright, Heyward had portrayed Black Americans in previous works. See conclusion for more information.

12. Throughout this essay, I am referencing the 2002 restored version of *The Emperor Jones* by the Library of Congress (originally released in 1933), unless otherwise noted.

13. In coining the phrase, the "Irish triumvirate," I am referencing the term "triumvirate," which was commonly used to describe the collaborations between Eugene O'Neill, Kenneth Macgowan, and Robert Edmond Jones after they left the Provincetown Players and formed the Experimental Theatre in 1924.

14. Ignatiev, *How the Irish Became White*, 2.

15. Ignatiev, *How the Irish Became White*, 3.

16. Roediger, *Working Toward Whiteness*, 7–8.

17. Ignatiev, *How the Irish Became White*, 3.

18. Monks, "'Genuine Negroes and Real Bloodhounds,'" 545.

19. O'Neill, qtd. in Robert M. Dowling, *Eugene O'Neill: A Life in Four Acts* (New Haven: Yale University Press, 2014), 91.

20. Declan Kiberd, "Losing Ireland, Inventing America: O'Neill and After," *Eugene O'Neill Review* 39, no. 1 (2018): 1–16, at 14.

21. O'Neill, *Selected Letters*, 475.

22. Dowling, *Eugene O'Neill*, 455.

23. Monks, "'Genuine Negroes and Real Bloodhounds,'" 549.

24. Murphy, qtd. in MacQueen, "Rise and Fall of *The Emperor Jones*," 39.

25. Creighton Peet, "The Emperor Jones Comes to the Screen," 1933, 40. Otherwise unidentified clipping, Folder: *T-CLP *The Emperor Jones* (Motion picture), Billy Rose Theatre Division, New York Public Library for the Performing Arts.

26. Susan Delson, *Dudley Murphy, Hollywood Wild Card* (Minneapolis: University of Minnesota Press, 2006), 130.

27. Murphy, qtd. in Delson, *Dudley Murphy, Hollywood Wild Card*, 125.

28. Garrett Eisler, "Backstory as Black Story: The Cinematic Reinvention of O'Neill's *The Emperor Jones*," *Eugene O'Neill Review* 32 (2010): 148–62, at 149.

29. For more about the significance of the Abbey Theatre on O'Neill, see Nelson O'Ceallaigh Ritschel, "Synge and the Irish Influence of the Abbey Theatre on Eugene O'Neill," *Eugene O'Neill Review* 29 (2007): 129–50; and Edward L. Shaughnessy's *Eugene O'Neill in Ireland: The Critical Reception* (Westport, CT: Greenwood, 1988).

30. "Paul Robeson in Emperor Jones," Souvenir Program, 1933. Clipping File, Series II: Personal/Corporate Names, Box 149, Robeson, Paul, 1922–1925, James Weldon Johnson Memorial Collection in the Yale Collection of American Literature, Beinecke Rare Book and Manuscript Library.

31. David Bordwell, *On the History of Film Style* (Cambridge, MA: Harvard University Press, 1997), 39.

32. William Lewin and Max J. Herzberg, "*The Emperor Jones* with a Study Guide for the Screen Version of the Play" (New York: Appleton-Century-Crofts, 1934), 56, 61.

33. Robinson, *Forgeries of Memory and Meaning*, 347.

34. Michael Malouf, *Transatlantic Solidarities: Irish Nationalism and Caribbean Poetics* (Charlottesville: University of Virginia Press, 2009), 10.

35. Taylor, *The Archive and the Repertoire*, 6.

36. Bazin, qtd. in Bert Cardullo, "André Bazin on Film Technique: Two Seminal Essays," *Film Criticism* 25, no. 2 (2000): 40–62, at 43.

37. Bazin, qtd. in Cardullo, "André Bazin on Film Technique," 44.

38. Bazin, qtd. in Cardullo, "André Bazin on Film Technique," 41.

39. The scenes in the forest, which included hallucination and double exposure scenes, were shot with Kodak tint #10, azure blue. The Library of Congress restored the tinting. See Jennie Saxena, "Preserving African-American Cinema: The Case of *The Emperor Jones* (1933)," contributions by Ken Weissman and James Cozart, *Moving Image* 3, no. 1 (2003): 42–58, at 55.

40. Toni Morrison, *Beloved* (New York: Alfred Knopf, 1987), 36.

41. Richard Watts Jr., "Review of *The Emperor Jones*," *New York Herald Tribune*, September 24, 1933. Folder: *T-CLP *The Emperor Jones* (Motion picture), Billy Rose Theatre Division, New York Public Library for the Performing Arts.

42. "New Films in London," *London Times*, March 19, 1934. Folder: *T-CLP *The Emperor Jones* (Motion picture), Billy Rose Theatre Division, New York Public Library for the Performing Arts.

43. Thornton Delehanty, "The New Film: Paul Robeson in the Screen Ver-

sion of 'The Emperor Jones' at the Rivoli," *New York Evening Post,* September 20, 1933. Folder: *T-CLP *The Emperor Jones* (Motion picture), Billy Rose Theatre Division, New York Public Library for the Performing Arts.

44. David Bordwell, "Jump Cuts and Blind Spots," *Wide Angle* 6, no. 1 (1984): 4–11, at 4.

45. Bordwell, "Jump Cuts and Blind Spots," 5.

46. Robinson, *Forgeries,* 349–50.

47. The quarry scene also anticipates the role Robeson would play in the 1940 musical *John Henry.* In the original screenplay of *The Emperor Jones,* there was supposed to be a reprise of the "John Henry" song in Scene 185 (when Jones first enters the forest), which was cut. Library of Congress Restoration Script, 85.

48. Ed Guerro, "Black Stars in Exile: Paul Robeson, O. J. Simpson, and Othello," in *Paul Robeson: Artist and Citizen,* ed. Jeffrey C. Stewart (New Brunswick, NJ: Rutgers University Press, 1988): 275–90, at 282 and 280. For more about Robeson's physicality and debates about the Black male performers and fetishism, see Stewart, "Black Body" ; Richard Dyer, *Heavenly Bodies: Film Stars and Society* (New York: St. Martin's, 1986); Stephens, *Black Empire*; and Callens, "'Black Is White, I Yells It out Louder 'n Deir Loudest.'"

49. Krimsky, qtd. in MacQueen, "Rise and Fall of *The Emperor Jones,*" 39. According to restoration notes, the sound of Jones hitting the prison guard on the head with the shovel was included on the studio print, though the visual footage was lost. Library of Congress Restoration Script, 37.

50. DuBose Heyward, "*The Emperor Jones* (shooting script)," 87. New York State Motion Picture Division License Application, Series #A1418, Case File #26195, Box 249, 1933. New York State Archives, Albany, New York.

51. Heyward, "*The Emperor Jones* (shooting script)," 89.

52. Saxena, "Preserving African-American Cinema," 47.

53. Jennie Dennis [Saxena] to Ken Weissman, "Emperor Jones Missing Scenes," January 31, 2001. From James Cozart's papers at Library of Congress (not catalogued).

54. Producer John Krimsky recounted that he and his coproducer Gifford Cochran "were determined to sign Paul Robeson, the most gifted actor and singer of the time" for the film version of *The Emperor Jones.* John Krimsky, "The Emperor Jones—Robeson and O'Neill on Film," *Connecticut Review* 7, no. 2 (1974): 94–99, at 94.

55. Richard Koszarski, *Hollywood on the Hudson: Film and Television in New York from Griffith to Sarnoff* (New Brunswick, NJ: Rutgers University Press, 2008), 529n38.

56. MacQueen, "Rise and Fall of *The Emperor Jones,*" 40.

57. Heyward, "The Emperor Jones (shooting script)," 91. The censorship of the slave auction scene is underscored by the fact that Heyward concocted *another* moment of slavery into his screenplay: Smithers buys Jones after Jones

lands on the island. This fabricated portion of the film occurs before O'Neill's text begins; it was also not cut.

58. Heyward, "The Emperor Jones (shooting script)," 91.

59. Anna Siomopoulos, "The 'Eighth o' Style': Black Nationalism, the New Deal, and *The Emperor Jones*," *Arizona Quarterly* 58, no. 3 (2002): 57–81, at 60.

60. "*Emperor Jones* Premiere," *The Crisis* 40, no. 10 (October 1933): 232–33, at 232.

61. Du Bois, *Souls of Black Folk*, 3.

62. "*Emperor Jones* Premiere," 232.

63. For more about how the film was screened for different audiences, see Eberhard Alsen, "Racism and the Film Version of Eugene O'Neill's *The Emperor Jones*," *CLA Journal* 49, no. 4 (2006): 406–22. Delson (*Dudley Murphy*), Koszarki (*Hollywood on the Hudson*), and MacQueen ("Rise and Fall of *The Emperor Jones*") also offer good summaries of the film's reception.

64. Delson, *Dudley Murphy, Hollywood Wild Card*, 141.

65. "Emperor Jones Has Premier[e] Tonight," *New York Sun*, September 19, 1933. Folder: *T-CLP *The Emperor Jones* (Motion picture), Billy Rose Theatre Division, New York Public Library for the Performing Arts.

66. "Harlem Also Gets Peek at Robeson," *Chicago Defender*, October 7, 1933, 5.

67. "'Emperor Jones' as Film Better Than Stage Play," *Chicago Defender*, September 30, 1933, 5.

68. "He's the Emperor," *New York Amsterdam News*, July 19, 1933, 1.

69. "'The Emperor' Is Held Over," *New York Amsterdam News*, September 27, 1933, 7.

70. "'The Emperor' Is Held Over," 7.

71. Saxena, "Preserving African-American Cinema," 47–48.

72. T. B. Poston, "Harlem Dislikes 'N——r' in 'Emperor Jones' but Flocks to See Picture at Uptown House," *New York Amsterdam News*, September 27, 1933, 9.

73. Cozart observes, "the premiere version of this film is probably lost." James Cozart, Memorandum, "Library of Congress QC Inspection Memo," undated but likely 2001. From Cozart's papers, shared with me by George Willeman from the Library of Congress Nitrate Vault. The restoration was a challenging process for the Library of Congress to piece together, involving footage from a variety of mediums (master prints, nitrate prints, 16 mm and 35 mm footage, and Vitaphone discs); lost reels (initially all of reel 1, parts of reel 7, and all of reel 8 were missing); and multiple geographical regions (the United States, United Kingdom, Canada, and Russia).

74. Koszarski, *Hollywood on the Hudson*, 529n39.

75. Saxena, "Preserving African-American Cinema," 47.

76. Jeffrey C. Stewart, audio commentary. *The Emperor Jones. Paul Robeson: Portraits of the Artist* (Criterion Collection, 2007): 44:19–37.

77. MacQueen, "Rise and Fall of *The Emperor Jones*," 39.

78. Alsen, "Racism and the Film Version of *The Emperor Jones*," 406. See also Saxena, "Preserving African-American Cinema," 47.

79. Ellen Scott, "Regulating 'N— —r': Racial Offense, African American Activists, and the MPPDA, 1928–1961," *Film History* 26, no. 4 (2014): 1–31, at 4.

80. Review of *The Emperor Jones*, directed by Dudley Murphy, *Variety*, September 26, 1933, 15.

81. Review of *The Emperor Jones*, 15.

82. William G. Nunn, "Private Preview at the Roosevelt Is Well Received," *Pittsburgh Courier*, October 21, 1933, A6.

83. Poston, "Harlem Dislikes 'N— —r' in 'Emperor Jones'," 9.

84. "Take Insult out of Movies," *Chicago Defender*, October 7, 1933, 1.

85. "33 Insults Cut Out of Paul Robeson's Film," *Afro-American* (Baltimore), October 7, 1933, 1.

86. For more about how Gilpin revised *The Emperor Jones* during performance, see Krasner, "Whose Role Is It Anyway?"; and Gelb and Gelb, *O'Neill*.

87. Thanks to film historian Scott MacQueen from UCLA's Film & Television Archive and George Willeman, manager of the Nitrate Film Vault at the Library of Congress National Audio-Conservation Center, both of whom shared with me their valuable insights and materials. Scott MacQueen, email message to author, February 7, 2018. See also MacQueen, "The Rise and Fall of *The Emperor Jones*, 1933." Willeman noted that his colleague James Cozart (now deceased) used the Black-house version "cut for African-American audiences" (among others) in restoring the Library of Congress version. George Willeman, email message to author, February 12, 2018.

88. A shorter version of *The Emperor Jones* (72:41 minutes) can be found at the Library and Archives Canada, accession number 1974–0195, item number 18295. *The Emperor Jones*, directed by Dudley Murphy, distributed by United Artists September 29, 1933, Peerless Films Collection.

89. MacQueen, "The Rise and Fall of *The Emperor Jones*," 36–37. The shooting script does not identify the policeman as Irish, but MacQueen's interpretation of the cop as Irish supports my argument about the intersections between the Black and Green Atlantics.

90. Notes from the Library of Congress restoration plan for *The Emperor Jones* confirm that portions from the shovel scene (scene 82 of the shooting script) were lost. James Cozart from the Library of Congress team was able to restore footage of Robeson picking up the shovel, but could not locate Robeson striking the guard. Restoration Plan Memo (likely 2001), Library of Congress Nitrate Vault.

91. MacQueen, "Rise and Fall of *The Emperor Jones*," 37. This search posse scene described by MacQueen appeared in yet another version of the film and the footage is lost; it is not in the version restored by the Library of Congress, nor in the Black house version I am using here.

92. DuBose Heyward, *The Emperor Jones* (shooting script), scene 115, page 56.

93. Judith Butler builds her argument on Toni Morrison's 1993 Nobel Lecture in Literature, wherein Morrison writes: "Oppressive language does more than represent violence: it is violence" (16). Qtd. in Butler, *Excitable Speech: A Politics of the Performative* (New York: Routledge, 1997), 6.

94. Butler, *Excitable Speech*, 15.

95. The azure color is also described as "tranquilizing to the point of becoming depressing." Saxena, "Preserving African-American Cinema," 55.

96. James Cozart, Memorandum to Library of Congress Restoration Team. "WRS." May 30, 2001.

97. Nunn, "Private Preview at the Roosevelt Is Well Received," A6.

98. "33 Insults Cut," 1. My count of the shooting script (which was missing eight pages) shows Smithers saying "n——r" four times and Jones saying it twenty-five times. Heyward DuBose, "*The Emperor Jones* Shooting Script."

99. "Theatrically Speaking," *Washington Tribune*, October 5, 1933, 15.

100. Krimsky, "The Emperor Jones—Robeson and O'Neill on Film," 97.

101. "33 Insults Cut," 1.

102. "33 Insults Cut," 2.

103. "33 Insults Cut," 2.

104. Thomas Cripps, "Paul Robeson and Black Identity in American Movies," *Massachusetts Review* 11, no. 3 (1970): 468–85, at 477.

105. See "Hollywood Likes 'Emperor Jones,'" *Washington Tribune*, December 7, 1933, 14.

106. John Lowe, "Creating the Circum-Caribbean Imaginary: DuBose Heyward's and Paul Robeson's Revision of *The Emperor Jones*," *Philological Quarterly* 90, nos. 2–3 (2011): 311–33.

107. Robert Garland mistakenly calls the leader "Jean Christophe." Henri Christophe fought in the Haitian Revolution and in 1807 he was elected as president of the State of Haiti. The Haitian Revolution, led by ex-slave Toussaint Louverture, is seen as a defining moment of triumph over colonial rule and slavery. See Garland, "Praise for Paul Robeson," *New York World-Telegram*, June 30, 1933. Folder: *T-CLP *The Emperor Jones* (Motion picture), Billy Rose Theatre Division, New York Public Library for the Performing Arts.

108. "Brutus Jones in Astoria," *New York Times*, July 16, 1933, X2.

109. Heyward, qtd. in Dowling, *Eugene O'Neill: A Life in Four Acts*, 517n242.

110. Ruby Cohn, "Black Power on Stage: Emperor Jones and King Christophe," *Yale French Studies* 46 (1971): 41–47, at 41.

111. Other scenes were shot on Jones Beach, Long Island and in a rock quarry in New Rochelle, New York. MacQueen, "Rise and Fall of *The Emperor Jones*," 38.

112. "In the Jungles of Astoria, L. I.," *New York Herald Tribune*, July 2, 1933. Folder: *T-CLP *The Emperor Jones* (Motion picture), Billy Rose Theatre Division, New York Public Library for the Performing Arts.

113. Eileen Creelman, "Pictures and Players: Dudley Murphy in Midst of Directing 'Emperor Jones' at Astoria Studio," *New York Sun*, July 5, 1933, 30. Folder: *T-CLP *The Emperor Jones* (Motion picture), Billy Rose Theatre Division, New York Public Library for the Performing Arts.

114. Unidentified clipping from the *New York Sun*, September 20, 1933. Folder: *T-CLP *The Emperor Jones* (Motion picture), Billy Rose Theatre Division, New York Public Library for the Performing Arts.

115. John C. Mosher, "Jungle in Astoria," *New Yorker*, July 2, 1933, 10.

116. Garland, "Praise for Paul Robeson."

117. Unidentified clipping from the *New York Sun*, September 20, 1933.

118. Thornton Delehanty, "The New Film: Paul Robeson in the Screen Version of 'The Emperor Jones' at the Rivoli," *New York Evening Post*, September 20, 1933. Folder: *T-CLP *The Emperor Jones* (Motion picture), Billy Rose Theatre Division, New York Public Library for the Performing Arts.

119. Garland, "Praise for Paul Robeson."

120. "Emperor Jones at Roosevelt," *New York Amsterdam News*, September 20, 1933, 7.

121. "Brutus Jones in Astoria," X2.

122. Don Wythe, "What a Headache!," *Shadow Play*, October 1933, 38. Eugene O'Neill Papers. Box 52, Folder 1057, Series III. Writings, Plays, *The Emperor Jones*. Yale Collection of American Literature, Beinecke Rare Book and Manuscript Library.

123. Murphy, qtd. in Wythe, "What a Headache!," 58.

124. MacQueen, "Rise and Fall of *The Emperor Jones*," 38.

125. "Emperor Jones as Film Better," 5.

126. Siomopoulos, "The 'Eighth o' Style'," 76n9.

CONCLUSION

1. Mervin Rothstein, "Robert Falls and His *Desire* for Eugene O'Neill," *Playbill*, January 17, 2009, accessed November 22, 2021, https://www.playbill.com/article/robert-falls-and-his-desire-for-eugene-oneill-com-157078

2. The Goodman Theatre, "A Global Exploration: Eugene O'Neill in the 21st Century," 2009, accessed November 22, 2021, https://www.goodmantheatre.org/season/0809/a-global-exploration-eugene-oneill-in-the-21st-century/

3. See David Thompson, "Shuffling Roles: Alterations and Audiences in *Shuffle Along*," *Theatre Symposium: A Journal of the Southeastern Theatre Conference* 20 (2012): 97–108; and Krasner, *A Beautiful Pageant*, 263–67.

4. "Stephen Sondheim Takes Issue with Plan for Revamped 'Porgy and Bess,'" *New York Times*, August 10, 2011, accessed November 28, 2021, https://artsbeat.blogs.nytimes.com/2011/08/10/stephen-sondheim-takes-issue-with-plan-for-revamped-porgy-and-bess/

5. Laura Collins-Hughes, "Review: Emperor Jones, Fearsome and Fearful in a Roaring Revival," *New York Times*, March 24, 2017, accessed November 23, 2021, https://www.nytimes.com/2017/03/24/theater/review-emperor-jones-fearsome-and-fearful-in-a-roaring-revival.html?smid=url-share

6. Pete Hempstead, "Review: *The Emperor Jones*," *TheaterMania*, March 12, 2017, accessed November 23, 2021, https://www.theatermania.com/off-broadway/reviews/the-emperor-jones_80333.html

7. Tony Kushner, "The Genius of O'Neill," *American Theatre*, February 2, 2015. Reprinted from the December 18, 2003 *New York Times* Literary Supplement, accessed November 22, 2021, https://www.americantheatre.org/2015/02/02/the-genius-of-oneill/

8. For more about the intersections between *"Anna Christie," The God of Vengeance*, and *Indecent*, see Katie N. Johnson and Sara L. Warner, "Indecent Collaborations and/in Queer Time(s)," in *Critical Perspectives on Contemporary Plays by Women: The Twenty-First Century*, ed. Lesley Ferris and Penelope Farfan (Ann Arbor: University of Michigan Press, 2021), 68–79; and Katie N. Johnson, *"'Anna Christie'*: A Repentant Courtesan, Made Respectable," *Eugene O'Neill Review* 26 (2004): 87–104.

9. Paula Vogel, *Indecent* (New York: Theatre Communications Group, 2017), 55.

10. Vogel, *Indecent*, 56.

11. Alex Roe, artistic director of the Metropolitan Playhouse, has written a superb essay on Zoom theater and its innovations and evolutions during the recent Covid pandemic. See Roe, "Port in a Storm: Arriving at a Virtual Theatre through the Pandemic of 2020," *Eugene O'Neill Review* 42, no. 1 (2021): 54–63.

Bibliography

"33 Insults Cut Out of Paul Robeson's Film." *Afro-American* (Baltimore), October 7, 1933, 1.

"6 ft. 4 in. Negro Actor's Triumph." *Star* (London), September 1925.

"Actress Quits Play with Negroes in Cast." *New York Times*, September 12, 1925, 9.

Ahmed, Shahed. "Evolution of Black Characterization in American Theater: Eugene O'Neill's *The Dreamy Kid* and Entrée into 'Authentic Negro' Experience." *SUST Studies* 15, no. 1 (2012): 21–33.

Alden, Whitman. "Paul Robeson Dead at 77." *New York Times*, January 24, 1976, 1.

"Algerian Star Thrills Paris in Gilpin Role." *Chicago Defender*, November 17, 1923, 3.

"'All God's Chillun.'" *Afro-American* (Baltimore), February 12, 1927, 8.

"'All God's Chillun.'" *New York Times*, December 5, 1948, E8.

"'All God's Chillun.'" *New York Times*, February 1, 1954, 22.

"All God's Chillun Got Feelings." *Arkansas State Press*, city ed., June 6, 1952, 5.

"All God's Chillum Got Wings." *Times* (London), March 17, 1933.

"*All God's Chillun Got Wings* Calls for White Actress to Kiss Negro's Hand." *Washington Post*, February 22, 1924, 3.

All God's Chillun Got Wings. T-Photo (B) file. Billy Role Theatre Collection, New York Public Library for the Performing Arts.

"'All God's Chillun' Makes Its Third Los Angeles Production." *Pittsburgh Courier*, June 25, 1927, A2.

"'All God's Chillun' in Broadway Revival." *Broad Ax* (Chicago), July 2, 1927, 2.

"'All God's Chillun' in Broadw'y Revival." *Afro-American* (Baltimore), June 25, 1927, 7.

Alsen, Eberhard. "Racism and the Film Version of Eugene O'Neill's *The Emperor Jones*." *CLA Journal* 49, no. 4 (2006): 406–22.

Ambrière, Francis. "Le 'Point 50.'" *Opéra*, February 15, 1950.

"Amsterdam Won by 'Emperor Jones.'" *New York Herald* [Paris edition], March 12, 1934.

"An einem 31. März." Accessed October 23, 2020. https://www.dhm.de/archiv/gaeste/luise/tagesfakten/tf03/0331.htm

"An Ill-Advised Performance." *New York World*, March 4, 1924.

Anderson, Harvey. "Race Stage Stars Are Numerous on Broadway." *Pittsburgh Courier*, October 29, 1927.

André, Antoine. Review of *L'Empereur Jones*. *L'Information* (Paris), November 12, 1923.

André, Naomi. *Black Opera: History, Power, Engagement*. Urbana: University of Illinois Press, 2018.

André, Naomi, Karen M. Bryan, and Eric Saylor, eds. *Blackness in Opera*. Urbana: University of Illinois Press, 2012.

[Annock], P. L. M. "Paul Robeson as Slave Leader." *Daily Herald* (London), March 17, 1936.

Atkinson, Brooks. *Broadway*. New York: Macmillan, 1970.

"At the Lafayette Theatre." *New York Age*, March 29, 1924, 6.

"Augustus Thomas Scores Casting in O'Neil [sic] Play." *Brooklyn Daily Eagle*, February 25, 1924, 9.

Austin, J. L. *How to Do Things with Words*. Edited by J. O. Urmson and Marina Sbisà. Cambridge, MA: Harvard University Press, 1975.

"Backstage with Stagestruck." *Inter-State Tattler* (New York), July 12, 1929, 9.

Barthes, Roland. *Camera Lucida*. New York: Hill and Wang, 1982.

Batiste, Stephanie Leigh. *Darkening Mirrors: Imperial Representation in Depression-Era African American Performance*. Durham, NC: Duke University Press, 2011.

Batson, Charles R. *Dance, Desire, and Anxiety in Early Twentieth-Century French Theater: Playing Identities*. Aldershot, UK: Ashgate, 2005.

Baughan, E. A. "Robeson in Play by Negro — Author Takes Part." *News Chronicle* (London), March 17, 1936.

"Belated Recognition." *Chicago Defender*, November 24, 1923, A12.

Bell, C. H. "Objects to Play." Letter to the editor. *Chicago Defender*, March 15, 1924, 12.

Bennett, Gwendolyn. "The Emperors Jones." *Opportunity* 8 (September 1930): 270.

Bernstein, Robin. *Racial Innocence: Performing American Childhood and Race from Slavery to Civil Rights*. New York: New York University Press, 2011.

B[est], M[arshall] A. "O'Neill in Paris." *New York Times*, November 18, 1923, X2.

Bhabha, Homi K. *The Location of Culture*. London: Routledge, 1994.

Bhabha, Homi K. "Of Mimicry and Man: The Ambivalence of Colonial Discourse." In "Discipleship: A Special Issue on Psychoanalysis," *October* 28 (Spring 1984): 125–33.

Bial, Henry. *Acting Jewish: Negotiating Ethnicity on the American Stage and Screen*. Ann Arbor: University of Michigan Press, 2005.

Bigsby, Christopher William Edgar. *Confrontation and Commitment: A Study of Contemporary American Drama 1959–66*. Columbia: University of Missouri Press, 1968.

Black, Cheryl. "After the Emperor: Interracial Collaborations Between Provincetown Alumni and Black Theatre Artists c. 1924–1946." *Journal of American Drama and Theatre* 20, no. 1 (Winter 2008): 5–26.

Black, Cheryl, and Jonathan Shandell. *Experiments in Democracy: Interracial and Cross-Cultural Exchange in American Theatre, 1912–1945*. Carbondale: Southern Illinois University Press, 2016.

"Black and Asian Performance in Britain, 1940–1969." Victoria & Albert Museum. Accessed November 20, 2020 (article is no longer posted). http://www.vam.ac.uk/content/articles/b/history-of-black-and-asian-performance-in-britain5/

"Black and White." March 30, 1922. Otherwise unidentified clipping from the Charles Gilpin Clipping File, James V. Hatch and Camille Billops Collection, New York City (now housed at Emory University as the Camille Billops and James V. Hatch Collection).

"Bledsoe Gets an Important Role in Play." *Chicago Defender*, June 30, 1934, 8.

Bledsoe, Jules. "The Emperor Jones [Opera Manuscript]." Jules Bledsoe Papers, 1931–1939, Box 4. Sc MG 255. Schomburg Center for Research in Black Culture, Manuscripts, Archives and Rare Books Division, The New York Public Library.

Bledsoe, Jules. "Has the Negro a Place in the Theatre?" *Opportunity* 6 (July 1928): 215.

Bledsoe, Jules. Letter to Nace [Naomi] Cobbs on February 4, 1934. Jules Bledsoe Papers, Accession #2086, Box 1, Folder 3: Correspondence 1934. The Texas Collection, Baylor University.

Bledsoe, Jules. Letter to Nace [Naomi] Cobbs, March 22, 1934. Jules Bledsoe Papers, Accession #2086, Box 1, Folder 3: Correspondence 1934. The Texas Collection, Baylor University.

Bledsoe, Jules. Letter to Nace [Naomi] Cobbs on November 9, 1935, Jules Bledsoe Papers, Accession #2086, Box 1, Folder 5: Correspondence 1935–36. The Texas Collection, Baylor University.

Bledsoe, Jules. Scrapbook. Jules Bledsoe Papers, Accession #2086, Box 23: Oversized Scrapbook, 1934–43. The Texas Collection, Baylor University.

Bledsoe, Jules. Travel Diary. Jules Bledsoe Papers, Accession #2086, Box 6, Folder 1: Literary Journals. The Texas Collection, Baylor University.

"Bledsoe Sings in N.Y. Opera Before Throng." *Chicago Defender*, July 14, 1934, 9.

"Bledsoe Will Sing Tuesday." *New York Amsterdam News*, July 7, 1934, 1.

Bogard, Travis. *Contour in Time: The Plays of Eugene O'Neill*. Oxford: Oxford University Press, 1988.

Boittin, Jennifer Anne. *Colonial Metropolis: The Urban Grounds of Anti-Imperialism and Feminism in Interwar Paris*. Lincoln: University of Nebraska Press, 2010.

Bond, Frederick Weldon. *The Negro and the Drama*. 1940. College Park, MD: McGrath Publishing, 1969.

Bordwell, David. "Jump Cuts and Blind Spots." *Wide Angle* 6, no. 1 (1984): 4–11.

Bordwell, David. *On the History of Film Style*. Cambridge, MA: Harvard University Press, 1997.

Bornstein, George. *The Colors of Zion: Blacks, Jews, and Irish from 1845 to 1945*. Cambridge, MA: Harvard University Press, 2011.

Botrot, Jean. "À l'Odéon *L'Empereur Jones*." November 3, 1923.

Bourdieu, Pierre. *Distinction: A Social Critique of the Judgment of Taste*. Translated by Richard Nice. Cambridge, MA: Harvard University Press, 1984.

Bourgeois, Maurice, trans. *L'Empereur Jones: Piece en 8 tableaux d'Eugene O'Neill*. Paris: Librarie Theatrale, 1953.

Bowen, Croswell. "The Black Irishman." *PM*, November 3, 1946, 13–17.

Bowen, Croswell. *The Curse of the Misbegotten: A Tale of the House of O'Neill*. New York: McGraw-Hill, 1959.

Bowen, Croswell. *O'Neill and His Plays: Four Decades of Criticism*. Edited by Oscar Cargill, N. Bryllion Fagin, and William J. Fisher. New York: New York University Press, 1961.

Braconi, Adrienne Macki. *Harlem's Theaters: A Staging Ground for Community, Class, and Contradiction, 1923–1939*. Evanston, IL: Northwestern University Press, 2015.

Brainwaithe, William Stanley. "The Negro in American Literature." In *The New Negro: An Interpretation*, edited by Alain Locke, 29–45. New York: Albert and Charles Boni, 1925.

Brannigan, John. *Race in Modern Irish Literature*. Edinburgh: Edinburgh University Press, 2009.

Brender, Richard. "Reinventing Africa in Their Own Image: The Ballets Suédois' 'Ballet nègre,' *La Création du monde*." *Dance Chronicle* 9, no. 1 (1986): 119–47.

"Broadway Gasps as Mary Blair, White Actress, Stars in Play Featuring Infatuation of Caucasian for Race Man." *Pittsburgh Courier*, June 19, 1926, 1.

Brooks, Daphne A. *Bodies in Dissent: Spectacular Performances of Race and Freedom, 1850–1910*. Durham, NC: Duke University Press, 2006.

Brown, Carlyle. *The African Company Presents Richard III*. New York: Dramatists Play Service, 1994.

Brown, Lloyd L. *The Young Paul Robeson: "On My Journey Now."* New York: Westview Press, 1997.

"Brutus Jones in Astoria." *New York Times*, July 16, 1933, X2.

Burns, Ken, dir. *Unforgiveable Blackness: The Rise and Fall of Jack Johnson*. 2004; Arlington County, VA: PBS, 2005. DVD.

Butler, Judith. *Excitable Speech: A Politics of the Performative*. New York: Routledge, 1997.

Callens, Johan. "'Black Is White, I Yells It Out Louder 'Deir Loudest': Unraveling the Wooster Group's *The Emperor Jones*." *Eugene O'Neill Review* 26 (2004): 43–69.

Carby, Hazel. *Race Men*. Cambridge, MA: Harvard University Press, 1998.

Cardullo, Bert. "André Bazin on Film Technique: Two Seminal Essays." *Film Criticism* 25, no. 2 (2000): 40–62.

Carlson, Marvin A. *The Haunted Stage: The Theatre as Memory Machine.* Ann Arbor: University of Michigan Press, 2003.

Carpenter, Faedra C. *Coloring Whiteness: Acts of Critique in Black Performance.* Ann Arbor: University of Michigan Press, 2014.

Castronovo, David, and Janet Groth. *Critic in Love: A Romantic Biography of Edmund Wilson.* Berkeley, CA: Counterpoint Press, 2005.

Catanese, Brandi Wilkins. *The Problem of the Color[blind]: Racial Transgression and the Politics of Black Performance.* Ann Arbor: University of Michigan Press, 2011.

Chalay, Sylvie. "Habib Benglia: Premier grand acteur noir en France." *Africultures.* Last modified March 31, 2000. http://africultures.com/habib-benglia-premier-grand-acteur-noir-en-france-1312/

Chonez, Claudine. "Bonne chance à Point 50." *Les Nouvelles Littéraires* (Paris), February 23, 1950.

Cixous, Hélène. "Fiction and Its Phantoms: A Reading of Freud's *Das Unheimliche* (The 'Uncanny')." *New Literary History* 7, no. 3 (1976): 525–645.

Cochrane, Claire. *Twentieth-Century British Theatre: Industry, Art and Empire.* Cambridge: Cambridge University Press, 2011.

Cohn, Ruby. "Black Power on Stage: Emperor Jones and King Christophe." *Yale French Studies* 46 (1971): 41–47.

Colbert, Soyica Diggs, Douglas A. Jones Jr., and Shane Vogel, eds. *Race and Performance after Repetition.* Durham, NC: Duke University Press, 2020.

Collins-Hughes, Laura. "Review: Emperor Jones, Fearsome and Fearful in a Roaring Revival." *New York Times,* March 24, 2017. Accessed November 23, 2021. https://www.nytimes.com/2017/03/24/theater/review-emperor-jones-fearsome-and-fearful-in-a-roaring-revival.html?smid=url-share

"Colored Artists Play Big Part in Workers' Dance in New York." *Washington Tribune,* October 12, 1933.

"Color Line in Art." *Chicago Defender,* April 24, 1926, A8.

Conquergood, Dwight. *Cultural Struggles: Performance, Ethnography, Praxis.* Ann Arbor: University of Michigan Press, 2013.

Cooper, Michael. "An 'Otello' Without Blackface Highlights an Enduring Tradition in Opera." *New York Times,* September 17, 2015. Accessed March 2, 2022. https://www.nytimes.com/2015/09/20/arts/music/an-otello-without-the-blackface-nods-to-modern-tastes.html

Corbin, John. "Among the New Plays." *New York Times,* May 18, 1924, XI.

Corbin, John. "'Emperor Jones' Revived." *New York Times,* May 7, 1924, 18.

"Cosmopolitan Opera Announces New Bill." *New York Amsterdam News,* November 24, 1934, 4.

"Cosmopolitan Opera Presents Gruenberg's 'Emperor Jones.'" December 8, 1934. Otherwise unidentified clipping, Louis Gruenberg, M Clippings File.

Billy Rose Theatre Division, New York Public Library for the Performing Arts.

Coutelet, Nathalie. "Habib Benglia, le 'nègrérotique' du spectacle français." *Genre, sexualité & société*. Posted online June 29, 2009. https://gss.revues.org /688#quotation

Cover of *The Crisis* 40, no. 10 (October 1933).

Cover of *Time Magazine*, January 16, 1933.

Cox, James H., and Alexander Pettit. "Black Indigeneity and Anti-Colonial Rebellion in Eugene O'Neill's *The Emperor Jones*." *Modern Drama* 64, no. 3 (Fall 2021): 259–82.

Cozart, James. Memorandum, "Library of Congress QC Inspection Memo." Undated but likely 2001.

Cozart, James. Memorandum to Library of Congress Restoration Team. "WRS." May 30, 2001.

Creelman, Eileen. "Pictures and Players: Dudley Murphy in Midst of Directing 'Emperor Jones' at Astoria Studio." *New York Sun*, July 5, 1933, 30.

Crewe, Regina. "Negro Actor Rises above All Else in O'Neill Play Film." *New York American*, September 20, 1933.

Cripps, Thomas. "Paul Robeson and Black Identity in American Movies." *Massachusetts Review* 11, no. 3 (1970): 468–85.

Crisis, November 1921. Otherwise unidentified clipping from the Alexander Gumby Collection of Negroiana, 1800–1981; Box 120, Negro in Drama 1, Rare Book and Manuscript Library, Columbia University Library.

Curtis, Susan. *The First Black Actors on the Great White Way*. Columbia: University of Missouri Press, 1998.

Darden, Robert. Interview. "Treasures of the Texas Collection: Jules Bledsoe." Script for KWBU-FM and Texas NPR Stations, January 9, 2010.

"Darktown Scandals to Play Columbia: Julius Bledsoe to Tour South in Emperor Jones." *Pittsburgh Courier*, July 16, 1927, A3.

Davis, Charles Belmont. "'Roseanne' Somber Study of Primitive Customs of Negro." *New York Tribune*, December 31, 1923, 6.

"Deems It an Honor to Play in Show with Negro, Says Mary Blair; Shows No Bias." *Brooklyn Daily Eagle*, February 22, 1924, 1.

De Jaffa, Kathleen. *The Emperor Jones: Opera in Two Acts (after Eugene O'Neill's Play)*. New York: Fred Rullman, 1932.

Delehanty, Thornton. "The New Film: Paul Robeson in the Screen Version of 'The Emperor Jones' at the Rivoli." *New York Evening Post*, September 20, 1933.

Delson, Susan. *Dudley Murphy, Hollywood Wild Card*. Minneapolis: University of Minnesota Press, 2006.

D[ent], A[lan]. "Mr. Paul Robeson as Toussaint: A Documentary Play." *Manchester Guardian*, March 17, 1936.

Deutsch, Helen, and Stella Hanau. *The Provincetown: A Story of the Theatre*. New York: Farrar & Rinehart, 1931.

Diawara, Manthia. "Black British Cinema: Spectatorship and Identity Formation in *Territories.*" *Public Culture* 3, no. 1 (1990): 33–48.

Display ad for *The Emperor Jones*. *New York Amsterdam News*, November 24, 1934, 10.

Dooley, Brian. *Black and Green: the Fight for Civil Rights in Northern Ireland and Black America*. London: Pluto Press, 1998.

Dossett, Kate. "Staging the Garveyite Home: Black Masculinity, Failure, and Redemption in Theodore Ward's 'Big White Fog.'" *African American Review* 43, no. 4 (2009): 557–76.

Douglas, Aaron. "The Emperor Jones Series." *Theatre Arts Monthly* 10, no. 2 (February 1926): 112–20.

Douxami, Christine. "Brazilian Black Theatre: A Political Theatre against Racism." *TDR/The Drama Review* 63, no. 1 (2019): 32–51.

Dowling, Robert M. *Eugene O'Neill: A Life in Four Acts*. New Haven: Yale University Press, 2014.

Downes, Olin. "'Emperor Jones' Triumphs as Opera." *New York Times*, January 8, 1933, 1 and 26.

Downes, Olin. "Gruenberg's 'Jones' in Premiere." *New York Times*, January 1, 1933, X6.

Downes, Olin. "Robeson Soloist with Orchestra: 'Emperor Jones' Excerpts Are Feature of the Philadelphia Organization's Program." *New York Times*, December 18, 1940, 32.

Duberman, Martin. *Paul Robeson: A Biography*. New York: Knopf, 1988.

Dubois, Laurent. Foreword to *Toussaint Louverture: The Story of the Only Successful Slave Revolt in History* by C. L. R. James. Durham, NC: Duke University Press, 2013.

Du Bois, W. E. B. "Krigwa, 1926." *The Crisis* 31 (August 1926): 134.

Du Bois, W. E. B. Letter to Eugene O'Neill, August 17, 1925. W. E. B. Du Bois Papers (MS 312). Special Collections and University Archives, University of Massachusetts Amherst Libraries.

Du Bois, W. E. B. Letter to Eugene O'Neill, September 16, 1924. W. E. B. Du Bois Papers (MS 312). Special Collections and University Archives, University of Massachusetts Amherst Libraries. http://credo.library.umass.edu/view/full/mums312-b168-i413

Du Bois, W. E. B. Letter to Esther E. Wilson, November 12, 1930. W. E. B. Du Bois Papers (MS 312). Special Collections and University Archives, University of Massachusetts Amherst Libraries.

Du Bois, W. E. B. "The Negro and Our Stage." Program for *All God's Chillun Got Wings*, Provincetown Players Season 1923–1924, No. 5, page 2.

Du Bois, W. E. B. "The Negro and Our Stage." *Sunday World*, May 4, 1924.

Du Bois, W. E. B. "Negro Art." *The Crisis* 22, no. 2 (June 1921): 56.

Du Bois, W. E. B. *The Souls of Black Folk*. 1903. Edited by Henry Louis Gates Jr., vii–x. Oxford: Oxford University Press, 2014.

Dupouy, Cécile. "Ce soir, pour l'inauguration de 'Point 50' les 'Argonautes' présentent 'Empereur Jones' et 'Bagatelles.'" *L'Aube* (Paris), January 7, 1950.

Dyer, Richard. *Heavenly Bodies: Film Stars and Society*. New York: St. Martin's, 1986.

Edwards, Brent Hayes. *The Practice of Diaspora: Literature, Translation, and the Rise of Black Internationalism*. Cambridge, MA: Harvard University Press, 2003.

Eisen, Kurt. "Theatrical Ethnography and Modernist Primitivism in Eugene O'Neill and Zora Neale Hurston." *South Central Review* 25, no. 1 (2008): 56–73.

Eisler, Garrett. "Backstory as Black Story: The Cinematic Reinvention of O'Neill's *The Emperor Jones*." *Eugene O'Neill Review* 32 (2010): 148–62.

"Electrifies French Capital." *Afro-American* (Baltimore), June 23, 1923, 8.

Elliot, Robin. "Blacks and Blackface at the Opera." In *Opera in a Multicultural World: Coloniality, Culture, Performance*, edited by Mary Ingraham, Joseph So, and Roy Moodley, 34–49. London: Taylor & Friends, 2015.

"Emperor." *New York Times*, August 28, 1960, X9.

The Emperor Jones. Directed by Dudley Murphy. Performances by Paul Robeson, Dudley Digges, Frank Wilson. United Artists Corporation, 1933.

The Emperor Jones. 1933. Directed by Dudley Murphy. Performances by Paul Robeson, Dudley Digges, Frank Wilson. National Film Preservation Foundation. Image Entertainment, 2003.

The Emperor Jones. Library of Congress Restoration Script. 2001.

"'Emperor Jones' as Film Better Than Stage Play." *Chicago Defender*, September 30, 1933, 5.

"Emperor Jones at Roosevelt." *New York Amsterdam News*, September 20, 1933, 7.

"'Emperor Jones' Bill at Hippodrome Tonight." *New York World Telegram*, November 24, 1934, 22.

"'The Emperor Jones' Did Not Go at the Lincoln." *New York Amsterdam News*, August 31, 1927, 13.

"'The Emperor Jones' Flops without C. Gilpin." *New York Amsterdam News*, November 7, 1923, 5.

"Emperor Jones Has Premier[e] Tonight." *New York Sun*, September 19, 1933.

"'Emperor Jones' in France." *Cleveland Gazette*, November 17, 1923, 1.

"'The Emperor' Is Held Over." *New York Amsterdam News*, September 27, 1933, 7.

"'Emperor Jones,' New American Opera Given Its Premier[e] Performance at Metropolitan." *Musical Courier*, January 14, 1933, 13.

"*Emperor Jones* Premiere." *The Crisis* 40, no. 10 (October 1933): 232–233.

"*The Emperor Jones* Reappears at Provincetown with a New Emperor." *New York Post*, May 7, 1924.

"'The Emperor Jones' with Bledsoe Is Next N.Y. Opera." *Chicago Defender*, July 7, 1934, 7.

"Emperor Jones with Negro Cast." *New York Times*, July 11, 1934, 20.

"Entertains Prisoners." *Pittsburgh Courier*, June 30, 1923, 4.

E[rvine], St. J[ohn]. Review of *The Emperor Jones*. *Observer* (London), September 15, 1925.

"Ethiopian Art Advances to Nine Plays in Season." *New York Amsterdam News*, June 15, 1927, 14.

"Eugene O'Neill in Paris." *New York Transcript*, January 14, 1923.

Farkas, Andrew, ed. *Lawrence Tibbett: Singing Actor*. Milwaukee: Hal Leonard, 1989.

Fernández, Oscar. "Black Theatre in Brazil." *Educational Theatre Journal* 29, no. 1 (1977): 5–17.

Fest, Kerstin. "Yesterday and/or Today: Time, History and Desire in Christa Winsloe's *Mädchen in Uniform*." *German Life and Letters* 65, no. 4 (October 2012): 457–71.

"Film Show Will Aid Babies." *New York Herald Tribune*, September 14, 1933.

Floyd, Virginia. *Eugene O'Neill at Work: Newly Released Ideas for Plays*. New York: Ungar Publishing, 1981.

Foster, Susan, ed. "The Ballerina's Phallic Pointe." In *Corporalities: Dancing Knowledge, Culture and Power*, 1–26. New York: Taylor & Francis, 2004.

Fraden, Rena. *Blueprints for a Black Federal Theatre*. Cambridge: Cambridge University Press, 1996.

Frank, Glenda. "Tempest in Black and White: The 1924 Premiere of Eugene O'Neill's *All God's Chillun Got Wings*." *Resources for American Literary Study* 26, no. 1 (2000): 75–89.

Freud, Sigmund. *Das Unheimliche*. Freiburg im Breisgau: Outlook Verlag, 2020. First published in 1919 by Imago Verlag (Vienna).

Friedman, Lester D. *Hollywood's Image of the Jew*. New York: Ungar, 1982.

"From Broadway to the Bowery." *Theatre Magazine* 7 (April 1907): 121.

Gabriel, Gilbert W. "*All God's Chillun*: First Scene of O'Neill's Play Reaches Public Performance At Last." Otherwise unidentified clipping, Series III, Writings, Plays, *All God's Chillun Got Wings*, Clippings of Reviews and Advertisements, 1925-68, n.d., Box 41, Folder 878. Eugene O'Neill Papers. Yale Collection of American Literature, Beinecke Rare Book and Manuscript Library.

Ganrey-Rety, Jean. "Empereur Jones et Bagatelles." *Le Soir* (Paris), February 11, 1950.

Gardner, Chappy. "White Actors Steal Your Art, Take Your Place and Your Job." *Pittsburgh Courier*, July 18, 1931, A8.

Garland, Robert. "Praise for Paul Robeson." *New York World-Telegram*, June 30, 1933.

Garrison, Jeffrey. "Aaron Douglas's *Emperor Jones Series*: The Illustrations." *Journal of Komazawa Junior College* 28 (March 2000): 253–94.

Gauss, Rebecca B. "O'Neill, Gruenberg and *The Emperor Jones*." *Eugene O'Neill Review* 18 (1994): 38–44.

Geary, Lynnette G. "Jules Bledsoe: The Original 'Ol' Man River.'" *The Black Perspective in Music* 17 nos. 1–2 (1989): 27–54.

Gelb, Arthur, and Barbara Gelb. *By Women Possessed: A Life of Eugene O'Neill.* New York: Marian Wood Books, 2016.

Gelb, Arthur, and Barbara Gelb. *O'Neill.* Rev. ed. New York: Harper and Row, 1973.

George, Maude Roberts. "'Emperor Jones' as Opera Wins Ovation in Chicago." *Chicago Defender,* May 6, 1933, 11.

"Giant Negro Actor." *Daily Mail* (London), September 11, 1925.

"Giant Negro-Actor on His Ambition to Sing." *Evening News* (London), September 11, 1925.

Gill, Glenda. "Eugene O'Neill and Paul Robeson: An Uneasy Collaboration in Three of O'Neill's Early Plays." *Laconics* 1 (2006).

Gill, Glenda. "Love in Black and White: Miscegenation on the Stage." *Journal of American Drama and Theatre* 10, no. 3 (Fall 1998): 32–51.

Gillespie, Michael Boyce. *Film Blackness: American Cinema and the Idea of Black Film.* Durham, NC: Duke University Press, 2016.

"Gilpin Dines." *Chicago Defender,* March 12, 1921, 5.

"Gilpin Play Read." *Chicago Defender,* March 8, 1924, 7.

"Gilpin Quits 'Roseanne,' Paul Robeson Takes His Place." *New York Age,* March 22, 1924, 1.

"Gilpin's Return in Old Role Hailed by Metropolitan Critics." *New York Amsterdam News,* February 24, 1926, 5.

Gilroy, Paul. *The Black Atlantic: Modernity and Double Consciousness.* Cambridge, MA: Harvard University Press, 1993.

Gonzalez, Anita. "Aldridge in Action: Building a Visual Digital Interface." *Theatre Journal* 68, no. 4 (2016): E1–E17. doi:10.1353/tj.2016.0136

Goodman Theatre. "A Global Exploration: Eugene O'Neill in the 21st Century." 2009. Accessed November 22, 2021. https://www.goodmantheatre.org/season/0809/a-global-exploration-eugene-oneill-in-the-21st-century/

Gregory, Montgomery. "The Drama of Negro Life." In *The New Negro: An Interpretation,* edited by Alain Locke, 153–60. New York: Albert and Charles Boni, 1925.

Gruenberg, Louis. *The Emperor Jones; Kaiser Jones Opera in Two Acts, a Prologue, an Interlude and Six Scenes (after Eugene O'Neill's Play).* Op. 36. New York: Cos Cob Press, 1932.

Guerro, Ed. "Black Stars in Exile: Paul Robeson, O. J. Simpson, and Othello." In *Paul Robeson: Artist and Citizen,* edited by Jeffrey C. Stewart, 275–90. New Brunswick, NJ: Rutgers University Press, 1988.

Gulden, Bruce. "Louis Gruenberg's Opera 'The Emperor Jones.'" *Dance Culture* (March 1933): 12.

Haine, W. Scott. "The Development of Leisure and the Transformation of Working-Class Adolescences, Paris 1830–1940." *Journal of Family History* 17, no. 4 (1992): 451–76.

Hamilton, Cicely. "The Theatre: Foreign Importations." *Time and Tide* (London), September 25, 1925.

Hammond, Percy. "The Mayor Interferes a Little Bit with *All God's Chillun Got Wings*." *New York Herald Tribune*, May 16, 1924, 10.

"Hands Across the Sea." Letter to the editor, *New York Amsterdam News*, October 9, 1929, 8.

"Harlem Also Gets Peek at Robeson." *Chicago Defender*, October 7, 1933, 5.

"Harlem's Finest Singers in Opera." *Chicago Defender*, July 7, 1934, 6.

Harrington, Dave. "All God's Chillun." *New York Amsterdam News*, July 18, 1936, 16.

Hart, Moss. *Act One*. New York: St. Martin's Press, 1959.

Hatch, James V., and Camille Billops, eds. "An Interview with Bruce Nugent." *Artists and Influences*. New York: James V. Hatch and Camille Billops Collection, 1982 (now housed at Emory University as the Camille Billops and James V. Hatch Collection).

Hatch, James V., Camille Billops, and Ted Shine, eds. *Black Theatre, USA. Revised and Expanded Edition, The Early Period, 1847–1938*. New York: Free Press, 1996.

Hayes, J. J. "An Irish 'Emperor Jones.'" *New York Times*, February 13, 1927, X4.

Hempstead, Pete. "Review: *The Emperor Jones*." *TheaterMania*, March 12, 2017. Accessed November 23, 2021. https://www.theatermania.com/off-broadway/reviews/the-emperor-jones_80333.html

"Hemsley Winfield [Obituary]." *New York Times*, January 17, 1934.

"Hemsley Winfield: Negro Actor Appeared in Opera 'The Emperor Jones.'" *New York Times*, January 16, 1934, 21.

Henderson, Mary C. *The City and the Theatre: New York Playhouses from Bowling Green to Times Square*. Clifton, NJ: James T. White, 1973.

"He's No Charles Gilpin." *Afro-American* (Baltimore), November 16, 1923, A1.

"He's the Emperor." *New York Amsterdam News*, July 19, 1933, 1.

Heyward, DuBose. "*The Emperor Jones* (shooting script)." New York State Motion Picture Division License Application, Series #A1418, Case File #26195, Box 249, 1933. New York State Archives, Albany, New York.

Hill, Errol, and James V. Hatch. *A History of African American Theatre*. Cambridge: Cambridge University Press, 2003.

Hirsch, Louis A., Gene Buck, and Dave Stamper. "It's Getting Dark on Broadway." 1922. Sheet Music Collection. 38. http://digitalcommons.ithaca.edu/sheetmusic/38

Hoffman, Warren. *The Great White Way: Race and the Broadway Musical*. New Brunswick, NJ: Rutgers University Press, 2014.

Høgsbjerg, Christian. Introduction to *Toussaint Louverture: The Story of the Only Successful Slave Revolt in History* by C. L. R. James, 1–39. Durham, NC: Duke University Press, 2013.

"Holland Goes Drama Dizzy as Bledsoe Plays 'Emperor.'" *Chicago Defender*, May 19, 1934, 9.

"Hollywood Likes 'Emperor Jones.'" *Washington Tribune,* December 7, 1933, 14.

Holton, Deborah Wood. "Revealing Blindness, Revealing Vision: Interpreting O'Neill's Black Female Characters in *Moon of the Caribbees, The Dreamy Kid* and *All God's Chillun Got Wings.*" *Eugene O'Neill Review* 19, nos. 1–2 (1995): 29–44.

hooks, bell. *Black Looks: Race and Representation.* Boston: South End Press, 1992.

"Horizon." *The Crisis* 26, no. 3 (1923): 130.

Houchin, John, ed. *The Critical Response to Eugene O'Neill.* Westport: Greenwood Press, 1997.

Hughes, Langston. *The Big Sea: An Autobiography.* New York: Alfred Knopf, 1940.

Hutchinson, George. *In Search of Nella Larsen: A Biography of the Color Line.* Cambridge, MA: Harvard University Press, 2009.

"Hylan Bars Scene in O'Neill's Play." *New York Times,* May 16, 1924, 1.

Ignatiev, Noel. *How the Irish Became White.* New York: Routledge, 2012.

IMDb. "Irving Pichel Biography." Accessed September 5, 2021. https://www.imdb.com/name/nm0681635/bio?ref_=nm_ov_bio_sm

"In Europe with J. A. Rogers." *New York Amsterdam News,* September 2, 1931, 10.

"In the Jungles of Astoria, L. I." *New York Herald Tribune,* July 2, 1933.

"Jack Goldberg, with Six Shows in Rehearsal, Gets Ready for Busy Fall and Winter Season." *Pittsburgh Courier,* July 30, 1927, A2.

Jackson, Paul. *Sunday Afternoons at the Old Met: The Metropolitan Opera Broadcasts, 1931–1950.* Portland, OR: Amadeus Press, 1992.

James, C. L. R. *Toussaint Louverture: The Story of the Only Successful Slave Revolt in History.* Durham, NC: Duke University Press, 2013.

Johns, Vere E. "Hemsley Winfield" [Obituary], *New York Age,* January 27, 1933, 6.

Johnson, E. Patrick. *Appropriating Blackness: Performance and the Politics of Authenticity.* Durham, NC: Duke University Press, 2003.

Johnson, E. Patrick. "Black Performance Studies: Genealogies, Politics, Futures." In *The Sage Handbook of Performance Studies,* edited by D. Soyini Madison and Judith Hamera. Thousand Oaks, CA: SAGE, 2006.

Johnson, James Weldon. *Black Manhattan.* New York: Alfred A. Knopf, 1930.

Johnson, Katie N. "'Anna Christie': A Repentant Courtesan, Made Respectable." *Eugene O'Neill Review* 26 (2004): 87–104.

Johnson, Katie N. "Black to Ireland: Circum-Atlantic Double Exposure and Racialized Jump Cuts in *The Emperor Jones.*" *MELUS* 44, no. 4 (Winter 2019): 147–76.

Johnson, Katie N. "Brutus Jones Remains: The Case of Jules Bledsoe." *Eugene O'Neill Review* 36, no. 1 (2015): 1–28.

Johnson, Katie N. "O'Neill's *Emperor Jones*: Racing the Great White Way." In *The Theatre of Eugene O'Neill: American Modernism on Stage,* edited by Kurt Eisen, 173–85. London: Bloomsbury Methuen, 2017.

Johnson, Katie N., and Sara L. Warner. "Indecent Collaborations and/in Queer

Time(s)." In *Critical Perspectives on Contemporary Plays by Women: The Twenty-First Century*, edited by Lesley Ferris and Penelope Farfan, 68–79. Ann Arbor: University of Michigan Press, 2021.

"Jules Bledsoe on Tour of Holland Singing 'The Emperor Jones.'" *New York Age*, April 14, 1934, 5.

Jules-Rosette, Bennetta. *Black Paris: The African Writers' Landscape*. Urbana: University of Illinois Press, 1998.

"Julius Bledsoe in First Straight Acting Part at the Provincetown." *New York Amsterdam News*, December 29, 1926, 11.

Kagan, Norman. "The Return of *The Emperor Jones*." *Negro History Bulletin* 34, no. 7 (1971): 160–66.

Kaplan, Lucy. "The Improbable Rise of the First African American Opera Impresario." *Classic Voice*, February 6, 2017. Accessed March 4, 2022. https://www.sfcv.org/articles/feature/improbable-rise-first-african-american-opera-impresario

Keelan, Harry. "The Emperor Jones." *Opportunity* 11 (February 1933): 45, 58.

Kiberd, Declan. "Losing Ireland, Inventing America: O'Neill and After." *Eugene O'Neill Review* 39, no. 1 (2018): 1–16.

Kibler, M. Alison. *Censoring Racial Ridicule: Irish, Jewish, and African American Struggles over Race and Representation, 1890–1930*. Chapel Hill: University of North Carolina Press, 2015.

Kommer, Rudolf. "Broadway in Central Europe." *New York Times*, September 28, 1924, X2.

Kommer, Rudolf. "O'Neill in Europe." *New York Times*, November 9, 1924, X2.

Komporaly, Jozefina. "The Gate Theatre: A Translation Powerhouse on the Inter-War British Stage." *Journal of Adaptation in Film & Performance* 4, no. 2 (2011): 129–43.

Konkobo, Christophe. "Dark Continent, Dark Stage: Body Performance in Colonial Theatre and Cinema." *Journal of Black Studies* 40, no. 6 (2010): 1094–1106.

Koszarski, Richard. *Hollywood on the Hudson: Film and Television in New York from Griffith to Sarnoff*. New Brunswick, NJ: Rutgers University Press, 2008.

Krasner, David. *A Beautiful Pageant: African American Theatre, Drama, and Performance in the Harlem Renaissance, 1910–1927*. New York: Palgrave, 2002.

Krasner, David. "Whose Role Is It Anyway? Charles Gilpin and the Harlem Renaissance." *African American Review* 29, no. 3 (1995): 483–96.

Krimsky, John. "The Emperor Jones—Robeson and O'Neill on Film." *Connecticut Review* 7, no. 2 (1974): 94–99.

Kringelbach, Hélène Neveu. "Moving Shadows of Casamance: Performance and Regionalism in Senegal." In *Dancing Cultures: Globalization, Tourism, and Identity in the Anthropology of Dance*, edited by Hélène Neveu Kringelbach and Jonathan Skinner, 143–60. New York: Berghahn Books, 2012.

Kushner, Tony. "The Genius of O'Neill." *American Theatre*, February 2, 2015.

Reprinted from the December 18, 2003 *New York Times* Literary Supplement. Accessed November 22, 2021. https://www.americantheatre.org/2015/02/02/the-genius-of-oneill/

[La Farge, John]. Letter to Eugene O'Neill, May 25, 1931. W. E. B. Du Bois Papers (MS 312). Special Collections and University Archives, University of Massachusetts Amherst Libraries. http://credo.library.umass.edu/view/full/mums312-b060-i215

"The Late Hemsley Winfield." *Harlem Heights Daily Citizen*, January 19, 1934, 4.

"L'Avante Scène." *L'Œuvre* (Paris), October 28, 1923, 7.

Ledger Sheet for Hemsley Winfield & Troupe. Folder: Clippings File, *The Emperor Jones*. Metropolitan Opera Archive, New York.

"Legislative League Acts." *Chicago Defender*, March 15, 1924, 6.

Lerminier, Georges. "A 'Point 50' Les Argonautes présentent 'Bagatelles' et 'Empereur Jones'." *L'Aube* (Paris), February 13, 1950.

Lewin, William, and Max J. Herzberg. "*The Emperor Jones* with a Study Guide for the Screen Version of the Play." New York: Appleton-Century-Crofts, 1934.

Lewis, David Levering, ed. *The Portable Harlem Renaissance Reader*. New York: Viking, 1994.

Lewis, Theophilus. "All God's Chillun Still Got Wings." *Messenger* 8, no. 11 (November 1924): 333–34.

Lewis, Theophilus. "Roseanne." *Messenger* 6, no 3 (March 1924): 73.

Liebling, Leonard. "Emperor Jones, New American Opera Given Its Premier[e] Performance at Metropolitan." *Musical Courier* 10 (January 14, 1933): 13.

Lindfors, Bernth. "'Mislike Me Not for My Complexion . . .': Ira Aldridge in Whiteface." *African American Review* 33, no. 2 (Summer 1999): 347–54.

Lipartito, Bob. Email message to author. October 8, 2021.

Lobby card. *The Emperor Jones*, featuring Paul Robeson, distributed by Screencraft Pictures, 1933. Collection of the Smithsonian National Museum of African American History and Culture, Washington, D.C.

Locke, Alain. "Broadway and the Negro Drama." *Theatre Arts* 25, no. 10 (October 1941): 745–50.

Locke, Alain. "The Negro and the American Stage." *Theatre Arts Monthly* 10, no. 2 (February 1926): 112–20.

Locke, Alain. "The Negro and the American Theatre." *Theatre Arts Monthly* 10, no. 10 (October 1926): 701–6.

Locke, Alain, ed. *The New Negro: An Interpretation*. New York: Albert and Charles Boni, 1925.

"London Applauds Robeson in 'Toussaint Louverture.'" *Negro Star* (Wichita, Kansas), March 27, 1936, 3.

"London Likes O'Neill Play: 'The Emperor Jones' and Paul Robeson Win Applause." *New York Times*, September 11, 1925, 20.

Londré, Felicia Hardison. *Words at Play: Creative Writing and Dramaturgy*. Carbondale: Southern Illinois University Press, 2005.

Lott, Eric. *Love and Theft: Blackface Minstrelsy and the American Working Class*. Oxford: Oxford University Press, 2013.

Lowe, John. "Creating the Circum-Caribbean Imaginary: DuBose Heyward's and Paul Robeson's Revision of *The Emperor Jones*." *Philological Quarterly* 90, nos. 2–3 (2011): 311–33.

Lubasch, Arnold H. *Robeson: An American Ballad*. Lanham, MD: Scarecrow Press, 2012.

Macgowan, Kenneth, Gilbert Seldes, Samuel J. Hume, Gilmor Brown, Everett Glass, Nina Moise, Paul Muni, Dudley Nichols, Josef von Sternberg, Robert G. Sproul, and Ralph Freud. "Irving Pichel (1891–1954): Wonderful to Have Had You with Us." *Quarterly of Film Radio and Television* 9, no. 2 (Winter 1954): 109–23.

MacQueen, Scott. Email message to author, February 7, 2018.

MacQueen, Scott. "The Rise and Fall of *The Emperor Jones*, 1933." *American Cinematographer* 71, no. 2 (1990): 34–40.

Madden, Will Anthony. "Why Did Eugene O'Neill Write 'All God's Chillun Got Wings'?" *Pittsburgh Courier*, April 12, 1924, 13.

Malouf, Michael. *Transatlantic Solidarities: Irish Nationalism and Caribbean Poetics*. Charlottesville: University of Virginia Press, 2009.

Mangéat, Jean. "Les Spectacles de la Semaine dans les Théâtres subventionnés." *La Rampe* (Paris), November 15, 1923, 10.

Mangéat, Jean. "Les Spectacles de la Semaine dans les Théâtres subventionnés." *La Rampe* (Paris), December 2, 1923, 14.

Mangéat, Jean. "Les Spectacles de la Semaine dans les Théâtres subventionnés." *La Rampe* (Paris), December 9, 1923, 12.

Mann, Frances Moss. "Music News." *New York Amsterdam News*, December 1, 1934, 4.

Manning, Susan. *Modern Dance, Negro Dance: Race in Motion*. Minneapolis: University of Minnesota Press, 2006.

Mantle, Burns. "*All God's Chillun* Plays without a Single Protest." *Chicago Daily Tribune*, May 25, 1924, F1.

Martin, Amy E. "Fenian Fever: Circum-Atlantic Insurgency and the Modern State." In *The Black and Green Atlantic: Cross-Currents of the African and Irish Diaspora*, edited by Peter O'Neill and David Lloyd, 20–32. New York: Palgrave Macmillan, 2009.

Martin, John. "The Dance: Russians in Paris." *New York Times*, June 15, 1930, X8.

"Mayor Still Bars Children in Play." *New York Times*, May 17, 1924, 18.

McAdoo, William. "Public Protests Ignored: O'Neill Play to Be Seen." *New York World*, March 3, 1924, 1 and 4.

McAllister, Marvin. *Whiting Up: Whiteface Minstrels and State Europeans in African American Performance*. Chapel Hill: University of North Carolina Press, 2011.

McClelland, L. S. "All God's Chillun Got Wings." *Pittsburgh Courier*, August 1, 1936, 15.

McClintock, Anne. *Imperial Leather: Race, Gender and Sexuality in the Colonial Context*. New York: Routledge, 1995.

McCloy, Shelby T. *The Negro in France*. Lexington: University Press of Kentucky, 1961.

McGarrity, Maria. *Washed by the Gulf Stream: The Historic and Geographic Relation of Irish and Caribbean Literature*. Newark: University of Delaware Press, 2008.

McGinley, Paige A. *Staging the Blues: From Tent Shows to Tourism*. Durham, NC: Duke University Press, 2014.

McKay, Nellie. "Black Theater and Drama in the 1920s: Years of Growing Pains." *Massachusetts Review* 28, no. 4 (Winter 1987): 615–26.

Merriam-Webster. "Fantee" and "Fanti." *Merriam-Webster.com Dictionary*. Accessed May 26, 2020, https://www.merriam-webster.com/dictionary/fa ntee

Metropolitan Opera. "World Premiere (The Emperor Jones)." Accessed March 2, 2022. http://archives.metoperafamily.org/archives/scripts/cgiip.exe/WSer vice=BibSpeed/fullcit.w?xCID=112640&limit=500&xBranch=ALL&xsdate= &xedate=&theterm=&x=0&xhomepath=&xhome=

Metzer, David. "'A Wall of Darkness Dividing the World': Blackness and Whiteness in Louis Gruenberg's *The Emperor Jones*." *Cambridge Opera Journal* 7, no. 1 (1995): 55–72.

Mielziner, Jo. "The Emperor Jones: Notes on Production." August 30, 1932. Folder: Edward Ziegler Correspondence, 1932–1933. Metropolitan Opera Archives, New York City.

Miller, Jeanne-Marie A. "The First Serious Dramas on Broadway by African American Playwrights." In *Experimenters, Rebels, and Disparate Voices: The Theatre of the 1920s Celebrates Diversity*, edited by Arthur Gewirtz and James J. Kolb, 71–81. Westport, CT: Praeger, 2003.

Mitchell, Loften. *Black Drama: The Story of the American Negro in the Theatre*. New York: Hawthorn Books, 1967.

Mitchell, Loften. "Harlem Has Broadway on Its Mind." *Theater Arts* 37 (June 1953): 68–69.

Monks, Aoife. "'Genuine Negroes and Real Bloodhounds': Cross-Dressing, Eugene O'Neill, the Wooster Group, and *The Emperor Jones*." *Modern Drama* 48, no. 3 (Fall 2005): 540–64.

Monroe, John Gilbert. "Charles Gilpin and the Drama League Controversy." *Black American Literature Forum* 16, no. 4 (School of Education, Indiana State University, 1982): 139–41.

Monroe, John Gilbert. "The Harlem Little Theatre Movement, 1920–1929." *Journal of American Culture* 6, no. 4 (1983): 63–70.

Monroe, John Gilbert. "A Record of the Black Theatre in New York City, 1920–29." PhD diss., University of Texas at Austin, 1980.

Morgan, Charles. "Mr. Robeson Tries an Experiment." *New York Times*, September 14, 1930, 108.

Morrison, Michael A. "Emperors Before Gilpin: Opal Cooper and Paul Robeson." *Eugene O'Neill Review* 33, no. 2 (2012): 159–73.

Morrison, Toni. *Beloved*. New York: Alfred Knopf, 1987.

Morton, Patricia A. "National and Colonial: The Musée des Colonies at the Colonial Exposition, Paris, 1931." *Art Bulletin* 80, no. 2 (1998): 357–77.

Mosher, John C. "Jungle in Astoria." *New Yorker*, July 22, 1933, 10.

Mosk, First name unknown. Review of *The Emperor Jones*, Paris, March 5, 1923. Otherwise unidentified clipping, *The Emperor Jones* Clipping File, Billy Rose Theatre Division, New York Public Library for the Performing Arts.

Moynihan, Sinéad. *Other People's Diasporas: Negotiating Race in Contemporary Irish and Irish-American Culture*. Syracuse: Syracuse University Press, 2013.

Mulett, Mary B. "Where Do I Go from Here?" *American Magazine* (June 1921): 54–56.

Mumford, Kevin J. *Interzones: Black/White Sex Districts in Chicago and New York in the Early Twentieth Century*. New York: Columbia University Press, 1997.

Murphy, Brenda. *The Provincetown Players and the Culture of Modernity*. Cambridge: Cambridge University Press, 2005.

Musser, Charles. "To Redream the Dream of White Playwrights: Reappropriation and Resistance in Oscar Micheaux's *Body and Soul*." In *Oscar Micheaux and His Circle: African American Filmmaking and Race Cinema of the Silent Era*, edited by Pearl Bowser, Jane Gaines, and Charles Musser, 97–131. Bloomington: Indiana University Press, 2001.

Musser, Charles. "Troubled Relations: Paul Robeson, Eugene O'Neill, and Oscar Micheaux." In *Paul Robeson: Artist and Citizen*, edited by Jeffrey C. Stewart, 80–103. New Brunswick, NJ: Rutgers University Press, 1998.

Musser, Charles. "Why Did Negroes Love Al Jolson and *The Jazz Singer*? Melodrama, Blackface and Cosmopolitan Theatrical Culture." *Film History: An International Journal* 23, no. 2 (June 2011): 196–222.

"Napoléon Noir." *L'Avenir normand* (Paris), January 15, 1947.

Neal, Nelson D. "Hemsley Winfield: First Black Modern Dancer." *Afro-Americans in New York Life and History* 36, no. 2 (July 2012): 66–85.

Neal, Nelson D. *Hemsley Winfield: The Forgotten Pioneer of Modern Dance, an Annotated Bibliography*. Scotts Valley, CA: CreateSpace Independent Publishing Platform, 2016.

Neal, Nelson D., and Diane Harrison. "Hemsley Winfield: First African American Modern Dancer Contracted by the Metropolitan Opera." *Afro-Americans in New York Life and History* 40, no. 1 (2018): 137–51.

"Negro as Dramatic Artist Finds Opportunity at Last." *World* (New York), May 13, 1923.

"The Negro in Opera." *New York Amsterdam News*, July 26, 1933, 6.

"Negro Opera Plans Debut." *New York Amsterdam News*, June 30, 1934, 17.

"Negro Theatrical Invasion of Europe." *New York Age*, May 19, 1923, 4.

"Negro Who Started Old Man River Buried on Brazos." *Dallas Morning News*, July 22, 1943, 5.

"A New Emperor." *New York World*, May 8, 1924.

"New Emperor Jones: A Bengali 'Discovery' Expected to Be a Sensation in Paris." *New York Times*, May 11, 1923, 20.

"New Films in London." *London Times*, March 19, 1934.

"New O'Neill Play and the Mayor." *New York Post*, May 16, 1924.

"New Racial Play Stirs Stage World: Mary Blair, White Actress, Revealed as Co-Star with Colored Actor." *Broad Ax* (Chicago), March 1, 1924, 2.

"News of the Stage." *New York Times*, May 29, 1941, 14.

Nollen, Scott Allen. *Paul Robeson: Film Pioneer*. Jefferson, NC: McFarland, 2010.

Norman, Dora Cole. "From Hattie's Point of View." *Messenger* 7, no. 1 (January 1925): 32–33.

Nunn, William G. "Private Preview at the Roosevelt Is Well Received." *Pittsburgh Courier*, October 21, 1933, A6.

Nyong'o, Tavia. *Afro-Fabulations: The Queer Drama of Black Life*. New York: New York University Press, 2019.

"N.Y. Raves over Bledsoe's Debut." *Chicago Defender*, July 21, 1934, 9.

"O'Neill Drama and 'Abie's Irish Rose,'" on Week's Calendar." *Los Angeles Times*, June 19, 1927, 17.

O'Neill, Carlotta Monterey. *Diary*. May 12, 1942. Copy at the Eugene O'Neill Foundation Archive, Tao House, Danville, California.

O'Neill, Eugene. *All God's Chillun Got Wings*. In *American Mercury* 1, no. 2 (February 1924): 129–48.

O'Neill, Eugene. *All God's Chillun Got Wings*. 1924. In *Complete Plays: 1920–1931*, edited by Travis Bogard, 278–315. New York: Library of America, 1988.

O'Neill, Eugene. "All God's Chillun Got Wings," draft, typescript and typescript carbon, corrected, n.d. Series III, Writings, 1914–1970, Plays, *All God's Chillun Got Wings*. Box 41, Folder 876. Eugene O'Neill Papers. Yale Collection of American Literature, Beinecke Rare Book and Manuscript Library.

O'Neill, Eugene. *The Dreamy Kid*. 1919. In *Eugene O'Neill: Complete Plays, 1913–1920*, edited by Travis Bogard, 278–315. New York: Library of America, 1988.

O'Neill, Eugene. *The Emperor Jones*. 1920. In *Complete Plays: 1920–1931*, edited by Travis Bogard, 1029–59. New York: Library of America, 1988.

O'Neill, Eugene. "Eugene O'Neill on the Negro Actor." *Messenger* 7 (January 1925): 17.

O'Neill, Eugene. *Eugene O'Neill Work Diary. Volume I, 1924–1933*. Transcribed by Donald Gallup. Prelim. ed. New Haven: Yale University Library, 1981.

O'Neill, Eugene. *Eugene O'Neill Work Diary. Volume II, 1934–1943*. Transcribed by Donald Gallup. Prelim. ed. New Haven: Yale University Library, 1981.

O'Neill, Eugene. Letter to Martin Birnbaum, March 26, 1942. Folder: Letters, Martin Birnbaum. Accession Number: BIM420326. Eugene O'Neill Foundation Archive, Tao House, Danville, California.

O'Neill, Eugene. Letter to W. E. B. Du Bois, September 24, 1924. W. E. B. Du Bois Papers (MS 312). Special Collections and University Archives, University of

Massachusetts Amherst Libraries. http://credo.library.umass.edu/view/full
/mums312-b060-i215

O'Neill, Eugene. Letter to Richard Madden, April 3, 1933. Folder: Letters, Madden, Richard, 1933–37. Accession Number for EOF: MAR330403-, Eugene O'Neill Foundation Library, Tao House, Danville, California.

O'Neill, Eugene. Letter to Richard Madden, on February 17, 1934. Folder: Letters, Madden, Richard, 1933–37. Accession Number MAR340217. Eugene O'Neill Foundation Archive, Tao House, Danville, California.

O'Neill, Eugene. Letter to Richard Madden, March 8, 1934. Folder: Letters, Madden, Richard, 1933–37. Accession Number: MAR340308. Eugene O'Neill Foundation Library, Tao House, Danville, California.

O'Neill, Eugene. Letter to Richard Madden, March 23, 1940. Folder: Letters, Madden, Richard, 1937–42. Accession Number: MAR400323. Eugene O'Neill Foundation, Tao House, Danville, California.

O'Neill, Eugene. Letter to Harry Weinberger, January 26, 1922. Folder: Letters, Weinberger, 1922–28. Accession Number: WEH220126. Eugene O'Neill Foundation Archive, Tao House, Danville, California.

O'Neill, Eugene. Letter to Harry Weinberger, June 4, 1933. Folder: Letters, Weinberger, 1932–37. Accession Number: WEH330604. Eugene O'Neill Foundation Library, Tao House, Danville, California.

O'Neill, Eugene. Letter to Harry Weinberger, July 9, 1933. Folder: Letters, Weinberger, 1932–37. Accession Number: WEH32330709. Eugene O'Neill Foundation Library, Tao House, Danville, California.

O'Neill, Eugene. *Selected Letters of Eugene O'Neill*. Edited by Travis Bogard and Jackson Bryer. New Haven: Yale University Press, 1988.

O'Neill, Eugene. Telegram to Richard Madden on May 15, 1930. Folder: Letters, Madden, Richard, 1919–32. Accession Number: MAR300515. Eugene O'Neill Foundation Archive, Tao House, Danville, California.

O'Neill, Eugene. Telegram to Richard Madden, July 21, 1940. Folder: Letters, Madden, Richard, 1937–42. Accession Number: MAR400731. Eugene O'Neill Foundation, Tao House, Danville, California.

"O'Neill in Paris." *New York Times*, November 18, 1923, X2.

"O'Neill into Opera." *Time Magazine*, January 16, 1933, 20.

"O'Neill to Rescue of 'All God's Chillun.'" *New York World*, March 19, 1924.

O'Neill, Peter D., and David Lloyd. Introduction to *The Black and Green Atlantic: Cross-Currents of the African and Irish Diaspora*, edited by Peter D. O'Neill and David Lloyd, xv–xx. New York: Palgrave, 2009.

"On the Air." *Washington Tribune*, May 24, 1934, 19.

"Opera Will Get Emperor Jones Early in Year." *Chicago Defender*, January 7 1933, 4.

Osborn, E. W. Review of *All God's Chillun Got Wings* by Eugene O'Neill, directed by James Light, Provincetown Playhouse. *New York Evening World*, May 16, 1924.

Ottley, R. Vincent. "Are You Listenin'?" *New York Amsterdam News*, February 1, 1933, 16.

Owen, Chandler. "New Opinion of the Negro." Editorial, *Messenger* 9, no. 6 (June 1, 1927): 191 and 207.

Packard, Paul. "'Emperor Jones' Gilpin's Last Stand." *New York Amsterdam News*, July 25, 1928, 7.

"Paris and 'The Emperor Jones.'" *The Crisis* 27, no. 5 (1924): 223.

"Paris Does 'Emperor Jones' with African Voodoo Troupe." 1950. Otherwise unidentified clipping, *The Emperor Jones* Clipping File. Billy Rose Theatre Division, New York Public Library for the Performing Arts.

"Passing the Grandstand." *Messenger* (New York) 6, no. 6 (July 1924): 224.

"Paul Robeson in Emperor Jones." Souvenir program, 1933. Series II: Personal/ Corporate Names, Box 149, Robeson, Paul, 1922–1925 Clipping File. James Weldon Johnson Memorial Collection in the Yale Collection of American Literature, Beinecke Rare Book and Manuscript Library.

"Paul Robeson in Negro Play — A Dignified Study: Toussaint Louverture, by C. L. R. James." *Morning Post* (London), March 17, 1936.

"Paul Robeson's Big Season in London." *Chicago Defender*, April 22, 1933, 5.

Peet, Creighton. "The Emperor Jones Comes to the Screen." 1933, 40. Otherwise unidentified clipping, Folder: *T-CLP *The Emperor Jones* (Motion picture). Billy Rose Theatre Division, New York Public Library for the Performing Arts.

Pennino, John. Email message to author. June 29, 2016.

Perpener, John O., III. *African-American Concert Dance: The Harlem Renaissance and Beyond*. Urbana: University of Illinois Press, 2001.

Perry, Twila L. "Race on the Opera Stage." In *The Routledge Companion to African American Theatre and Performance*, edited by Kathy A. Perkins, Sandra L. Richards, Renée Alexander Craft, and Thomas F. DeFrantz, 77–82. London: Taylor & Francis, 2019.

Perucci, Tony. *Paul Robeson and the Cold War Performance Complex: Race, Madness, Activism*. Ann Arbor: University of Michigan Press 2012.

Peterson, Bernard L. *Profiles of African American Stage Performers and Theatre People, 1816–1960*. New York: Greenwood Press, 2001.

Pickens, W[illiam] M. "O'Neill's Drama Supports Race Discrimination." *Chicago Defender*, March 22, 1924, 8.

Playbill, *The Emperor Jones*. Salem, MA, February 7, 1938. Library of Congress. Accessed May 20, 2020, https://www.loc.gov/item/musftpplaybills.200220 584/

Playbill, *The Emperor Jones* with Paul Robeson at the Provincetown Playhouse, NY. Season 1923–24.

Pollock, Arthur. Review of *All God's Chillun Got Wings*. *Brooklyn Daily News*, May 16, 1924, 5.

Pool, Rosey E. "The Negro Actor in Europe." *Phylon* 14, no. 3 (1953): 258–67.

Poston, T. B. "Harlem Dislikes 'N——r' in 'Emperor Jones' but Flocks to See Picture at Uptown House." *New York Amsterdam News*, September 27, 1933, 9.

P. P. "Eugene O'Neill's Plays." *Evening Standard* (London), September 11, 1925.

"Program of Negro Music" featuring Paul Robeson with Lawrence Brown on the piano at the Greenwich Theatre, New York. Clippings File of the James Weldon Johnson Memorial Papers. Series II: Personal/Corporate Names, Box 149, Folder: Paul Robeson File, 1922–25. Yale Collection of American Literature, Beinecke Rare Book and Manuscript Library.

Programme for 'All God's Chillun Got Wings' by Eugene O'Neill (1944) at the Mercury Theatre, Colchester, UK. Posted February 11, 2020. Accessed November 21, 2020. https://www.mercurytheatre.co.uk/mercury-voices/pr ogramme-for-all-gods-chillun-got-wings-by-eugene-oneill/

"Prologue of 'All God's Chillun' Is Read, as Child Actors Are Barred." *New York World*, May 16, 1924.

"Public Protests Ignored." *New York World*, March 3, 1924.

P. V. "At the Provincetown." *New York Morning World*, May 7, 1924.

"Race Strife Seen if 'God's Chillun' Is Staged." *New York American*, March 15, 1924, 1.

Ranald, Margaret Loftus. *The Eugene O'Neill Companion*. Westport, CT: Greenwood Press, 1985.

Ransan, André. "Empereur Jones." *Le Matin-Le Pays* (Paris), February 11–12, 1950.

Rea, E. B. "Encores and Echoes." *Afro-American* (Baltimore), March 4, 1950, 8.

Redmond, Shana L. *Everything Man: The Form and Function of Paul Robeson*. Ann Arbor: University of Michigan Press, 2019.

Review of *L'Empereur Jones*, translated by Maurice Bourgeois, directed by Sylvain Dhomme. Maison de la Pensée Française, Paris, France. *L'Aurore* (Paris), February 12, 1950.

Review of *The Emperor Jones* by Eugene O'Neill, Ambassadors Theatre, London, 1925. V&A Collections, Department of Theatre and Performance.

Review of *The Emperor Jones* by Eugene O'Neill. *New York Herald Tribune*, August 4, 1940.

Review of *The Emperor Jones*, directed by Dudley Murphy. *Variety*, September 26, 1933, 15.

"Reviews: Paul Robeson." *Chicago Defender*, October 31, 1925, 7.

Rhambo, Clarence. *The Life of Jules Bledsoe*. Lima, OH: Fairway Press, 1989.

"Rialto Gossip." *New York Times*, January 4, 1925, X1.

"Rialto Gossip: The Theatre Guild Also Has Its Casting Problems." *New York Times*, April 2, 1933, X1.

Rich, B. Ruby. "From Repressive Tolerance to Erotic Liberation: *Mädchen in Uniform*." *Gender and German Cinema: Feminist Interventions*, vol. 2, edited by Sandra Frieden, Richard McCormick, Vibeke Petersen, and Laurie Melissa Vogelsang, 61–96. Oxford: Berg, 1993.

Ries, Frank William David. *The Dance Theatre of Jean Cocteau*. Ann Arbor, MI: UMI Research Press, 1986.

"Riots Feared from Drama." *New York American*, March 18, 1924, 1.

Ritschel, Nelson O'Ceallaigh. "Synge and the Irish Influence of the Abbey Theatre on Eugene O'Neill." *Eugene O'Neill Review* 29 (2007): 129–50.

Roach, Joseph. *Cities of the Dead: Circum-Atlantic Performance*. New York: Columbia University Press, 1996.

"Robeson a Success in Drama by Negro." *New York Times*, March 16, 1936, 21.

Robeson, Paul. "The Black Emperor." Conducted by Eric Ansell, recorded May 21, 1936. EMI Classics, track number 5–8 on *Paul Robeson: The Complete EMI Sessions, (1928–1939)*, 2008, CD box set.

Robeson, Paul. "I Want Negro Culture." *News Chronicle* (London), May 30, 1935.

Robeson, Paul. *Paul Robeson Speaks: Writings, Speeches, and Interviews, a Centennial Celebration*. New York: Citadel Press, 1978.

Robeson, Paul. "Reflections on O'Neill's Plays." *Opportunity* 2, no. 25 (December 1924): 368–70.

Robeson, Paul, Jr. *The Undiscovered Paul Robeson: An Artist's Journey, 1898–1939*. New York: John Wiley & Sons, 2001.

"Robeson 'Recaptures' Chicago." *Chicago Defender*, July 1940.

"Robeson to Form London Repertory: Plans to Organize Permanent Company as Soon as His Engagements Permit." *New York Times*, October 28, 1932, 22.

"Robeson Wins Plaudits: Hailed in London in O'Neill's 'All God's Chillun.'" *New York Times*, March 14, 1933, 19.

"Robeson Wins Praise of Critics in London." *Pittsburgh Courier*, October 10, 1925.

Robinson, Cedric J. *Forgeries of Memory and Meaning: Blacks and the Regimes of Race in American Theater and Film before World War II*. Chapel Hill: University of North Carolina Press, 2007.

Robinson, Cedric J. "Ventriloquizing Blackness: Eugene O'Neill and Irish-American Racial Performance." In *The Black and Green Atlantic: Cross-Currents of the African and Irish Diaspora*, edited by Peter O'Neill and David Lloyd, 49–63. New York: Palgrave, 2009.

Rodgers, Nini. *Ireland, Slavery, and Anti-Slavery: 1612–1865*. New York: Palgrave Macmillan, 2007.

Roe, Alex. "Port in a Storm: Arriving at a Virtual Theatre through the Pandemic of 2020." *Eugene O'Neill Review* 42, no. 1 (2021): 54–63.

Roediger, David R. *The Wages of Whiteness: Race and the Making of the American Working Class*. London: Verso, 1991.

Roediger, David R. *Working Toward Whiteness: How America's Immigrants Became White: The Strange Journey from Ellis Island to the Suburbs*. New York: Basic Books, 2006.

Rogers, J. A. "O'Neill's Masterpiece, 'The Emperor Jones,' Flayed by J. A. Rogers as Portraying False Negro Type: Appeals to Nordic Prejudice." *Pitts-burgh Courier*, September 30, 1933, 11.

Rogin, Michael. *Blackface, White Noise: Jewish Immigrants in the Hollywood Melt-ing Pot*. Berkeley: University of California Press, 1998.

Román, David. *Performance in America: Contemporary U.S. Culture and the Per-forming Arts*. Durham, NC: Duke University Press, 2005.

Romeyn, Esther. *Street Scenes: Staging the Self in Immigrant New York, 1880–1924*. Minneapolis: University of Minnesota Press, 2008.

Rothstein, Mervin. "Robert Falls and His *Desire* for Eugene O'Neill." *Playbill*, January 17, 2009. Accessed November 22, 2021. https://www.playbill.com/ar ticle/robert-falls-and-his-desire-for-eugene-oneill-com-157078

Russell, Richard Rankin. "The Black and Green Atlantic: Violence, History, and Memory in Natasha Trethewey's 'South' and Seamus Heaney's 'North.'" *Southern Literary Journal* 46, no. 2 (2014): 155–72.

Said, Edward W. *Orientalism*. New York: Pantheon Books, 1978.

Salini, Formose. "Le grand acteur noir: Habib Benglia." *La Rampe* (Paris), December 1, 1931, 43–44.

Savran, David. *Highbrow/Lowdown: Theater, Jazz, and the Making of the New Mid-dle Class*. Ann Arbor: University of Michigan Press, 2009.

Saxena, Jennie. Letter to Ken Weissman. "Emperor Jones Missing Scenes." Jan-uary 31, 2001. James Cozart's Papers, the Conservation Center of the Library of Congress (not catalogued).

Saxena, Jennie. "Preserving African-American Cinema: The Case of *The Emperor Jones* (1933)." Contributions by Ken Weissman and James Cozart. *Moving Image* 3, no. 1 (2003): 42–58.

Schechner, Richard. *Between Theatre and Anthropology*. Chicago: University of Chicago Press, 1985.

Schneider, Rebecca. *Performing Remains: Art and War in Times of Theatrical Reen-actment*. London: Routledge, 2011.

Scott, Ellen. "Regulating 'N——r': Racial Offense, African American Activists, and the MPPDA, 1928–1961." *Film History* 26, no. 4 (2014): 1–31.

Scott, Freda. "Five African-American Playwrights on Broadway, 1923–1929." PhD diss., City University of New York, 1990.

"Seeking Play for Gilpin." *New York Amsterdam News*, November 24, 1926, 13.

Shack, William A. *Harlem in Montmartre: A Paris Jazz Story between the Great Wars*. Berkeley: University of California Press, 2001.

Shaughnessy, Edward L. *Eugene O'Neill in Ireland: The Critical Reception*. West-port, CT: Greenwood, 1988.

Shaughnessy, Edward L. "O'Neill's African and Irish-Americans: Stereotypes or 'Faithful Realism'?" In *The Cambridge Companion to Eugene O'Neill*, edited by Michael Manheim, 148–63. New York: Cambridge University Press, 1998.

Sheaffer, Louis. *O'Neill: Son and Artist*. Boston: Little, Brown, 1973.

Simmons, Lisa. "The Negro Theater Project, 1935–1939." *Boston Black Theater: Its Golden Era*. Accessed on March 22, 2020. http://academics.wellesley.edu/AmerStudies/BostonBlackHistory/theatre/theatreproject.html

Siomopoulos, Anna. "The 'Eighth o' Style' Black Nationalism, the New Deal, and *The Emperor Jones*." *Arizona Quarterly* 58, no. 3 (2002): 57–81.

Smalls, James. *The Homoerotic Photography of Carl Van Vechten*. Philadelphia: Temple University Press, 2006.

Smith, Jessie Carney. *Black Firsts: 4,000 Ground-Breaking and Pioneering Historical Events*. Detroit: Visible Ink Press, 2012.

Sollors, Werner. *Neither Black Nor White Yet Both: Thematic Explorations of Interracial Literature*. Cambridge, MA: Harvard University Press, 1991.

Somerville, Siobhan B. *Queering the Color Line: Race and the Invention of Homosexuality in American Culture*. Durham, NC: Duke University Press, 2000.

Southern, Eileen. *The Music of Black Americans: A History*. New York: W. W. Norton, 1997.

"Spotlight Highlights." *Philadelphia Tribune*, September 3, 1931, 7.

"Stage Society: 'Toussaint Louverture' by C. L. R. James." *Times* (London), March 17, 1936.

Stallybrass, Peter, and Allon White. *The Poetics and Politics of Transgression*. London: Methuen, 1986.

"Stay Is Extended of 'Tobacco Road.'" *New York Times*, August 8, 1940, 23.

Steen, Shannon. "Melancholy Bodies: Racial Subjectivity and Whiteness in O'Neill's *The Emperor Jones*." *Theatre Journal* 52, no. 3 (2000): 339–59.

Steen, Shannon. *Racial Geometries of the Black Atlantic, Asian Pacific and American Theatre*. New York: Palgrave Macmillan, 2010.

Steichen, Edward. "Paul Robeson as 'The Emperor Jones,' New York." Library of Congress, Prints and Photographs Division, PH—Steichen (E.), no. 15 (B size) [P&P].

"Stephen Sondheim Takes Issue with Plan for Revamped 'Porgy and Bess.'" *New York Times*, August 10, 2011. Accessed November 28, 2021. https://artsbeat.blogs.nytimes.com/2011/08/10/stephen-sondheim-takes-issue-with-plan-for-revamped-porgy-and-bess/

Stephens, Michelle Ann. *Black Empire: The Masculine Global Imaginary of Caribbean Intellectuals in the United States, 1914–1962*. Durham, NC: Duke University Press, 2005.

Stewart, Jeffrey C. "The Black Body: Paul Robeson as a Work of Art and Politics." In *Paul Robeson: Artist and Citizen*, edited by Jeffrey C. Stewart, 134–63. New Brunswick, NJ: Rutgers University Press, 1988.

Stewart, Jeffrey C. *The Emperor Jones*. In *Paul Robeson: Portraits of the Artist*. Audio commentary. Criterion Collection, 2007.

Stovall, Horalde R. "The 'Emperor Jones' Hailed at the Metropolitan Opera." *New York Amsterdam News*, January 11, 1933, 8.

"Take Insult out of Movies." *Chicago Defender*, October 7, 1933, 1.

Taylor, Diana. *The Archive and the Repertoire: Performing Cultural Memory in the Americas*. Durham, NC: Duke University Press, 2003.

"Ted Hammerstein Gets Saratoga Post: Will Operate the Spa Theatre, Which Plans 8-Week Season." *New York Times*, June 17, 1941, 24.

"The Theatre: *All God's Chillun* Monday." *Time Magazine*, March 17, 1924.

"The Theatre in France." *Forum* 72 (1924): 798.

"Theatres and Performers—Big and Little." *New York Amsterdam News*, April 24, 1929, 13.

"Theatrically Speaking." *Washington Tribune*, October 5, 1933, 15.

"This Week's Summer Bills." *New York Times*, July 13, 1941, X2.

Thompson, David. "Shuffling Roles: Alterations and Audiences in *Shuffle Along*." *Theatre Symposium: A Journal of the Southeastern Theatre Conference* 20 (2012): 97–108.

Thompson, Debby. "Is Race a Trope? Anna Deavere Smith and the Question of Racial Performativity." *African American Review* 37, no. 1 (2003): 127–38.

Thompson, Mary Francesca. Email message to author, June 2010.

Thompson, Mary Francesca. "The Lafayette Players, 1915–1932." PhD diss., University of Michigan, 1972.

Tolliver, Cedric R. *Of Vagabonds and Fellow Travelers: African Diaspora Literary Culture and the Cultural Cold War*. Ann Arbor: University of Michigan Press, 2019.

"To Open in Old Role." *New York Times*, July 26, 1941, 18.

Trask, C. Hooper. "Berlin Calls It a Season." *New York Times*, June 15, 1930, X6.

Trask, C. Hooper. "Berlin's Year at the Spring." *New York Times*, May 25, 1930, 1 and 2.

Triolet, Elsa. "'Empereur Jones' la célèbre pièce." *Lettres Française* (Paris), February 16, 1950, 7.

Turner, Kristen M. "Class, Race, and Uplift in the Opera House: Theodore Drury and His Company Cross the Color Line." *Journal of Musicological Research* 34, no. 4 (2015): 320–51.

Unidentified clipping from the *New York Sun*. September 20, 1933. Folder: *T-CLP *The Emperor Jones* (Motion picture). Billy Rose Theatre Division, New York Public Library for the Performing Arts.

Untitled clipping from the *New York Herald Tribune*. July 2, 1933. Folder: *T-CLP *The Emperor Jones* (Motion picture). Billy Rose Theatre Division, New York Public Library for the Performing Arts.

"U.S. Coaches Declare That Tolan Conditioned Himself." *Afro-American* (Baltimore), August 13, 1932, 15.

Van Gyseghem, Andrew. *Paul Robeson: The Great Forerunner*. New York: Dodd, Mead, 1978.

Vogel, Paula. *Indecent*. New York: Theatre Communications Group, 2017.

Vogel, Shane. *The Scene of Harlem Cabaret: Race, Sexuality, Performance*. Chicago: University of Chicago Press, 2009.

Wainscott, Ronald H. *Staging O'Neill: The Experimental Years, 1920–1934*. New Haven: Yale University Press, 1988.

Walker, Ethel Pitts. "Krigwa, a Theatre By, For, and About Black People." *Theatre Journal* 40, vol. 3 (1988): 347–56.

Walton, Lester A. "Evelyn Preer Would Make Good 'Ella Downey' in 'All God's Chillun Got Wings.'" *Pittsburgh Courier*, March 15, 1924, 10.

Walton, Lester A. "'Roseanne,' with All Negro Cast, Strike Higher Average Than When Given by White Co." *New York Age*, March 15, 1924, 6.

Walton, Lester A. [Title unknown.] *New York Age*, January 17, 1920.

Washington, Booker T. "Why Not a Negro Drama for Negroes by Negroes." *Current Opinion* 72, no. 5 (May 1922): 639–40.

Watkins, Mary F. "With the Dancers." *New York Herald Tribune*, January 15, 1933.

Watts, Richard, Jr. Review of *The Emperor Jones. New York Herald Tribune*, September 24, 1933.

Wearing, J. P. *The London Stage 1920–1929: A Calendar of Productions, Performers, and Personnel*. New York: Rowman & Littlefield, 2014.

Weinstein, Katherine. "Towards a Theatre of Creative Imagination: Alexander Tairov's O'Neill Productions." *Eugene O'Neill Review* 22, nos. 1–2 (1998): 157–70.

Weisenfeld, Judith. *Hollywood Be Thy Name: African American Religion in American Film, 1929–1949*. Berkeley: University of California Press, 2007.

Weixlmann, Joe. "Staged Segregation: Baldwin's *Blues for Mister Charlie* and O'Neill's *All God's Chillun Got Wings*." *Black American Literature Forum* 11, no. 1 (Spring 1977): 35–36.

Whelan, Kevin. "The Green Atlantic: Radical Reciprocities between Ireland and America in the Long Eighteenth Century." In *A New Imperial History: Culture, Identity, and Modernity in Britain and the Empire, 1660–1840*, edited by Kathleen Wilson, 216–38. Cambridge: Cambridge University Press, 2004.

"White Actress to Play Opposite Negro 'Lead.'" *Washington Post*, February 22, 1924, 3.

White, Walter. "The Negro Renaissance" (1926). In *The New Negro: Readings on Race, Representation, and African American Culture, 1892–1938*, edited by Henry Louis Gates and Gene Andrew Jarrett, 231. Princeton, NJ: Princeton University Press, 2007.

Wiktionary. "Herp." Accessed May 20, 2020, https://en.wiktionary.org/wiki/%D0%BD%D0%B5%D0%B3%D1%80

Wiegman, Robyn. *American Anatomies: Theorizing Race and Gender*. Durham, NC: Duke University Press, 1995.

Wikipedia. "Ida Shepley." Accessed November 20, 2020. https://en.wikipedia.org/wiki/Ida_Shepley#cite_note-3

Wikipedia. "Irving Pichel." Accessed September 5, 2021. https://www.imdb.com/name/nm0681635/bio?ref_=nm_ov_bio_sm

"Will Play 'Emperor Jones' in Paris." *New York Amsterdam News*, May 16, 1923, 4.

Willeman, George. Email message to author, February 12, 2018.

Williams, Gary Jay. "*The Dreamy Kid*: O'Neill's Darker Brother." *Theatre Annual* 43 (1988): 3–14.

Williams, Steven. "Robeson as Negro Leader." *Evening Standard* (London), March 17, 1936.

Willis, Deborah. "The Image and Paul Robeson." In *Paul Robeson: Artist and Citizen*, edited by Jeffrey C. Stewart, 61–80. New Brunswick, NJ: Rutgers University Press, 1998.

Wilson, James F. *Bulldaggers, Pansies, and Chocolate Babies: Performance, Race, and Sexuality in the Harlem Renaissance*. Ann Arbor: University of Michigan Press, 2010.

"Winfield Dead at 27; 'Emperor Jones' Dancer." *New York Herald Tribune*, January 16, 1934.

Winz, Cary D. *Black Culture and the Harlem Renaissance*. Houston: Rice University Press, 1988.

Wisner, René. "La Semaine Théatrale." *La Rampe* (Paris), November 11, 1923, 7–11.

Wisner, René. "Théâtre de l'Odéon." *La Rampe* (Paris), November 11, 1923.

Woollcott, Alexander. "*All God's Chillun Got Wings*: O'Neill's Play Tranquilly Produced in Macdougal Street." *New York Sun*, May 16, 1924, 24.

Woollcott, Alexander. "Second Thoughts on First Night." *New York Times*, November 9, 1919, XX2.

Wright, Michelle M. *Physics of Blackness: Beyond the Middle Passage Epistemology*. Minneapolis: University of Minnesota Press, 2015.

Wythe, Don. "What a Headache!" *Shadow Play*, October 1933, 38.

Young, Harvey. *Embodying Blackness: Stillness, Critical Memory, and the Black Body*. Ann Arbor: University of Michigan Press, 2010.

Young, Stark. "*All God's Chillun* Again." *New York Times*, August 19, 1924, 9.

Ziegler, Edie. Letter to Edward Ellsworth Hipsher. March 25, 1924. Folder: Edward Ziegler Correspondence File (F–G), 1932–1933. Metropolitan Opera Archives, New York City.

Ziegler, Edie. Letter to Louis Gruenberg, June 7, 1933. Folder: Edward Ziegler Correspondence File (F–G), 1932–1933. Metropolitan Opera Archives, New York City.

Index

Notes: Page numbers in italics indicate figures.